Essay Index

FREEDOM IN THE MODERN WORLD

FREEDOM IN THE MODERN WORLD

EDITED BY

HORACE M. KALLEN

*Lectures Delivered at the New
School for Social Research by:*

WALTON H. HAMILTON
REV. JOHN A. RYAN, D.D.
F. J. FOAKES-JACKSON
ZECHARIAH CHAFEE, JR.
CLARENCE DARROW
SILAS BENT
MAX EASTMAN
ROBERT MORSS LOVETT
JOSEPH JASTROW
JOHN DEWEY
HORACE M. KALLEN

Essay Index

Essay Index Reprint Series

BOOKS FOR LIBRARIES PRESS
FREEPORT, NEW YORK

First Published 1928
Reprinted 1969

STANDARD BOOK NUMBER:
8369-1085-0

LIBRARY OF CONGRESS CATALOG CARD NUMBER:
70-84313

CONTENTS

PREFACE

IT is now several generations since "the interests" have become a permanent figure of our political and social world. Both the forum and the study have recognized them as powerful monopolies of fundamental goods or services, concerned, as a part of the upkeep of their establishments in our national economy, to crush competition, to suppress or abort invention, to debauch the government and to prostitute the press. Recently, one such "interest" has been exposed insinuating itself into school and university, bribing investigators and teachers to create and to expound a doctrine advantageous to its purposes. Among those who had taken its money were counted the most ancient and prosperous academies of the land. The public has had an object lesson of how the vested interest of an economic establishment gets extended to the free fields of thought, and how it works to subvert to its own ends impartial research and scientific truth.

This modern instance is, however, but a latest item in an ancient tradition, a special case of a predicament of the spirit which has been universal and endemic, time out of mind. Indeed, the world of thought has had its doctrinal monopolies long before those of the modern economic order were born. Freedom to think and to teach has ever been limited by the prevailing orthodoxy and the ruling passions of place and time. These have always imposed a grammar of assent where a technique of doubt was required; they have demanded conformity where the call was for dispute. Truth has always been for them the rehearsal of some advantageous lie. The monopoly has been most notorious in the field of religion, where every question used to be literally a burning question and every competitive teaching becomes automatically an issue of life and death. But monopoly is just as eager and just as rapacious in the fields of the political and social sciences. Willy-nilly the prevailing orthodoxies and ruling passions of the community are weighted against competing doctrines. The competing doctrines certainly receive no favor; and at least as certainly do not get a fair field. In a thousand subtle, unconscious ways, they are deprived of a fighting chance, so that the issue against them is a foregone conclusion. Even where they are expounded and taught, the teacher is without faith in them—if he did believe in them he could not long hold his post in the usual institution of the higher learning—and his interest is to deny and defeat them, somehow, anyhow. With respect to the social and political sciences the institutions of higher learning show themselves to be as definitely, if more subtly, seats of monopolistic orthodoxy as any sectarian theological school. They make the same demands upon conformity; they take the same attitude toward dissidence and heresy. The consequence is that much of what goes for research within their walls is a kind of statistical scholasticism; all of what goes for education is not an enrichment of the future but a reproduction of the past; heresies, banished without candor from the field of scientific fair play, become cults of the mind on their own account, without regard to their actual merits as scientific hypotheses or social programs.

This situation, which is chronic in the world of school and college, had come to one of its recurrent crises ten years ago, at the close of the Great War. Then orthodoxy seemed more rigidly compulsive than ever, ruling passions more fiery. The free, open confrontation and mutual testing of opposed ideas upon a fair field without favor seemed more remote than ever as an academic enterprise. Free thought in the political and social sciences seemed more than ever seriously endangered. It then occurred to a group of high-minded men and women, much concerned over the integrity of the intellectual life in the United States, that there might be created at least one institution of the higher learning in the social sciences where these dangers to free thought and intellectual integrity could not obtain. In such an institution there would be no prevailing orthodoxy and no ruling passion. It would provide, in the spirit of scientific fair play, for social and political theories that fair field and no favor which the conventional academies did not provide. It would bring together as a student body men and women of mature mind, whose formal training has already been completed, and who are now more concerned to doubt and to inquire than to believe and to assent. No subject should be taboo; none should be taught by a teacher who did not believe in it. The faculty should consist, as nearly as possible, of the masters in their fields, innovators and adventurers in the social sciences. There were to be no entrance requirements, no examinations, no degrees. The work of the school was to consist of a cooperative endeavor of faculty and pupils in study and research.

With this program of adult education and scientific impartiality for its objective, the New School for Social Research opened its doors in the Spring of 1919. Among its faculty were John Dewey, Wesley Clair Mitchell, James Harvey Robinson, Graham Wallas, Charles A. Beard, Thorstein Veblen. Among its students have been distinguished physicians and lawyers, journalists and social workers, business men and artists, trades-union leaders and plain working-men, outstanding feminists and simple shopgirls. In the ten years since its establishment, more than twelve thousand persons have been students within its walls. Without endowment, dependent for the upkeep of its work on students' fees and annual gifts and contributions, it has maintained its difficult and precarious existence amid many vicissitudes, some to the very verge of closing its work, and it has labored unflinchingly to realize the ideals set by its founders—to provide an academic forum where honest scholarship in the social sciences should be free and untrammelled, where theories and ideas should find a fair field and no favor, where those that prevailed in the struggle for intellectual survival might prevail by inward scientific merit, not by outer reenforcement from a vested interest of the spirit or the flesh.

The present course of lectures has been given in harmony with these ideals. The general topic is one of unsurpassed importance for our times. The lecturers are masters distinguished in their special fields. Each is the exponent of a different theory of freedom, the spokesman for a different social and political point of view. One is a protagonist of the modern school of institutional economics, another is an outstanding Roman Catholic moralist; a third is a notable Protestant theologian; a fourth professes law—soundly, safely, as the eminent president of his university would assure you—in the Law School at Harvard; a fifth is a well-known criminal lawyer of the widest experience before bench and bar; a sixth is a journalist who has not only learned the newspaper in all its intricate structure and relationships, but is widely experienced in politics and publicity and the publicity of politics; the seventh is a notable apostle of communism, the friend of Trotsky, and a critic of the present regime in Russia; the eighth is the foremost professor of English literature in the middle west and one of the country's outstanding literary critics; the ninth is among the pioneers of scientific psychology in the United States; the tenth is America's foremost philosopher, a teacher acknowledged and revered by the whole civilized world.

Pragmatist, materialist, capitalist, communist, catholic, protestant, republican, democrat, conservative, and liberal, each made his deliverance not knowing what those had said who had preceded him, unaware of what those were going to say who should follow. If, in spite of this diversity in point of view and this mutual independence of reflection and utterance, there appears among these authorities a consensus concerning the problem of freedom in the modern world, a certain repetition and overlapping, this can derive from no collusion of opinion, but must rest upon correct observation of the facts themselves. These have been reached, as it were, concentrically and convergently, and auscultated at their very heart. The occurrence of a consensus under such circumstances is the establishment of a truth, and it is the truth about freedom which this book in no small degree so signally records.

H. M. KALLEN

THE NEW SCHOOL FOR SOCIAL RESEARCH
20 August 1928.

WHY FREEDOM IS A PROBLEM

Horace M. Kallen

I

IN the decade since the world has been made
safe for democracy, it seems to have been made
very unsafe for freedom. Freedom has become a
paramount topic of liberal discussion. The Eternal
Vigilance which is notoriously its price seems to be
once more aroused, and the wakefulness of a thinking and tiny minority hopes to extend itself to the
sleeping masses. Certainly, the minority is beating
loud enough alarms. See, they cry, all our ancient
liberties are being taken from us, directly or by indirection; we may neither assemble nor speak nor write
freely; we may not choose what to drink or what to
eat; what play to go to or what book to read: government works more and more by coercion and less
and less by consent; privileged and organized special
interests impose upon us the service of their limited
causes; religion shackles us; the state shackles us; the
economic order shackles us; justice exploits us. And
science and philosophy aid and abet them by insisting
that the spirit of man falls under the determinations
of natural law; that we live as we must, not as we
may; that our freedom is at best an illusion.

Since the champions of Freedom are at the same time—like Mr. Bertrand Russell—believers in scientific determinism, they champion, it would seem, something that in the nature of things cannot exist anyhow. Thus they are out of their own mouths convicted of folly. Yet one need only to name the champions of Freedom to know that they are no fools; that, on the contrary, they are among the wisest and best of our times, at once humanists and humanitarians. If their view appears to be involved in contradiction and paradox, it is because the freedoms they care for are known only by the restraints that negate them: speaking and eating and drinking are not freedoms until someone tries to prevent their happening: someone, and not something: we do not ordinarily regard a blister on the tongue or a sour stomach as an interference with an ancient liberty.

But a Freedom which is known by the influences that keep it back can hardly be said to be known at all, any more than a man can be known by the key that locks him in. The fact is, no political or social scientist has yet produced, so far as I know, a description of freedom as a positive, intrinsic quality of the course of nature or the life of man. Such positive descriptions as exist are the work of psychologists and philosophers like William James or Henri Bergson; and of theologians, especially of orthodox theologians, to whom the reality of "free-will" is momentous, and who are thus professionally preoccupied with showing what it is, and that it exists. But their accounts of the intrinsic character of freedom are usually very involved with other matters and very abstract in themselves; indeed, one cannot understand what a thinker like, say, Thomas Aquinas positively means by "freewill" unless one understands his whole system. And then it develops, all too often, that save by reference to the contrasting notion of necessity or coercion, the qualities of choice and chance, of fiat and unpredictability which usually go into every positive account of freedom, lose all concreteness and almost all meaning.

Thus the champions of Freedom may be justified after all. Freedom seems of all our notions most idiosyncratic. We seem to require the presence of its opposites and enemies in order to experience its intrinsic character. Positively, Freedom seems to involve the way you feel when you are let go—whether in talking, eating, drinking, fighting, moving, or what you will. Without the restraint and its relaxation this feeling does not seem to occur; and as feeling is always an individual experience, the social definition of Freedom involves prohibiting interference, forbidding or removing obstruction or restraint, rather than characterizing a feeling. Bills of rights and the like prohibit or nullify certain types of action: they command non-interference; they could be described, in fact, as curbing or destroying one kind of freedom to enlarge or create another. Hence Freedom, as an ideal at work in any society, seems always to have a revolutionary implication; seems always to require the dissolution of systems of thought and principles of behavior; the overthrow of existing power, privilege or institutional rule. Wherever men agitate for liberty, they agitate for the

elimination of one thing or another from the conjunctions of public or private life.

How such elimination takes place defines to a very
great degree the locus and the quality of the Freedom that is aspired to. For example, the modes of
liberation which began with the industrial revolution,
one hundred and seventy-five years or so ago, and
developed into institutions of our modern world,
define a kind of freedom the ancients wouldn't understand at all. The Greeks of the time of Pericles or
of Aristotle wouldn't mean by Freedom the same
thing that you and I mean, because they were under
different compulsions from ours. Those that
troubled them most deeply are such as little concern
us; those against which we are most breathlessly on
the watch they could hardly understand as compulsions at all. To Aristotle, for example, slavery and
war, which are to us the enemies of Freedom, were
its indispensable foundations. We see finitude as a
limitation and restriction, custom and law as obstructions, form as fatality. To Aristotle finitude was
the definitive quality of progress, custom and law
the opportunity for the good life, form the differ-
entia of excellence. Existence could be free only by
acquiescence in them, where for us moderns Freedom
comes mainly by rebellion against them. Indeed,
the Freedom which the prophets and philosophers of
the ancient world preached and expounded is a function of the security which comes from acquiescing
in the established order of society, in the necessary
structure of the world. This Freedom is something,

in fact, quite positive, a quality of feeling, not the withdrawal of an obstruction. To feel free is to be free, so far as you can be free at all. Even though in fact your way in any direction is blocked, you are free if you do not feel blocked. So you may, like Epictetus, be a slave and nevertheless free, or like Marcus Aurelius, an emperor and not free until you accept the compulsions of your place. The philosopher or wise man of antiquity is known as the free man. And he is the free man because he neither rebels nor struggles. He accepts the universe and his place in it, his condition in his place, and the tasks of his condition. He does not pull against the stream of existence, he goes with it. He is like a person tied to a moving automobile. So long as he wants to go to another place than that the automobile is headed for, he resists its motion but goes with the automobile nevertheless. And his resistance exhausts him, body and soul; it makes his life a struggle with its ground. He is a slave because he resists. To become a free man he needs only to cease resisting. Let him instead hop on the car, and permit it to carry him; let him ride like a prince instead of running reluctantly backward like a pauper. So with the universe. Since we cannot escape it, let us accept it; let us conform to its laws and acquiesce in Nature and Destiny. By ceasing to resist we cease to be bond. Effortlessness, non-resistance is freedom. It is the whole sum of wisdom.

This wisdom, to a certain degree, was carried over into Christianity. It is there complicated by cer-

tain notions of freewill and its surrender, summed up
in the expression, "God's will, not mine, be done."
Thence it emerges into the great tradition of philosophy, where it continues to be advocated by such
types of mind which temperamentally prefer it.
Spinoza's great Ethics is a survey of human bondage
and a program of human freedom: and what human
bondage distils to is wanting things impossible to get;
and what human freedom amounts to is accepting
those that are inevitable to our lot, identifying oneself with the courses of nature which determine one's
character, one's status and one's destiny. This is the
Freedom which scientific naturalism points to when it
considers Freedom at all—the feeling we have when
we make no effort and take no trouble, when we
accept and acquiesce. But it is not the kind of Freedom which the modern world has in mind. The
Freedom we are anxious about involves effort and
trouble, rejection and denial. It is a function of
dissent, insecurity and disestablishment. It would
rather slow up the world-machine than exercise no
influence whatever upon it. It is rebellion, not
patriotism, and it defies not merely the powers that
rule the home, but the laws of nature and the
ordinances of God: the greatest poet of Protestantism, mourning the loss of Paradise, makes of the
Rebel of Heaven who caused the loss an incom-
parable hero; Milton's Satan turns out as greater of
soul than Milton's God.

II

Modern liberty begins in revolt—revolt in the church, revolt in the state, revolt in the workshop and studio, in the counting-house and study. Its history is a battle royal with authority in these various domains of civilized life. To rationalize the revolt, men elaborate the legend that they are possessed of natural and inalienable rights which no authority can infringe, no power destroy. The legend reaches an imaginative perfection in the principal apothegm of the American "Declaration of Independence." It is a compendium of the whole modern philosophy of rebellion, invoked as much by the champions of dictatorships as by the enemies of authority. All men, it asserts, are created equal. They are endowed by their Creator with certain inalienable rights. Among these rights it names especially life, liberty and the pursuit of happiness. It further asserts that government is only an instrument to make these rights secure; that if the instrument becomes subversive of the end for which it was created, it is to be abandoned and replaced by another which will be loyal to these ends. And the assertions are pronounced "self-evident truths."

How revolutionary and rationalizing this whole philosophy is, may be inferred from the fact that the sacred oracle of American history which embodies it is one that you cannot read in many another place besides Passaic, New Jersey, or Chicago, Illinois, without running the risk of being thrown into jail. It is revolutionary, because it conceives human nature abstractly and sets up the abstractions against the

living establishments of living society and against the
dogmas and doctrines which rationalize that, and
enable its beneficiaries—the military and the religious
castes, the hereditary nobility and the like—to direct
the appetites and activities of men in their own
interest. Thus rights are conceived as "natural" in
order to nullify rights claimed to be divine. They
are called inalienable, because they had been utterly
alienated and a struggle was afoot to naturalize the
alien. This struggle is to a large degree the problem of freedom in the modern world. It recognizes
that there is not a single right of man which cannot
be taken from him, that his "inalienable rights" are
those more completely subject to alienation than any
he lays claim to. Consider "life, liberty and the pursuit of happiness." A human life is today perhaps
somewhat more inviolable than it used to be in the
eighteenth century. Liberty: eighteenth-century mankind as a whole was altogether without any; it
was a class privilege and the claim that it was inalienable to all men was the claim to share the privilege. Some division has taken place since this claim
was made but if the division had been adequate Freedom would not have been a problem. As for the
pursuit of happiness: antiquity assumed that the
generality of mankind were incapable of happiness;
the Christian world inherited the tradition of
antiquity. Whatever happiness may mean—and its
definitions all carry stigmata from metaphysics—the
pursuit of it, when the Declaration of Independence
was composed, was a class privilege. Judge for
yourselves if it be any less so now. . . .

If it be, if the pursuit of happiness, together with
life and liberty have in fact undergone a change of
status and distribution and been transformed in any
degree from privileges of the few into rights of the
many, it is because they were the shadows cast before,
of a new and growing power. This power was the
power of wealth won in trade; it expressed the
changing economy of the times. It upset the balance
of the classes. Its dimensions measured the freedom
of those who possessed it. Toward the middle of the
eighteenth century there became noticeable, in different spots in Europe, a shift in the caste incidence of
real property. It began to pass from the hands of the
hereditary nobility into the hands of merchants and
master-workmen, who made up in gold and goods
and credit what they lacked in lands. With it moved
social and political power, consequently liberty. Not
simply, not easily. One by one, and each only after
sharp and bitter struggles, the privileges of inherited
caste became the liberties of the acquiring class.
One by one the restrictions upon their activities in the
economic establishment and the social and cultural
structure of their countries broke down before their
power. In England toward the middle of the nineteenth century their attitude became definitive, their
program generalized and grounded in a philosophy.
Attitude, program and philosophy may be summed
up in the term *Liberalism*. With few exceptions the
advocates of Liberalism were members of the non-
hereditary propertied classes. They were persons
who had something to gain from the loosening of
the social structure and were possessed of the power,

if not the technique, to bring that loosening on. They were persons who would be able, in the looser society, to move more freely, to breathe more fully, to eat more and better things, to wear more and better clothes, to try out their powers and expand their lives in other respects. Their philosophic voices were J. S. Mill and Herbert Spencer.

In France the shift of social and political power developed into an avalanche with the usual accompanying catastrophes. The event is called the French Revolution and among professional libertarians and revolutionaries is the theme of endless scholastic discussions. It is French, of course, only geographically; only because the process of social change of which it is a phase took on an acuter form in France than in other countries. Morally, the French Revolution is international. It ran its course through Europe and America. It petered out only in the canalizations of machine industry. In England, for example, the social process of which the French Revolution is a phase, was far slower, and with consequences more genuinely revolutionary. Liberalism became the *credo* of a party, which began by seeking to lay open, first to its own class, and then to wider and wider ranges of the masses of men, ways of living and doing and thinking that had until then been shut to them. Liberalism is a libertarian movement thus: a breaking of bonds, an opening of doors—in politics, in industry and commerce, in art, in learning, in education, in play and in work—which men and women had hitherto been forbidden to pass through. You may gather something of the import of this movement if you recall that all over nine-teenth-century Europe, and in England to this very day, the gentleman's sport is the workingman's crime; the gentleman hunts and the workingman poaches; the gentleman gets drunk "like a gentle-man" but a drunken worker is an immoral and irre-ligious beast. The difference, which is deep-rooted in the British social code and has its projections in the vaunted common law, is in the end one of wealth. Poverty in fact implies crime; wealth in fact implies privilege. Wealth is power. Without wealth in-herited privilege is an empty form. With wealth it becomes an effective right. The poor man takes a liberty, he makes free; the rich man exercises a pre-rogative, he holds an advantage. The hereditary nobility required force to impose and sustain the recognition of their inheritances in prerogative and advantage. This force in the end was wealth. Once it could be met by equal or superior force, the in-heritances ceased to be favoring differentials: they lost their pull. A generalized "law and order" re-placed private authority; personal security became a right of the masses of the poor and an objective in the program of their liberation. Their endeavor to participate in the privileges of their betters lost the stigma of criminality.

III

The hunt, especially the fox hunt, is the gentle-man's last stand—for a plain man to kill a fox is still the most heinous of abominations; much else that my lord was born to, he has allowed to become common by sharing. Take the franchise. Voting is a privilege. Universal manhood suffrage is far from being the rule even today; and it took many bitter struggles to enfranchise the unprivileged whose franchise is now regarded as a right, an exercise of their power as free men. The enfranchisement of women is a recent extension of this freedom, compelled by force and the fear of it far more than persuasion and goodwill. Both are achievements of liberalism. Both consist in the removal of obstructions which kept masses of human beings from behaving in ways which were the privilege of classes. By the act of voting, men suppose themselves to render effective that dictum of the Declaration of Independence that government rests on the consent of the governed. To exercise the suffrage is to set down your consent that the persons you vote for shall be your rulers, if elected. You consent to their looking after those public affairs that you can't or won't look after for yourself.

Such is the theory. It prevails even though the only connection it has with the event of voting is to rationalize in it the desire of the unprivileged to conduct themselves like the privileged. In naked truth, the notion that government is a just and rational power exercised on reasonable grounds or that the state is a rational association of men in order to secure the best life, is not borne out either by the conduct of individuals or the behavior of states. As an effective working establishment, the state is no more and no less than a group of individuals who by hook or by crook are in a position to use political in-

stitutions for the purpose of controlling and manipu-
lating other groups and other institutions and individuals: government is such a use; and political
theory is the analysis of what so happens, and how.
The libertarian ideal of government has simply confused the theory without genuinely altering the facts.
It is a rationalization.

The same is true of the economic establishment
and its theories. Today we scorn *laissez-faire*. We
give the expression the same opprobrium that we
give "Victorian." We won't tolerate what it means
in our progressive economic speculations. Yet its
history and accomplishment is that of a libertarian
endeavor. As a theory it was invented to vindicate
and to justify an economic practice seeking to free
itself from very complete restrictions by church and
state. Church prohibited interest; state enacted all
kinds of sumptuary laws, manipulated currencies,
regulated markets, and what not. It behaved very
much as intelligent American politicians try to behave
today, and for worse reasons. So the rising middle
class said, as their American descendants say after
them. "Hands off! Let government not meddle
with business! Let business men alone! *Laissez-
faire!* Business will take care of its own!" *Laissez-
faire* meant then the abolition of stupid and avid interference by privilege with the processes of the
national economy. Its consequences were the abolition of the corn laws, the opening up of the
economic domain as a free field without favor to
anybody who had courage enough to risk his property in new enterprises, the establishment of Free

Trade as the basic mercantile policy of Great Britain. And this had for consequence the rise of great business.

Great Business emerged as an entirely new form of economic endeavor because it made use of automatic machinery. Machinery generated the factory and the factory town. Whether or not these would have established themselves undefended by the principle of *laissez-faire,*—in the United States they depended on "protection"—certain of the evils they brought would not have. The implications of the factory system for the lives of workers have been so often repeated that they are trite; nevertheless . . . automatic machinery imposes the regimentation of all lives that have any contact with it. Men cease to be regarded as men. They are called hands. These hands manipulate specific knobs or levers or wheels of a great machine. The movements they execute are the same throughout the day, and repeated thousands of times. They are infinitely monotonous. They catch the mind in the clutch of their rhythm, repeating, repeating, without pause and without change. Under their obsession, everything is deindividualized, reduced to repetitive standard and rule. The man himself becomes an automatism. Beyond the machine his hours are also measured off. He wakes when a bell rings or a whistle blows. He punches a time-clock. He starts work and stops on signal.

From him this automatism, this regimentation of mechanical repetions spreads to the whole of society. Human nature struggles against it. We may observe the major aspects of this struggle in the spread of neurasthenia, in the arhythmic and tuneless character of modern music, in the glare and formlessness of the modern graphic arts, in the prominence of sex and crime as themes for literature. These are all endeavors after freedom and they are all problems.

With the automatism of repetition, imposed by the machines, goes also the automatism of organization. Take shoes. Before the rise of the machines of the United Shoe Machinery Company, one cobbler working at his craft would make all of two shoes—fitting, cutting, stitching, nailing—everything. Since machinery, it takes, I have been told, in all about two hundred people to make one pair of shoes. The shoe-worker in a factory is only one two-hundredth of a cobbler. He is utterly unable to make a pair of shoes without the collaboration, each in a fixed inevitable place, at a fixed inevitable phase, of one hundred and ninety-nine other people. Should any of these fail to do his part at precisely the time the process calls for it, the whole process breaks down. Because each phase of factory production is determined by automatic relations to the other phases, workers are no longer free individuals. The factory imposes upon them a mechanical interdependence. It robs them of personality without making them truly cooperative. Thus it exposes them to a new type of privileged manipulation, justified on the theory of "liberty of contract," and grounded in the philosophy of *laissez-faire*. Industrial freedom is thus made a problem through that which began by bringing it into existence. *Laissez-faire* is invoked

not only in the exploitation of "hands," but to fore-
stall and keep off any interference whatsoever with
oppressive and tyrannical abuses of economic power
won through *laissez-faire*. Recent American history
stinks with such abuses. And this is why today
laissez-faire is anathema among lovers of liberty;
we see it invoked to vindicate tyranny and injustice:
we forget that its first calling was to be a battle cry
of freedom.

IV

The intellectual world presents an analogous spectacle. With liberalism there came to Europe, and
first to England, a plan for secular public education
at public cost. Those of us who have been brought
up in the tradition of the free public school of
America cannot easily realize just what this means.
To get its full import you would need the contrast
of some country like Spain or any other clerically-
dominated European or South American country
or locality. In places of that kind the clergy have
entire charge of education. Consequently what is
taught the new generations is not how to invent and
enrich the future, but how to repeat and conserve the
past. They learn neither to seek nor to inquire; they
learn to accept and to assent. Dogmas are transmitted as for eternity; doubt is discouraged and
punished. Independent thinking is treated as rebellion; confrontation of the sanctioned "truth" with
forbidden fact or outlawed thought is treated as
blasphemy or heresy and punished accordingly.
So the intellectual life had been managed in

Europe, from the day the Byzantine emperor closed the classic schools and gave the advancement of learning over into the hands of the Christian clergy. All schools, from the parish primary to the university, became then what we call today Sunday schools, religious schools, transmitting an infallible doctrine which could not successfully meet competition with teachings as much less infallible as they were more correct. For a long time education was a privilege of clergy; later, the military caste shared it spontaneously, because it had the power. But the masses of men won it as a right only through a bitter struggle against the clergy and their allies. The right is not yet entirely established as a fact. Clerical control has thinned down to theological influence; the free public secular school advances slowly and still has far to go. Its great propulsion comes from the rise of machine industry, with the great cities that it brought into being, and its need of a literate working class. Because of this propulsion, the free public school of industrial countries has become a national institution. It has driven the church-school down to a part-time industry. It holds a practical monopoly of its competitive field. But because of its size, it has had to revert to the standardized technique; because of its origins and backing, it has become the medium for the transmission of a new grammar of assent. The infallible dogmas of theology have given way to the sacred dogmas of patriotism and Big Business. These now provide the sanctioned "truths" which must not be confounded with forbidden fact and outlawed thought.

In one place the vocation of teacher is closed to you unless you swear you believe in the present form of government and the present state of society. In another you must not be a German, or a Pole, or a Jew, or whatever. In still another Evolution is anathema, or a certain conception of God: in still another, religion itself. Candor about the economic mechanism and its ways with the agencies of government is everywhere a menace to livelihood and limitation upon freedom of movement and expression. The American Constitution is now a most sacred law, hedged around with sanctifications. To discuss it as Charles Beard showed us how to is of the nature of blasphemy and sacrilege, and like so much going by those names, is both veracious and important. The variety of bounds set for the intellect is endless, and endlessly minute. Truths unpleasant to possible benefactors become academic pariahs. Truths unpleasant to voters and legislators controlling appropriations become Untouchables. Vested interests of the heart and the mind present themselves as perennial obstructions to free thought. Recall how so practically remote a speculation as the theory of relativity met in Germany with denunciation and organized assault on the score that it was a Semitic attack on the foundations of Christian and Nordic physics; how it was excommunicated in Russia because it was in conflict with dialectic materialism and the Marxist dogma.

To conclude this point: Free secular public education, which began as a libertarian enterprise whereby the masses of men might be enabled to consider and to use the knowledge that had been kept from them, has become an instrument whereby they are confined to such knowledge as the rulers of education think safe.

From the problem of free thought to the problem of free press is a natural, an inevitable, step. Indeed the first could not really be a problem unless the second were. Freedom to print and to publish is also a modern "right," and seems like other freedoms a function of power. It is a fundamental right, for without honest communication through the press we should be in entire isolation from the work of the world; we should know nothing of what is happening in science or religion or art or politics or sport or business; we should remain natural boors, limited to the gossip of our own home towns. Printing thus, Milton's "unlicensed printing," was from the first a privilege for which men sought the status of a universal right, and its history shows the paradoxes of the other rights. Publishing, especially the publishing of newspapers, became big business with the advent of great printing machines. Returns on investment became thus more important than excellence of service. News came to be gathered, not because it was an accurate record of what happens, but because it would enhance return on investment. News is that which can be sold to readers in large quantities, not that which is significant as event. Newspapers, consequently tend to contain a minimum of news and a maximum of entertainment. They tend to present both in standard form—the former as reports from a single source, the latter as "boiler-plate." They tend to avoid anything that will cut down circulation, alienate advertisers or otherwise exercise a negative influence on income.

These tendencies are all away from a correct record of events, all toward systematic and persistent distortion of the news. So well-known is this that an experienced and reflective journalist like Silas Bent gives serious thought to the proposal of a public censorship of the press, to neutralize the private censorship exercised by the owner of the invested capital. Thoughtful people have become suspicious of the press. If they see a thing, they say, in the papers, they doubt that it is true.

They say, and, I believe, they think they do what they say. But they don't really do it. Doubting is an arduous task, difficult to learn, painful to practice. It underlies the whole art of free thought. But we are not born to free thought. We are born to believe. The grammar of assent is our natural grammar. We spontaneously resist the upsetting of established ways by their confrontation with alternatives and competitors. We resent insecurity whether of mind and body. Hence the press, like the school, shuts us in; it confirms us in that grammar of assent which the school teaches. We not only endure it, we like it and demand it—until at last the time comes when the datum ignored, the event misrepresented, the truth falsified have won the power to challenge us. Then we feel the bonds. We say we must be free. And freedom of the press is a problem then.

V

Next consider the churches.

Our modern world is apt to pride itself on its religious tolerance, but this tolerance is surely a compensatory ideal beside the practical tolerance which prevailed in the ancient world. To the princes of the Christian Church, who are the guardians of an infallible revelation, religious liberty is an inconceivable idea. Every variant is of necessity a falsehood and heresy, and must be extirpated. Consequently, the Christian Church, in all its many forms, has ever been a persecuting church. But persecution is possible only where its victim is submissive or weak. Prior to the Protestant Reformation the Church was always stronger than the schismatic. After the Reformation, there were schismatics who could hold their own against the Church, and in the course of time, against each other. As each grew in numbers and in power, it became too strong to fight. In the course of time a sort of theological balance of power took form among them. In this balance the mutual fears and hatreds are still alive but inactive. On occasion they break out like volcanoes. The occasion is usually a new sect or another "subversive" idea. The current occasion is what is called Modernism. The rise of Modernism has made clear once more the depth of intolerance in the religious life. It has emphasized anew that tolerance, which we assume to rest on recognition of the right of another to live and move and have his being in his own way, according to his own vision, is in fact a fear of the power of the other to enforce his right against interference. Tolerance, in other words, is not a virtue in him who tolerates but a power in him who is tolerated. Freethinkers, for example, are still so few that no one who publicly declares himself such—not an atheist or an agnostic but simply a free thinker—could be elected to the presidency of the United States; a Roman Catholic not too close to the Church might be. Liberty of conscience and of worship, which is the ultimate implication of tolerance, had everywhere to be won by a series of enabling acts. Where, as in the United States, this liberty is guaranteed by a written constitution, the guarantee receives the same deference as the eighteenth amendment; bootleg intolerance develops in the form of secret orders, hooded fraternities, commercial boycotts and the like. These orders carry out unlawfully, but as champions of the law, the actions which the law forbids.

The law forbids! Here is the whole point of the libertarian movement of the nineteenth century which is the immediate ancestor of our contemporary ardors about Freedom. The movement prescribes little; it forbids much. It works in the main as a loosener of bonds, a spirit that denies. Its import is revolutionary, the while its ideal is law and order. As organic and self-conscious Liberalism it is involved in paradoxes, and seems in the end to be self-defeating.

VI

And this is why, on the whole and in the long run, Freedom is a problem to us moderns. The present generation feels that the freedom of the age's beginnings has become the slavery of its passing. All that has been established in its name and has taken root has grown into a heavy burden and a tyranny, oppressive almost to the limit of endurance. There is in the air, even among the Babbitts and the sons of Babbitts, the spirit of a vague rebellion. This spirit is the descendant, in a straight line, of the revolutionary Liberalism that constructed the Open Door to all those institutions which hem in and thwart the occidental mind today.

But it is not only angered by the oppression which these institutions have learned to practice, it is disgusted with their hypocrisy and shamed by their postures and pretenses. The great grandchildren of the American Revolution, for examples, are finding the Daughters of the American Revolution to be snobs and bounders. They are confronting professions with practice, maxims with conduct. The Freedom they look to now is set over against the institutions of democracy. The powers they rebel against are of tremendously greater range and subtler influence than the Liberalism that bred them ever conceived of. They are the powers of the "Great Society," the institutions of an industrial economy. In this economy a thousand miles is no more than ten were a hundred years ago; one hour now is as long as a thousand then. At this moment a millennium of homes in

New York are "listening in" to the same music as another millennium of homes in San Francisco and still another in London. At this moment a hundred newspapers in Chicago, in Paris, in Rome, in Berlin, in Jerusalem, are receiving a photograph being radioed from Pekin, which their readers will look at in their breakfast papers. All the people of all the Main Streets of the industrial world will be seeing this same picture, reading the same story with reference to it, and believing the same editorial comments about it.

In the Great Society the human environment, the environment of dress and diet and amusement and opinion, takes on an appalling uniformity. Never has there been an age in which the institutions and practices of civilized society were so much alike over such wide and varied areas. Never has there been an age in which the unity of the social structure and the social purpose has so clamped down upon the individual and so blurred and distorted his individuality. Because the machine cannot grow a different thing but only reproduce an identical one, the Great Society imposes like-mindedness upon us. During the Renascence, Rome and Naples, or Florence and Milan varied far more from one another than Paris and London or London and New York do today. And herein, perhaps, is the ultimate seat of the problem of Freedom in the modern world—in this overwhelming unification and repetition against which everything individual, spontaneous, variant and new is by its very nature condemned to raise a rebellious head.

FREEDOM AND ECONOMIC NECESSITY

By WALTON H. HAMILTON

I

THE ideal of freedom is the holy grail of social progress. It is the blessed state towards which we would have our changing culture move, yet it is forever just out of reach. We cannot set down the ends of our strivings, we cannot consider wherein our institutions need mending, we cannot contrive ways and means for improving the condition of mankind without using some such dynamic word as freedom. Yet, for all our knowledge and understanding, we can no more define freedom than we can realize it. It is a general term the core of which is an opportunity for man to make the most of himself in the fragment of the world about him. When translated into the reality of here and now, or of then and there, or of presently and over yonder, it becomes a multitude of particulars which have been and may be put together in endless permutations. What it is, what it means, what it promises vary with the circumstances of society, the institutions under which we live, and the thoughts which variously lie within our several heads.

There are, in fact, as many freedoms as there are persons to declaim its greatness or to invoke it in the name of humanity. To the ordinary man "free-

dom" means getting rid of something that interposes
a barrier between some desire of his and its attainment. It is a big word that justifies at least a Simian
protest in speech against some grand or petit institution which "cramps his style" or impinges upon his
personal conduct. To the negro in the South it
means the abolition of the restraints which have been
set up to keep him in his place; to the industrial
worker in the North, a desire to escape the daily
grind of his workaday life. The farmer in the West
sees freedom in an active relief by the government
of his acute economic distress; the business man
means by freedom getting rid of governmental restrictions, or at least of such of them as do not seem
to have been contrived for his advantage. The free
thinker protests against the dogma of the church, the
scholar against the power of boards of trustees, the
reformer against political machines. The epitome
of freedom to the New Yorker is the right to drink;
to the Kansan, the right to impose his antibibulous
notions upon others. At times freedom means getting rid of the Pope, the party in power, Wall Street,
labor agitators, or whoever or whatever should
straightway begin a *descensus Averno*. At others it
signifies rather the indefeasible and inalienable right
of the individual to go to the devil by whatever prim-
rose path that leads most gaily to the everlasting
bonfire. Only the annals of man's feverish activities
can show the many particular desires which he identifies with the cosmic urge to freedom.

Nor is it strange that this should be so. Man is a
rationalizing animal; he must have grand reasons

for his petty acts; he must use big words to describe
his little desires and the small circumstances of his
life. Yet the big words carry very different meanings
to men in different circumstances; for, in spite of
their abstractness and their grandeur, general words
cannot escape a likeness to the particulars which call
them into being. In England for centuries freedom
meant the maintenance of the established perquisites
and privileges of a social caste. It was a late day,
and one of some importance in the history of ideas,
when for the first time the adjective "individual" was
joined with the noun "'freedom." The specific
events of the English struggle with monarchy in the
seventeenth century, of the American war for independence, and of the American Civil War have given
to the word freedom a specific meaning. To us who
are in "the great tradition" the word is not easily
dissociated from the particular protests against King,
crown, and slavery which it was used to sanctify. To
Blackstone freedom meant being out of jail; to the
Supreme Court justices of the eighteen hundred and
nineties, "liberty of contract." Our freedom has been
called "wage-slavery" by men of importance in
Russia, and men of substance and standing among us
think that bondage is a mild term to apply to Russian
freedom. The word "freedom," in whatever language it be spoken or written, is a poor word for
communication between the peoples of the East and
the West.

Not only is there an Oriental and an Occidental
freedom, but there is a distinctively British and a
distinctively American freedom. As we look at the

tangle of human affairs from several angles of vision, there is religious freedom and political freedom,
legal freedom and economic freedom, personal freedom and group freedom, freedom to teach and
freedom to escape being taught, freedom to do
and freedom not to be done, freedom as current fact
and freedom as utopian promise. As useful as words
of ample sound, as broad as the stuff of philosophies,
as varied as the ways in which ideas may be put together, so is the utility, the breadth, and the variety
of freedom.

II

It is this capacity of the word for variety in meaning that endows freedom with a hazardous promise.
The word suggests opportunities for individual
attainment not yet realized; its broad confine has a
place which the constructive imagination and the conscious strivings of man can fill with institutions which
develop human capacities and give them more ample
scope. But the chance at a greater freedom is beset
with hazards which are inseparable from the use of
the term. For the circumstance which has been
crowded into the word, the particulars which have
gone into its making, the specific ends and issues
which it calls up in the mind narrow its meaning and
restrict its use. Men are prone to see the desirable
in terms of the historical, to reargue outworn questions, to fight again over issues long ago settled. The
word invites maintenance of freedom if the adversary
can be pictured as a military dictator, a monarch, or
a pope; it commits to an attack if the cause can be

paraded as against arbitrary taxation, the interference with trade, chattel slavery, or the pleasure of
an irresponsible king. It is, in fact, a summons to a
struggle like those which have already been fought
in its name. What has been is specific, what may
come to pass is not yet so; if the idea of freedom is
to find constructive use, it must be emancipated from
the particular content which makes it an intellectual
instrument for looking backward.

If freedom is to be put to constructive use, the
word must be freed from its negative connotation.
It must employ institutions rather than escape them.
As it has come down to us, the word liberty has been
closely associated with a struggle against autocratic
power in high places. The quarrels in which it has
been used to give sanctity to a cause have quickly
passed beyond inquiry and discussion into militant
procedure and often to armed hostility. The authority, against which there has been protest, has
generally been stripped of its power and ofttimes has
been overthrown. The dramatic or even catas-
trophic eclipse of an old institution, rather than the
slow and little controlled growth of a new one to re-
place it, has been the subject of conscious attention.
Hence the idea of freedom has come to be associated
rather with the process by which old controls are put
off than with the less conspicuous procedure by which
new ones are put on.

As a result there has grown up a theory that the
individual and the institution—unlike as they are—
are complementary and antithetical; that individual
freedom is to wax with the waning of political

authority; that an abridgment of the sovereignty of church or state means an enlargement of the sovereignty of man. The Constitution of the United States doles out its powers to the federal and to the state governments and reserves the residuum to the individual. The social thought of the second half of the nineteenth century divides the realm of human control into the domain of individual freedom and the province of government. In its terms, moreover, the authority of government can be increased only at the expense of personal liberty; and there is a sacred minimum of individual freedom which under no circumstances must be invaded.

However useful such a negative freedom is for an attack upon the lords of earth who attempt formally to rule mankind from Olympus, it fails to serve the constructive thought of today. To us the individual and the institution, personal discretion and social organization, are so very unlike that there can be no antithesis between them. However cabined and confined the individual, however iniquitous the institution, however we may despise the one and seek to dispense with the other, our condemnation is specific and not general. For, whatever their character, we cannot if we are to have individuals possessed of discretion, dispense with institutions of control in general. Man comes into the world, not as an embryo which time and an innate something will magically convert into an enlightened and rational human being; instead he is a bundle of very adaptable potentialities some of which chance and environment will convert into capacities. The development of his aptitudes for enjoyment and for attainment is dependent upon the richness and the variety of the opportunities about him. The breadth, the variety, the quality of this world of opportunity comes from the character of the social organization and what it can extract from the material and human resources at hand.

Accordingly, there must be institutions of control if there is to be a capacity for individual freedom. In a society in which individuals live isolated lives, there is no real freedom, even though there is no authority to forbid anything that men may choose to do; such liberty to do as one pleases has been aptly called "the freedom of the wild ass." In a society, in which institutions are inchoate and social organization backward, the dearth of authority does not improve the individual's capacity for wise choice. On the American frontier, which has already become a by-gone utopia to liberals, the individual was free of formal restraint and yet well-nigh without opportunities which invited choice. His occupation had to be selected from a scanty list, the limited chances at recreation he could take or leave, and the world of ideas was almost closed to him. The plain truth is that there must be developed capacity within and organized opportunity without or there can be no choice; the range of conscious discretion is the measure of personal freedom.

If freedom be positive, it belongs to tomorrow and not to today; if its essence be the capacity of wise choice, it must be attained. In its quest no one agency or institution is sufficient; the whole complex of arrangements which make up the government of society must be employed. It is the sequence of events in the Western world which has brought to the front church and state as conspicuous agencies of control. But even their reach is no narrow one; the church of "the age of science" is not the church of the Middle Ages; the state of a rising competitive nationalism is not the state of the era of big business. Never has the church been all church, never has the state performed all the functions of the state. The control in society can be distributed between its institutions in many ways, and the discretion which lies with a particular agency is a changing one.

Moreover, beyond church and state, there are many institutions which may abridge, deny, or enlarge the individual's freedom. The organization of family life gives the child's potentialities their first start towards capacities. The educational system may or may not "improve" the growing mind; but, in its true sense of controlled exposure, it gives or denies to the developing person a chance to find out what he can and what he cannot do. Likewise it furnishes opportunities for practice in the liberal art of personal choice. The law, which in a world full of a number of tangled things has an organic growth that transcends legislation, gives at least a crude form to human activities, and sets rough limits within which the individual must order his life. The press, the institutions for recreation and culture and parade, the organization of the frivolities of life, all have their places as factors in the making of the individual. One and all, in accordance with their characters and qualities, they give or withhold the stuff out of which personal freedom is made.

Not the least among the institutions which give or withhold the chance of freedom is the economic system. For many decades the industrial order has been advertised as a great cooperative enterprise carried on by a scheme of voluntary agreements among free individuals. Liberty of contract has been made the be-all and the end-all of personal freedom; buying and selling has been regarded as a process by which individuals have voluntarily kept industrial activity going; the domain of business has been defended against control from without in the name of freedom. Yet the economic system is as much a scheme of human arrangements as is the church or the state; its control over what individuals are and what they do is just as continuous and just as compelling. At its basis lie usages respecting property, the use of labor, contract, and purchase and sale; it is carried on under a code of rules called competition. Its practices of dubbing goods and services with prices, using profits as the bait to get goods produced, and centering discretion in "executives" are as conventional as the ways of the family or the state. Business is not business because a pecuniary motive is a part of an innate human nature; rather, in response to the constraints of business usage, man's industrial actions are impelled towards pecuniary ends. These institutions have grown up in response to various needs; each of them has a long and checkered history; more than one of them has been made over in our own lifetime; the scheme as a whole falls far short of a conscious social provision for human needs.

Nor is the scheme of control "automatic." The empire of business moves by personal discretion and the exercise of formal authority. In every business it is the judgment of the few who compose the administration which counts for most. In the great industrial system there are a few places of great strategic importance; those who chance to occupy them make judgments the results of which run out to the fringes of industry and down the generations. Because of the exalted place which business has in our culture, and because of the high values we impute to material things, the arrangements which make up the economic order are of supreme importance. With us, as with perhaps no other people, they may advance or stay the development of freedom.

From all of this it follows that a constructive freedom has its roots in the informal controls of society. Its attainment may demand a curbing of formal authorities, their abolition, or their remaking to meet its needs. But it demands even more that the usages of life, the convention and traditions, the ways of thought and action which are institutions be of a kind to produce individuals with the capacity for freedom. Our common-sense, our ways of using our resources, our habits of organizing our activities into the life of the folk are more compelling and more lasting than officers of state, or legislative enactments, or business policies. Those who order us to do their wills are here for a moment and give place to others; their mite of discretion is pent in by the ceremonials of the places they hold and by the demands of the institutions they serve. We who obey are creatures of the ways of thought and the order of life about us. Had the circumstances of our lives been different, we know not who we would be, what universes would lie beneath our hats, what things of life we would choose to serve. Whether we be among those who give or among those who receive orders, our folk-ways create within us a folk-thought which we take to be our own and obey.

So it is that the quest for the sources of freedom runs back of formal authority to the informal controls which are constantly making and remaking us in their own likeness. If we are to be free, it must be by the grace of a social organization which has been made to serve the ends of freedom.

III

It is quite the fashion among those who discuss freedom to make "economic necessity" the villain in the piece. The professors of the dismal science expel man from Eden, condemn him to eat his bread in the sweat of his brow, and keep him too close to starvation to allow the stirrings of liberty within him. In a doctrine of scarcity, which they have invented, they make his world one of limited resources, erect a barrier of costs between man and the wherewithal of life, and keep social affluence afar by multiplying his numbers.

The preachers of the gospel of socialism keep man in bondage in Egypt, give him only enough to sustain his life as an animated implement of toil, and have

his surplus product expropriated by a class of opulent
and parasitic masters. Lest there be a chance of an
easy escape into the Promised Land, they contrive a
system which they call Capitalism in which they keep
him shut fast.

A group of young Americans, who are far from
being spoken of as authorities, endow man with a
bit of rationality and a lot of muddle-headedness,
place him in a Simian world, surround him with a
tangle of social arrangements which are none too
purposive, and make his bondage to ignorance and
poverty a product of his inability to solve his own
problems. They find him a prey to habit and a creature of circumstance, not because his resources are
scanty or his technology is backward, but because he
has never learned to organize industry in such a way
as to make the means of life serve its ends. Differ
as they may in all else, the expounders of the several
theories are agreed that there can be no genuine
freedom until the constraints of the economic system
are relaxed.

The compulsions of economic necessity require no
elaborate parade. A few paragraphs, set down in the
methodical manner of a catalogue, will cause them to
live afresh in the reader's mind. A heavy volume
could not be made to hold them in all their colorful
variety.

First, and most conspicuous, is the ordinary man's
bondage to the making of a living which is never
quite made. Whether he be tinker or tailor, advertiser or bond salesman, realtor or mortician, he must
make such terms with an industrial system as his

immediate necessities will allow. The institutions of business consign him to a groove or catapult him restlessly from job to job, take a first mortgage upon his time and energy, and make the other values of life residual claimants upon his attention.

Second, is the tyranny of the system of prices; from this there may be respite, but there is no lasting escape for farmer or broker, wage-slave or industrial baron. Each must order his affairs as best he may with one eye upon income and the other upon the outgo associated with what he would have or do or be. An established way of life and a standard of living has already imposed its own terms upon the bulk of expenditure, and the surplus of income which invites discretion is small. Would one have a dinner at the shore, a trip to Europe, a new car, the prestige which comes from an elaborate entertainment, the matter is referred for approval or disapproval to the dictates of the price-system. The church is no longer the overlord of our private lives, the law we meet only on occasion, a contact with the processes of state is an occurrence; but the price-system, sovereign and insidious, is insistently with us always.

Third, the necessities which we call economic take our thought into bondage. It is our personal and immediate interest which we serve rather than the long-time interests of the larger groups to which we belong. The receipt of the next pay envelope, the meeting of the next installment on the car, the size of the next dividend, the renewal of the expiring contract, the maintenance and enlargement of the cur-

rent market becomes objectives of great importance.
As Simians we are not content to strive for little
things as little things; we must endow the objects
of our efforts with values larger than themselves. So
as bakers, trainmen, crusaders, and professors we
create our lay philosophies whose cosmic terms cannot quite escape the particular interests which they
justify. Thanks to economic necessity, "my interest"
becomes "mon droit" which in time becomes "dieu."
So our strivings are not for ourselves, but in behalf
of principles.

Fourth, our economic institutions make the big
things of life wait upon the little things. In cotton-
planting, in lumbering, in coal-mining whole industries are in disorder because all who are concerned
act as immediate circumstances dictate. As day follows day, owners, managers, workers, and consumers
settle the petty questions which come their way as
best they can. They make decisions the wisdom of
which cannot be tested for months or even for years;
yet the incident of their combined judgments makes
the jumble of affairs in the industry what it is.
There is no organization of the industry as a whole;
there is no procedure by which questions which are
of concern to all can be consciously considered and
deliberately settled. Such questions as the claim of
the industry upon the human and material resources
of the community, the efficiency or inefficiency with
which it is run, its service to consumers, and the liv-
ings which it gives to workers are settled, not by
planning and guidance, but as a mere by-product of a
medley of little decisions addressed to a multitude of

passing matters. It all makes for a squandering of thought, of which there is hardly enough to go round, upon the little things of the moment.

Fifth, and perhaps most important of all, are the compulsions which lurk in the process known as economic development. The elements of a changing culture are many and tangled, and as yet we know far too little of the impact of institution upon institution to be sure of getting what we want. A valiant crusader, determined to improve the conditions of the masses, elaborates some principles of wage-determination which promise to make for better incomes,—only to discover that as applied by a commission a generation later they tend to keep earnings down. A good Samaritan launches a campaign to increase the span of human life,—and is so successful as to aggravate the problem of unemployment. A group of coal operators, with no more angelic intention than reducing their costs, resolve to make their mines more efficient, to find out when it is too late that the increased capacity which they have created threatens to drive them into bankruptcy. A small group of men took a few centuries to contrive the price-system, accountancy, and the other devices of pecuniary calculation—little thinking how many, even of the intangible values of life, would eventually be reduced to its commensurable terms. An even smaller group of men, aiming at nothing more disturbing than pursuing their intellectual problems and increasing their profits, gave an innovation called the machine process the run of their shops,—and started a social revolution. All because of their curiosity, trades have been remade into a crude and gigantic industrial system, cities have been piled up, and a heritage of common-sense slowly accumulated has been divorced from the facts of an industrialized world. In long-time willing and striving, the march of events still holds the trumps. It happens as a consequence that intent is one thing and event quite another. The resulting inability of man to control the long-time circumstances which make him what he is is hardly to be thought of as freedom.

Such a catalogue of the many and devious ways in which economic necessity holds our thought and actions in bondage might be continued indefinitely. The items which have been set down and the many others which may be made to keep them company may be grouped under almost whatever heads you will. There is, and so far as we can see the course of human events there can be, no escape from the constraints of the industrial system; economic necessity must continue to play the role of villain in the drama of personal freedom. But villains are not all alike, and the quality of villainy is subject to amendment. Our economic arrangements, however much we would keep them intact, are changing. They are far too strongly entrenched and far too stubborn to give up their wills entirely. But so far as it is possible, they should be kept in their places as instruments, and be made to serve the ends of life. Surely economic institutions may be reshaped to make a greater contribution towards the development of individuals with a broader and more discriminating capacity of choice.

IV

Rich man, poor man, preacher, salesman, economist, socialist, Philistine, and intellectual are champions of a newer and a better freedom. They seem to be agreed that its coming is dependent upon some relaxation of the pressure of economic necessity. Since each has come to his conclusion in his own way, there is no agreement about the economic necessity which must be domesticated. Since each has his own notion of the freedom which is desirable, there can be no common route to very different destinations. A brief presentation of the more dominant views may serve to clarify the issue of personal freedom and economic institution. Even an overdogmatic appraisal of them will fail to resolve the question.

A group which we have with us always would relax the pressure and free the individual by calling upon mankind to mend their personal ways. They preach the doctrine of thrift and industry; men must make and keep themselves more efficient, save all they can, and prudently keep their numbers down. In all of this there is probably nothing that is wrong; its shortcoming is in what is overlooked. In its terms the arrangements which make up the economic order are immutable and beneficent; it is only man who is vile and should be called to repentence. In its terms the problem is ended by man's being blessed with more of the good things of life; either their enjoyment is the whole of freedom, or in some automatic way the overplus of goods and services gets itself commuted into enriched human capacities and into opportunities for their employment. Seek first the gains of industry and thrift, and all other good and unspecified things will be added unto you.

Another group, less reverant but more vocal, would achieve freedom for all by a single concerted act of revolution. They are conscious that the constraints of the economic system impinge upon the individual; they attribute all the narrowness and poverty of human bondage to wage-slavery; they seek the millennium through an overthrow of capitalism. Once the institutions of iniquity are destroyed, they depend upon the action of economic forces to set the other aspects of man's life and the other institutions of society to rights.

Again, the trouble seems to be with what is not taken into account. The analysis and the program look very much like economic orthodoxy turned wrong side out. Instead of casting the devil of indolence out of man, the institution of greed which embodies his satanic majesty must be destroyed. A great moral victory for the proletariat, like the individual's triumph in the battle of thrift, will be followed by whatever is essential to freedom. In its wake there will come a proletarian law, a proletarian literature, a proletarian morality. Again, the theory is established upon a negative conception of freedom. The revolution over, liberty will come as an unfolding of the human spirit. There seems to be no need for an establishment of a scheme of social arrangements which will develop the aptitudes of man and make him in reality what potentially he is.

Most important of all, revolution is not the surest

and most delicate tool in the kit of social reform. Its use is attended by grave hazards; it has the habit of missing its objective and doing violence where it was never intended to go. The technique of wielding it towards a fixed and specific objective has not yet become a fine art, and its competent practitioners are not yet licensed. This is not to say that it should never be employed, for there may be occasions of great need when no other weapon is available. But, since time has an incurable habit of interposing between what we intend and what we accomplish, revolution is only for those who want something better, without caring overmuch what it is in particular, and are willing to take very long chances. But even at best it is only a clearing of the ground for the development of new institutions; in and of itself it falls far short of producing a culture in which men may be free.

Between the right and the left there are innumerable positions. Few of these are unoccupied by individuals or groups, each of which knows quite beyond peradventure the road that leads away from human bondage. The procession is too long and its numerous members too loquacious to be passed in review; hence a single group, and a badly-assorted one, must represent the heterogeneous legion of apostles. The common tie that binds its members together is their belief that the tyranny of things economic can be broken by the abolition or the revision of some one agency of control; they differ in that they select for the sacrifice very different institutions. The single root of all industrial evil may be an arbitrary system of taxation, some monetary system that holds debtors in bondage, some one of the many institutions of property, an iniquitous system of marketing, or the business practice of treating human labor as a commodity. It is unfortunate that so hopeful and so heroic a procedure should amount only to economic priestcraft; it finds a single source for all industrial malady, and exorcises it by the use of a panacea. But none can say that the administration of the nostrum is of no avail, for economic arrangements are so sensitive and so interwoven that, whatever is tried, there are bound to be results. But what comes has little relation to what is planned, and the cause of freedom must sooner or later be championed by other crusaders.

Another and a subtler danger lies in this attempt to establish the conditions of liberty by circumventing some dastardly institution. Its champions naïvely come to think that they can make simple words stand for the abuses of which they complain and by outlawing the words get rid of the abuses. Once few there were who doubted that if chattel slavery were abolished, men would be free. At the end of the Civil War new institutions were created which left the former slaves in the state of life to which they had been accustomed. Even today the art of controlling the black man by getting him in debt is well understood, and as yet a final chapter cannot be written to "the end of involuntary servitude in the South." The American Federation of Labor poured out heroic effort to write into the law of the land "a charter of freedom" specifying that the labor of a human being is not a commodity, and won only a great rhetorical victory for its pains. Instances might be multiplied; but unless those who would mend things push their thought beyond words, it is usually possible for those who are attacked to furbish up the diabolical institutions and tuck them away behind newer and nicer names.

In addition, one economic institution shades off into another so imperceptibly that the villain has an easy chance of escape. Slavery may cease to be a mark of degradation and become an insignia of caste. In the ante-bellum South there were slaves who found compensation for bondage in lording it over other negroes who were their own personal property. In Rome, with the gradual development of the imperial system, slaves of the Emperor came to be ministers of state, possessed of great authority and buttressed about with high social position. More than once a wages-system has been employed with slavery, and profit-sharing, industrial government, and other modern fads were not unknown in the Cotton Kingdom. Likewise a system of free labor may mask involuntary servitude. In a country in which industry is depressed and unemployment is rife, one who has jobs to dole out may have workers upon his own terms. They obey him as if they were legally his own property; the difference is that he is put to no expense to keep his employees from running away.

So it is, too, with other economic institutions. Very slowly, but quite unmistakably, in these United States, public equities are being established in what

is still known as private property. Someday some
one will win immortality by showing how private
equities are being established in what in Russia continues to be called public property. After all, words
are easy things; they are loose terms that describe
bundles of particulars that seldom exist in the same
combination. They belong rather to the forms that
we love to think human relationships take than to the
variable reality which analysis discloses. The route
towards freedom must start from the substance of
things; no reform of words is sufficient.

What we need, then, is a realistic, an intelligent,
and a persistent attempt to recreate economic institutions to make them serve the ends of freedom. The
tyranny of economic necessity comes, not from the
wrongfulness of economic arrangements, but from
their backwardness. The pressure of economic compulsion is to be relieved, not by the abolition of institutions which impinge upon human development, but
by consciously bringing the scheme under which our
industries are organized up-to-date.

A helpful approach to the problem is a conception
of three closely related arts, that of the way of life,
that of industry, and that of economic control. The
art of the way of life in its development furnishes us
with our ends. The art of industry, which is technology, converts human and material resources into
goods which we can use. The role of the art of
economics is mediation between the means of living
and its objectives; its task is to contrive a scheme of
organization whereby our industries are made to
serve the ends of life. Since these arts exist together

in a changing world, the development of each of them is conditioned by the others, and yet they can never be in accord.   There has in a short span in history been a moral evolution; the idea of the fulness of life has come to dominate our ethical values. In even a shorter period there has occurred a technological revolution which has multiplied the potential means of life many fold.   Likewise of late there have been devised many ingenious institutions of economic control.   Yet, compared with the art of industry, and possibly with the art of the way of life, the art of economics is woefully backward.   To a large extent we still use the devices and procedures of petty trade to subdue a great industrial system and make it serve our needs.   This is the real reason for the great economic paradox; that the masses of men lack the material means for personal development and for the fulness of life, yet society possesses a great unused surplus capacity to produce.

There may, elsewhere, be a place for a scientific economics, which boldly sets out to study objectively the means of life without raising questions about the ends they serve.   But there is also a place, whether it be economics or something else, for a conscious improvement of the institutions under which our industries are organized.   Such an attempt must make the best terms it can with the machine-process, for technology is a powerful thing and has a habit of having its own way.   Such an art of control has to do with the making over of a tangled scheme of institutions; it can, no more than art or engineering or medicine, reduce its procedure to a simple formula; it must, like every art and every technique, grow slowly at the hands of its practitioners. Its development must come with difficulty; for those who must push it forward are creatures of its backwardness and can by no means escape the necessities of the moment by which they are beset. But it must, if it is to mediate between technical processes and the uses of wealth, serve ends which are beyond itself, and among the most important of these is the development of a society in which a rich choice is possible and of individuals possessed of a discriminating capacity to choose. The age of magic is past; we must pay for what we are to have; and there is no easy price for even so much of freedom as Simians may hope to possess.

v

All of this falls short of an answer to the question of freedom and economic necessity. It states the issue rather than resolves it; it raises more questions than it settles. Freedom has been cried in the name of rebellion and in that of authority; it has been the goal of the crusader who has gone forth to find the promised land and of the stalwart who has sought a return to the flesh-pots of Egypt. Surely it may be invoked in the cause of a conscious reorganization of the institutions of society to make them serve our needs. Its nature, its promise, its hazards cannot be revealed in an essay; else it would not be the great human adventure.

So it is that the quest for freedom is concerned, not with the fact of restraint, but with its quality;

not with the fact that institutions close in upon man and mould him in their likeness, but with their character and the kind of stamps which they leave; not with the fact that tyranny has its seat in social arrangements, but with their peculiar incidence upon the human lives which are their products. Freedom is not to be found by so easy a trick as toppling a few potentates over, voting an administration out, or sending the most titanic of titans to their eternal reward. It demands the slow, tortuous, painful recreation of the institutions under which we live and think and do.

But the ideal of freedom is a thing we cannot do without. It stands, more than any other word, for the possibilities of human attainment. It invites to efforts at its realization, because we know that it may come to have a content with which our minds cannot now endow it. If it can never be attained, it can at least point the way from human bondage. In the conscious striving after social improvement freedom is and must remain the holy grail.

HOW A CATHOLIC LOOKS AT FREEDOM

By Rev. John A. Ryan, D.D.

LIBERTAS praestantissimum naturae bonum[1] are the opening words of the original text of Pope Leo XIII's "Encyclical on Human Liberty." While the great Pontiff used these words specifically of freedom of the will, they may not inappropriately be applied to the whole realm of free action. In its most general comprehension liberty means immunity from restraint. To the extent that man is restrained by any forces, whether psychological or physical, he is incapable of deliberate and purposeful action. Without action of this character there can be no achievement, no self-determination, no development of personality. Freedom may be conveniently classified under eight heads.

1. Psychological Freedom

By this is meant freedom of the will. It may be defined as the power to act or to refrain from acting in a certain way in a given set of circumstances. Not all actions of man are free. His physiological acts or processes are, of course, determined by forces that are only indirectly or not at all under the control of his will, for example, respiration, digestion

[1] "Liberty, the most outstanding gift of nature."

50

and heart action. It is only what the Scholastic philosophers called "human acts" that are, or may be, free: namely, those which are performed with advertence of the intellect and consent of the will. All these are potentially free, but not always actually free. Acts which are performed in relation to only a single motive, in response to a sudden and sharp stimulus, such as slapping at a mosquito that has inflicted a bite, are not free in any adequate sense of the term, although they might be if a contrary suggestion or motive had entered consciousness during the interval between the bite and the initiation of the impulsive reaction. Many of our habitual daily actions are actually indeliberate, or performed in relation to only one motive and without advertence to any other course of action than the one which takes place in consequence of the habit and its related circumstances. To be sure, both these classes of acts are potentially free, and in most cases would be actually free if an alternative motive, or action should come into the consciousness.[2]

Freedom implies choice between or among motives. Hence, there is no such thing as "motiveless volition" which has been attributed to believers in freedom by some determinists. Obviously we cannot will anything unless it is apprehended by, and appears to, the intellect as good. *Nihil eligitur nisi sub specie boni*—"nothing is chosen except under the appearance of good"—is the traditional formula

[2] The Reverend Michael Maher, S. J., goes so far as to say that "a very large part of man's daily action is indeliberate, and therefore merely the resultant of the forces playing upon him; . . ." *Psychology*, p. 397.

by which Catholic philosophers have expressed the fact that a motive is always a prerequisite to any act of the will.   Therefore, there is no such thing as causeless volition.   In free acts the adequate cause is always the will itself choosing between alternatives.

The proofs that the will is free, in the sense and to the degree just explained, cannot be stated here at length.   The most important arguments are those drawn from the testimony of consciousness and the ethical notions of responsibility, desert, blame, and remorse.   Our consciousness assures us that some of our acts are free, and that they proceed from us in a manner totally different from acts that we perform under compulsion.   In the exercise of freedom we act; we are not acted upon.   There is no more reason for rejecting the testimony of consciousness when it assures us that our wills act freely than there is for rejecting its reports concerning external objects.   It is no more trustworthy in the second case than in the first.

If the will be not free, our moral perceptions concerning responsibility, desert, blame and remorse should all be completely changed.   We should have to think of ourselves in relation to our deliberate acts in the same way that we now think of the performances of hurricanes and brute animals.   Even the most convinced determinists are unable to look at their acts in that light.   The unique character of our notions of responsibility, desert, blame and remorse implies freedom in the acts to which they are imputed.   The universality and persistence of these ethical notions cannot adequately be explained on any other hypothesis except that these convictions represent psychical facts.

2. Moral Freedom

By some writers this term is used to designate freedom of the will. However, it is more properly applied to the moral lawfulness of an action. As freedom of the will means absence of psychic restraint, moral freedom means absence of restraint by the moral law. The Christian holds himself morally free to do everything that is not forbidden by the precepts of Revelation and of the natural law. Under the former head the Catholic includes the Commandments of the Church, and under the latter head, the laws of the state, the ordinances of the family, and of every other society to which he owes ethical allegiance. The man who rejects the Christian Revelation may, nevertheless, feel bound by the precepts of the natural law; or he may regard the state as the only power having moral authority to limit his freedom of action. That school of thought which is sometimes known as Continental Liberalism does not accept the Christian Revelation, nor any commands issuing from organized religion. In its more extreme form it refuses to be bound by divine law, for it holds that man is morally autonomous; that is, he is his own legislator and is under obligation to obey only the dictates of his autonomous will. His moral freedom is not limited by any commands from without or from above.[3] Such, at any rate, is

[3] The extent to which men can go in rejecting the authority of God, as regards both conduct and belief, is strikingly exemplified

the view of Kant and his followers. While they would not claim the right to do as they like, they do assert the moral lawfulness of all acts which are not forbidden by the autonomous reason, or the autonomous will.

3. FREEDOM OF CONSCIENCE

Under this phrase we understand freedom of thought and of opinion. It implies absence of restraint upon one's assents, judgments, opinions and conclusions. In this domain every person is psychologically free, for thoughts and judgments cannot be restrained either by external forces or by any internal influence, except that of reason itself.

Immunity from interference with the profession or the propagation of thought or opinion is sometimes called freedom of conscience, particularly in matters of religious belief. It is more properly designated as freedom of speech or expression. Sometimes a distinction is made between expression in the sense of mere avowal of belief and expression in the sense of propagating one's views and urging them upon others. Freedom in the former province is sometimes called freedom of conscience; in the latter, freedom of teaching. These are purely questions of usage.

While thoughts, judgments, and opinions are, for the most part, psychologically free, they do not all

in the following proposition, which is No. 3 in the Syllabus of Errors condemned by Pope Pius IX: "Human reason, utterly regardless of God, is the sole judge of true and false, good and evil, is a law unto itself, and by its own natural powers is adequate to safeguard the welfare of men and peoples."

enjoy moral freedom. One is not morally permitted to hold opinions that one knows to be false. Since the mind seeks truth, such an attitude is clearly irrational. However, this matter has practical importance only where the false opinion has a direct bearing upon conduct. Under the influence of prejudice or inclination men can and do adhere to doctrines and systems which they know or at least suspect to be false. They dislike to face the obligations of conduct which are involved in acceptance of the true doctrine.

Is one morally free to hold false opinions which one believes to be true? One is not morally free to do otherwise. The final guide of belief and conduct is conscience. Actions, whether of the mind or of the external faculties, which go contrary to one's conscience, necessarily appear to the doer as wrong. To disregard the verdict of conscience implies a willingness to violate the moral law. The judgments pronounced by conscience may indeed be false and wrong, but there is no rational alternative. Even when a person doubts his own judgment and accepts instead the judgment of others, he is obeying his own conscience as the final arbiter.

Conscience as understood in the preceding paragraph, conscience endowed with this final authority, is not a judgment or opinion or prejudice which one is morally free to manipulate according to one's desires and inclinations. It is a judgment sincerely and courageously formed on the basis of all the information that one can obtain. Freedom of conscience is not freedom to think what one will, but to think what one ought. Cardinal Newman's eloquent description may appropriately be quoted here: "Conscience is not a long-sighted selfishness, nor a desire to be consistent with oneself; but it is a messenger from Him who, both in nature and in grace, speaks to us behind a veil, and teaches and rules us by His representatives. Conscience is the aboriginal Vicar of Christ, a prophet in its informations, a monarch in its peremptoriness, a priest in its blessings and anathemas, and, even though the eternal priesthood throughout the Church could cease to be, in it the sacerdotal principle would remain and would have a sway." [4]

Since no one is morally free to reject the known truth, a Catholic is not permitted to hold opinions which are contrary to the teachings of the Church. He cannot do so with a right conscience. If, however, a Catholic comes sincerely to disbelieve in the Church he will, of course, be morally free to follow his false conscience. It is the only one that he has. On the other hand, any person who believes that the Church was founded by the Son of God, and by Him endowed with the prerogative of infallibility, cannot reasonably reject His teachings any more than he can reject the multiplication table. Even those formal doctrines and decisions of the Church and the Roman Congregations which are not infallible, must in ordinary cases receive the assent of the loyal Catholic. Such assent is not, indeed, absolute and unconditional as is that given to infallible propositions, but it is at least as reasonable as the assent

[4] *Letter to the Duke of Norfolk,* Chapter V.

commonly accorded to the hypotheses propounded by scientific authorities. In passing it might properly be observed that this so-called scientific age of ours is quite as addicted to receiving doctrines and opinions on the sole authority of great names as any age since the invention of letters. To the easy objection that Catholics were once obliged to give internal, although conditional, assent to the decree of the Holy Office condemning the teaching of Galileo about the rotundity of the earth, etc., the equally easy reply is that this is the one exception which proves the rule that even the non-infallible pronouncements of the Church command the assent of Catholics with complete reasonableness.

Freedom of conscience to reject the revealed truth is intelligible when it is asserted by those who honestly believe that no Revelation has been made, but it is difficult to understand when asserted merely on the basis of autonomous reason; for example, when men say that even though an infallible authority exists it must not be accepted. To accept the multiplication table limits and restricts the autonomous reason quite as definitely. Yet none of the defenders of the autonomous conscience in matters of religion apply their principle to the sphere of mathematics.

4. Freedom of Investigation and Research

The same principles apply here as under freedom of conscience. A Catholic enjoys full liberty of investigation and research in the sciences, both physical and social, except where they have moral or religious

implications. There can obviously be no conflict between the conclusions of science and the principles of
faith and morals. Where conflicts seem to exist
between the teachings of the Church and that of
science the latter will be found to consist, not of
demonstrated conclusions, but merely of hypotheses;
for example, the hypothesis of materialistic evolution. Materialistic science starts with certain presuppositions, such as, that man has no spiritual soul
and that there is no causality in the universe except
that proceeding from natural forces. Obviously this
is not science but philosophy—of a certain sort.
Questions of this kind are entirely beyond the reach
of the methods of science. When the Church con-
demns such doctrines it is rejecting, not scientific conclusions, but philosophical speculations. Catholics
likewise start from certain presuppositions. We are
convinced that Christ is God, and that He would not
and could not deceive us, when He endowed His
Church with infallibility. Our belief in this matter
is founded upon our examination of the historical
facts concerning the life of Christ on earth. This
method of establishing our presuppositions is entirely
scientific. Materialistic scientists and non-Christians
do not always take the trouble to examine the facts
dispassionately in order to ascertain whether our
presuppositions are worthy of acceptance. Frequently they reject the whole Christian system on the
basis of an *a priori* assumption, such as, "miracles
do not happen." This is clearly unscientific.

While it is true that some of the non-infallible
decisions of the Church authorities concerning Scrip-

tural, scientific and social questions have, to some extent, discouraged freedom of investigation and research among Catholics, this was and must remain inevitable. In the long run it has done much more good than harm. On the one hand it has placed a salutary check upon misdirected investigation; on the other hand it has not seriously nor practically interfered with the pursuit and acquisition of knowledge.

The antagonism which scientific men sometimes profess to find between science and faith is frequently due to a misconception of the latter. They think of faith as some kind of feeling, a subconscious yearning for the ideal of the divine, an inner experience. They do not understand it as an act of the intellect, as an assent to truths ultimately known from history. Accordingly they look upon faith as utterly different from knowledge. Their conception is essentially that of the poet Tennyson, who wrote: "We have but faith, we cannot know; for knowledge comes of things we see." Of course, this is not faith as understood by Catholics. Our faith *is* knowledge.

5. Freedom of Expression and of Teaching

Just as there is no moral right to think or believe what one knows to be false, so there cannot be unlimited freedom of teaching or of expression. Obviously one can have no reasonable ground for desiring to publish what one knows to be false. Neither has one a valid moral claim to teach that which one thinks to be truth, but which is objectively erroneous. All rights are but means to some rational end. No such end is promoted through the propagation of error. Therefore, when the state or any other authority prevents the dissemination of false doctrine it promotes the interests of truth and it does not deprive the individual of any valid right of reasonable freedom. When the state is incompetent to decide whether a doctrine be true or false, whether it be helpful or harmful to the community, it acts irrationally and tyrannically if it attempts a policy of repression. The only instances in which the state is competent to decide this question are those involving violations of good morals and direct incitements to riot or revolution. Even in the case of obviously false teaching toleration of freedom may be, and frequently is, the lesser evil.

6. Civil Freedom

This phrase covers freedom of expression and teaching, and also freedom of contract, occupation, association, education, movement, and all the other immunities for arbitrary interference either by individuals or by the state, which are guaranteed in the constitutions of most modern states.

7. Political Freedom

In as much as it implies absence of restraint asserted by a foreign government or by a despotic domestic government, political freedom has a close affinity to civil freedom. As regards its positive content, it denotes the power of the citizen to participate in the activities of his government through the electoral franchise, office holding, and determining the political constitution.

Concerning political freedom and political rights the traditional Catholic theory is fundamentally democratic. It holds that the right to rule comes ultimately from God through the people. The latter have the right to determine the form of the government and to select its ministers. From the Middle Ages until comparatively recent times Catholic writers on this subject were practically unanimous in teaching that the people were also the depository of the civil authority which they received from God and transferred to the rulers whom they designated. Even if we hold with the minority of Catholic political writers that authority is conferred directly by God on the persons chosen by the people to govern, we still attribute to the people the decisive political power, both as to rulers and to the Constitution.

When a constitution has once been established its terms, of course, define the right of the people to participate in the government. In a republic they are empowered to select the officials at regular intervals. Generally speaking, they have no right to change such a government between elections. Nor have they a right violently to overthrow even a monarchical form of government, unless it has degenerated into a persistent and obstinate tyranny. The decisive factor in all questions of political freedom is the welfare of the people. Any form of government which safeguards this purpose is legitimate. Any change which is necessary to attain it is likewise legitimate, provided that it is carried out by methods which are not contrary to the moral law.

8. Economic Freedom

This category is relatively new in political discussion. To a considerable extent it is identical with civil freedom. The rights enumerated in the decision of the Supreme Court in *Allgeyer* v. *Louisiana* describe both civil and economic freedom. The liberty guaranteed by the Due Process Clause of the Fourteenth Amendment comprises, said the Court, "Not only the right of a citizen to be free from the mere physical restraint of his person, as by incarceration, but the term is deemed to embrace the right of the citizen to be free in the enjoyment of all his faculties, to be free to use them in all lawful ways, to live and work where he will, to earn his livelihood by any lawful calling, to pursue any livelihood or avocation, and for that purpose to enter into all contracts which may be proper, necessary and essential to his carrying out to a successful conclusion the purposes above mentioned."

Economic freedom, however, has positive elements which are not contained in the foregoing or any other formulation of civil freedom. This positive element stresses opportunity rather than absence of restraint. It includes all those social and economic conditions which are necessary for a reasonable livelihood and a reasonable development of personality. Chief among these conditions are: legal protection against extortionate economic contracts and the various forms of economic oppression to which these frequently give legal authorization, and adequate opportunity to form and conduct the kind of unions and associations which are desired by the various economic groups. This measure of economic freedom is not yet secured by law in any modern state.

The foregoing survey of the various kinds of human freedom has been too brief to constitute a comprehensive and complete description. Nevertheless, it is sufficient, I think, to show that the Catholic's view of freedom is adequate to the attainment of all the rational ends of human action.

THE PROTESTANT VIEW OF FREEDOM

By F. J. FOAKES-JACKSON

YOU have invited me to speak upon a subject which is very difficult to me for two reasons. First, except that I am not a member of the Church of Rome, I do not know how far I am entitled to be called a Protestant; and in the second place, what Protestant can speak for such a heterogeneous body as is comprised under the name? A Roman Catholic can speak with a certain definiteness. To him a man, as far as his duties as a citizen are concerned, can live under any form of government, provided it does not try to force him to act contrary to his religious obligations. As an individual he has the right to order his life as he pleases, provided he does nothing contrary to the laws of Christian morality. But as a member of the Church he is expected to be guided by the authority of those who are set over him in the Lord. Even then he is allowed a right to his own opinions, though he may not question certain things which the Church considers to be essential to the Christian Faith.

Then the main difference between the Catholic and the Protestant is that of authority. The Catholic priest claims and often exercises the right to regulate the conduct and habits of those committed to

his care. He can still enforce his commands by refusing absolution; and has, perhaps, other means
of bringing pressure upon the recalcitrant. But, except for his personal authority and his influence with
the members of his congregation the Protestant minister has little or no authority. The average church
member claims the right to direct his life as he
pleases, uninfluenced by the sanctions or prohibitions
of his minister. To take a concrete example. In a
Catholic city if the bishop were to warn his flock
not to purchase or advertise in a newspaper because
it published what was injurious to faith or morals,
its fate would probably be sealed. Suppose, however, one of our great Protestant preachers were to
denounce a publication in this city, he would almost
certainly give it a good advertisement. There are
still ministers who object to dancing, and would prevent members of their congregations from indulging
in it, nay, it is contrary to the principles of some very
large churches. But people see no harm in dancing,
and they dance. In a certain sense conscience is that
which restrains a Protestant, and authority a
Catholic; and so far as this goes the Protestant religion is the freer of the two. Yes: freer because
its power is more limited; but is it more free in
Spirit? To decide this one must appeal to history.

We must go back to the times just before what is
known as the Reformation, more than four centuries
ago. There we find the Catholic Church with power
greater than can now be conceived. It controlled
every act of life, the clergy claimed, and were believed to have the salvation of each man dependent

on their will. To question their authority meant
death: the man who thought for himself literally
took his life in his hands. This is not mere Protestant
declamation—it is simple truth. Catholics may re-
gret the Reformation, and declare that Luther did
infinite harm by his protest; but not one of them
today would tolerate what went on at the time; and
there was a Catholic as well as a Protestant reformation. We are apt to forget that the period
before the Reformation was a widespread moral
anarchy, which despite the powers it claimed, the
Church was powerless to restrain. The newly revived knowledge of the ancient world caused much
the same reaction against religion as the new science
of our day is thought to be doing in this generation.
As the one had made many forsake and despise
(often wrongly) the old scholastic learning, so the
new scientific teaching is discrediting the Bible with
us; and men, free from what they supposed to be the
sanctions, on which morality was assumed to be
based, revolted against all restraint. The state of
the late Medieval Church though nominally united
under one government was well nigh as chaotic as is
the Christianity of today. In Rome the great ec-
clesiastics, despairing of saving the Church by religion, strove to preserve it by making its capital the
center of art and culture. So widely is the pagan
tone and character of some of the popes of the late
fifteenth century admitted, that when a few years
ago the Anglican bishop Creighton tried to excuse
the conduct of such popes as Alexander VI, he was
severely taken to task by the Roman Catholic his-

torian Lord Acton for in any way trying to palliate the sin and infidelity of the time. Luther had many sympathizers among avowed supporters of the old order. In Rome the order of the Theatines resolutely set themselves to combat the secularity of the Church, and later St. Ignatius Loyola was a stern reformer. The Council of Trent was a reforming council, and though it refused to listen to Protestant complaints, it reformed some of the most flagrant abuses of the pre-Reformation Church. Indeed it would have been impossible for the Church in the condition it was in at the beginning of the sixteenth century to win back to Catholicism all save the Northern nations of Europe. The so-called Catholic Reformation is almost as surprising as the Protestant.

But let us pass over this controversial topic and come to undoubted facts. The Reformation was a revolution: it destroyed an authority which had unbounded possibilities for good as well as for evil. The clergy—for it was against them even more than the See of Rome that popular indignation was directed,—lost their power, and what was there to take its place? I suppose that never in all its history was there more oppression, cruelty, injustice in England than in the reign of Edward VI when the Reformation was at its height. It was the same throughout Europe, for anarchy, at any rate for a time, must always follow revolution. The story of the Reformation is remarkably analogous to the great secular revolutions of our time. There were antagonists to all reform; conservatives who wanted a few moderate changes, but did not desire to go too far; reformers who wished the Church to return to what they deemed to be primitive simplicity; and anarchists who desired to break up the whole fabric of Christian society as it then existed. Luther had to contend with the most violent of fanatics and aimed at a cautious and moderate removal of serious abuses. Calvin with masterly skill created a new church polity. Some Anabaptists were guilty of the wildest excesses. In Scotland the so-called reforming nobility would have reduced the Church to a position of utter poverty and servile dependence and religion and education were both saved by the inflexible courage of John Knox. In England one has only to read Latimer's sermon to realize how frightful was the state of greed and immorality into which the country fell when its king, Edward VI, was a boy under the influence of his successive guardians; and the preacher, a fanatical anti-Romanist, was quite as unsparing a critic of the corruption of the Protestant governors. J. R. Green, the historian, frankly described the period as the Protestant Misrule. The leaders in this great revolt against priestly claims soon found that they had before them the task of finding a substitute; but before I attempt to relate how they endeavored to do so, let us consider what the Reformers meant by liberty.

I think they meant what St. Paul in writing to the Galatians calls "the liberty in which Christ hath made us free," and this had little or nothing to do with what we consider to be political or even religious freedom. The medieval Churchman was, in fact, far more interested in political liberty than many of the reformers. The schoolmen were many of them keenly interested in what we call political science and constantly discussed problems of government. And it should be noticed that in theory at least all rulers were elected and acknowledged by the people. The Pope and the Emperor, the two who in a particular sense were considered to be divinely appointed, were elected. Kings were not, as a rule, recognized as such till they had been solemnly crowned, when they were presented to their people and acclaimed as their lawful governors. By the end of the thirteenth century Western Europe was prolific in theories of government. The idea that any European monarch possessed divine authority to govern wrong is medieval is absolutely wrong. The coronation service in England to this day does not recognize hereditary right; and, till the sovereign had been crowned, he was not supposed to have any authority. The ceremony was not, as it has been for a long time, a pageant: it was a necessity. The nobility had to accept their monarch individually by their homage, and the people by their acclamations, when presented to them. In the Spanish kingdoms the power of the kings was severely limited. When the crusaders set up a model kingdom at Jerusalem in the twelfth century the king's authority was defined and the rights of every class of his subjects asserted. The only secular sovereign who could claim divine authority was the Emperor, and this was only in theory. Practically he was often almost powerless. Every school of thought had its own political theory. Thomas Aquinas claimed that all sovereigns were subject to the Pope; Dante, that secular power was vested in the Emperor. The Italian, Marsilius of Padua, the Englishman William of Occam, the French John of Jandun, elaborated theories of government and of the rights of the people. Even in matters of religion the papal autocracy and its claims were often sharply questioned.

There was further no idea of an irresponsible ruler: on the contrary the duties of the King towards his subjects were strongly insisted upon, as was their right to repudiate a tyrant.

With the Reformation a great change came over the scene. Feudalism had made way for monarchic absolutism. In Germany the princes had espoused the cause of the Reformation in opposition to the Emperor, and Luther, in gratitude for their support, had declared that subjects ought to follow their prince in the matter of religion. The power of the Pope was transferred to the territorial sovereign; and when, after Luther's death, a peace was made in Germany it was on the basis of each principality having the right to embrace Lutheranism or Catholicism, and its ruler authority to compel the inhabitants to adopt the state religion. Thus we get the germ of the theory of the divine right of kings. The king becomes a Messiah, the anointed of the Lord, and disobedience to him a sin against God. It is due in a great measure to Protestantism that the rights of the subject had to yield to the arbitrary power of the government. The Pope's power had apparently been broken, not that men might be free but that they might be subjected to monarchs. It is noteworthy that Luther, a man of the people, took the side of the nobles against the peasants, whose lot in Germany was far from enviable; but this was because his doctrine was in peril if he lost the support of the princes of the Empire. Out of the Reformation there arose the principle *cuius regio eius religio,* i.e., that the sovereign might determine the religion of his subjects.

A contrast, however, between the Tudor monarchs of England and their successors, the Stuarts, is instructive as has already been pointed out by Lord Macaulay. Henry VIII and his two daughters Mary and Elizabeth ruled as well as reigned. To all outward appearances they might seem to alter the religion of their subjects at pleasure, and no one who disputed their authority could hope for a long life. They rated their Parliaments as if they were composed of refractory schoolboys, and were served by their nobility on bended knees. But their title to the throne was always questionable; and both Mary and Elizabeth had been declared by Parliament to be illegitimate. Yet they interpreted the wishes of their people generally, and their religious policy was carried out constitutionally. Henry's persecuting acts were strictly legal; Mary resumed relations with Rome with the consent of a Parliament which successfully demanded some important modifications; and Elizabeth could yield with grace to the remonstrances of her Commons. Their 'divine right' was due to their strong wills and power of interpreting the national

will.   The idea of the divine right of kings as a
principle came in with the Stuarts, and was formu-
lated by the theologians in opposition to the claim
of 'divine right' by the papacy.   The failure of this
dynasty was due to the beliefs of its representatives to be above the law.   Insistence upon the duty
of 'passive obedience' by the clergy was in part due
to the Great Rebellion (1640-1660) in which
Church, King and Constitution had been involved
in a common ruin.   It was essentially Protestant, till
James II interpreted it as authorizing him to re-
introduce Romanism.   In its early stages in Europe
the great opponents of the arbitrary government of
kings sanctioned by religion were the Jesuits.   The
whole subject has been brilliantly treated by my late
lamented friend Dr. Figgis in his *Divine Right of
Kings*.

The ancient Church had claimed the right of dis-
ciplining its members, and had exercised it unspar-
ingly.   But just before the Reformation it had come
to pass that the temporal penalty for any sin might
be commuted for money.   This is what is meant by
the 'sale of indulgences' against which Luther had
protested.   The Protestant leaders, disgusted with
the laxity of the old régime, insisted upon a stern
discipline under which no sin should be unpunished,
and no satisfaction accepted in lieu of the ecclesiastical penalty.   In this way they sought to limit the
power of the Crown by making the king or the lay
magistrate the officer to carry out their decrees.
James I of England and VII of Scotland when he
ascended the English throne is said to have uttered

the pithy saying 'No bishop, no king.' His preference for bishops may have been in part due to his
theological knowledge, but was principally caused by
his experience as King of Scotland where the presby-
teries treated him with scant civility. Hooker in
England supports the Church as recognized by the
government because the Puritan discipline would be
well nigh unsupportable by the majority. Thus
Protestantism stood for restrictions of liberty
greater than those of the pre-Reformation period;
for absolute monarchs, to whom Scripture com-
manded unquestioning obedience; and for a Church
whose discipline could not be tempered by mercy.
Moreover the old Church had at least taken human
nature into consideration. It had recognized the
need of mankind for enjoyment, and had encour-
aged innocent and manly forms of amusements. Protestantism, where dominant, condemned all pleasure,
and sought to make life a gloomy preparation for a
hereafter of saintly rapture for the few, and eternal
torment for the many. Puritanism, when it was
dominant in England and Scotland, certainly did not
encourage liberty; its régime was a tyranny, none
the less endurable because it was efficient. It frowned
upon all enjoyment, however innocent in our eyes,
and when it condemned the sport of bear-bating it
was, as Lord Macaulay says, not out of consideration for the bear, but because it gave the spectators
pleasure.

But Protestantism threatened the world with a
tyranny far more terrible than that of a king or a
church assembly. The popular conception of God

among its staunchest of adherents was that of an absolute ruler, with all the inferences which can logically be drawn from such a definition of His power. For if God is omniscient, He must know what will happen in the future, and must always have known it; and if he is the omnipotent Creator, he must have made all things, knowing exactly what their fate was to be. As therefore the Scripture tells us some after leaving this world will hereafter enjoy happiness and others misery, God must know who are saved and who are lost. The consequence of this is that the eternal destiny of each one was settled before Creation, and nothing we can do can change the divine decree, made in the eternal ages of the past. We are therefore nothing but automata, our every act as well as our ultimate fate having been determined. Science has made and is making an attempt similar to that of theology by showing that our lives and actions are due to purely physical happenings to the complex machinery of our bodies in a past over which we have had no control. I may be wrong but I imagine that, if I were a theologian, I should call this theory 'predestination' and if a scientist, 'determinism'. It is remarkable that both are Latin words since the Greek Church left the question severely alone. I must freely admit that I would like to imitate the wise silence of the East, rather than follow the interminable disputings of the West on this difficult if not unsoluble problem, had I not been specially requested to speak about it. The logical consequences of accepting the conclusions of the doctrine of predestination would be that men should fold their hands and accept the situation. They might well argue that if few are saved and many lost, they themselves can do nothing to prevent it and had better trust to God and leave things alone. But by a strange paradox the most active and energetic Christians have been those who are credited with believing that the future has been predetermined by God. St. Paul's belief in the election of those who were to be saved did not prevent his indefatigable efforts to add to their number. St. Augustine, who pushes Paul's statements to a terribly logical conclusion was preeminently a Shepherd of Souls. Calvin has the credit of being harsher even than Augustine, but his personal life and conduct was not in keeping with the theology imputed to him. Pascal and his friends, for the Roman communion has been divided on the subject as well as the Protestant, were followers of the gentler virtues as well as of the severe theology of Augustine. The fact that a man regards himself as an instrument in the hands of God to do His will tends to make him more and not less energetic in His service.

Protestantism, therefore, left little room for freedom whether in politics or in theology; and, had it been consistent, it would at least have robbed hell of one of its terrors, as it would have made the world so uncomfortable that the lost would have at least been spared the bitterness of remembering happier things. But with a commendable inconsistency these theories, having been elaborated by logic, have been disregarded by reason; and Protestantism, instead of becoming a yoke of slavery, has done great things in promoting active exertion in the cause of political liberty and freedom of thought. This was particularly true of England, where Protestantism was established with many of the externals of the ancient religion. This was naturally displeasing to the extremists of either faction; and the Puritans, as the ultra reformers were called, opposed the Crown in the name of religion. When the Stuarts came to the throne the Puritans, finding that the national Church was in favor of the divine right of kings, ranged themselves on the side of the Parliament, and became the champions of the liberty of the subject, for on the whole the opposition to the arbitrary policy of Charles I was fully as much political as religious; and it was Archbishop Laud and his friend the Earl of Strafford who identified the bishops with the king's illegal attempts to enforce taxation and to quarter troops on his subjects. This made many who had no particular enmity to the Church join the Puritans, who formed the nucleus of the Parliamentary opposition to the Court. The civil war was at first conducted with equal incompetence by both factions, till Cromwell and Fairfax created their formidable army and threw the whole power into the hands of the victorious Independents. To this party, religious liberty meant the right to suppress religious opposition, and to exercise an unscrupulous inquisition into the habits of every individual; and neither Cromwellian England, nor Puritan New England enjoyed enough liberty of thought and action to be endurable to any person today. In England a violent reaction followed; but the country settled down in the end to a more sober way of living, and enjoyed more liberty of thought than elsewhere in Europe. Still those Protestants who seceded from the national Church were always inclined to the so-called liberal party; and upon the whole the trend of Puritanism has been in the direction of democracy. Religious liberalism has been fostered by the claim of Protestants to read the Bible for themselves, and to be independent of church authority in interpreting it. This is the right of private judgment.

That Protestantism has, whether wittingly or unwittingly, done a great service to freedom is undeniable. The countries which are predominantly Protestant enjoy more liberty than any other, and, generally speaking, are the most law-abiding; and when statistics show a preponderance of lawless crime, serious offences are rare among its Protestant inhabitants. As a rule prosperity accompanies Protestantism. Hitherto the protagonists of civil liberty have professed its tenets. Yet in view of its history it cannot be said that it is naturally disposed to take the side of freedom, nor even that it is the inevitable champion of religious liberty. No form of Christianity engenders a more vigorous type of humanity; but it is very hard for people with strong virility to tolerate, not merely error, but slackness or idleness in others, let alone what they consider to be immorality. Protestant legislation is apt to be intolerant and interfering. Blue laws, prohibition, sumptuary measures are frequently its outcome. The tendency is to force people to be

moral whether they like it or not. What is now
called Liberal Protestantism is far from encouraging
freedom in thought. It relaxes the obligation to
subscribe to creeds and to accept all Scripture as
the literal law of God, but has little or no sympathy
with what it considers to be superstition. The most
intolerant men I have known have been clergymen
of outstanding ability who are as ready to jettison
the leading articles of the Creed, as they would, if
they had the power, be to punish those who want to
believe a little more than the formularies of the
church to which they belong seem in their eyes to
warrant.

I once heard a paper on the beauty of a town
in which all the Protestant churches lived in complete
harmony. No one tried to force his religious belief
on his neighbor, but labored with all his might to
convert him to a program which made for social
righteousness. One of those present when the paper
was read was asked to give his opinion. He said,
"Bad as it is to be asked to assent to that which reason tends to condemn as improbable, it is worse to be
asked to assent to schemes which experience is proving to be fallacious."

In fact, Protestantism, not only in its narrowest,
but in its most liberal form, may at any time become
a foe to liberty. But what predominant power is to
be trusted? A tyranny is not the less odious because
of the adjective prefixed. Whether we call it Catholic
or Protestant, monarchical or democratic, socialistic
or communistic, it is a very ugly thing; and, with the
modern passion for setting things right by reorgan-

izing the world, tyranny of one kind or another is a serious menace. For the liberty any sensible man demands is to be let alone to hold his own opinions, and to order his own life in such a way as not to interfere with the welfare of other people. The danger of Protestantism becoming a tyranny is the propensity of its leaders to adopt the rabbinical injunction to 'make a fence round the law,' that is, to forbid everything, however innocent in itself, which may lead to a violation of a commandment. The old Puritans sought to do this by draping ancient statues, breaking the images placed by pious men of old in or outside cathedrals and churches, and cutting down May-poles. In this way they hoped to make immorality, superstition and paganism impossible. The modern Puritan taboos beer in order to make it impossible for the workingman to be intoxicated by ardent spirits, and consequently to be of less value to his employer. Not that I wish to express approval or disapproval of what is called 'Prohibition'. As a stranger I have no right to do so. But such legislation may be the precursor of much which will rob the individual of freedom and initiative and this is proving true especially in the sphere of education.

Hitherto I fear I have played the part of an *advocatus diaboli* to Protestantism by showing how it has not consistently supported liberty in the past, and may well become a serious menace to it in the future. Now I wish to change my note and to try to indicate how Protestantism, if indeed it means "pure religion and undefiled before God and the Father," can effect

in the future. Since no man can live to himself, no
man can claim to be really free. He is fettered by
responsibilities he may never avoid, to his own self-
respect, to his family, to his country, to his fellow-
men, to his God. All these cause him to exercise
self-denial which in a certain sense is a renunciation
of liberty. He is not free to commit wilful sin, he is
not free of responsibility to obey the law or to defend his native land, he is not free by exercising his
own liberty to injure or even to infringe the liberty
of others. He is not free even to complain of the
dispensations of his Makers, when he suffers sor-
row or bereavement. He is a responsible agent, and
all responsibility implies a limitation of liberty.

Protestantism's chosen hero is St. Paul. Three
words of his translated into English, 'justification
by faith,' were the keynote of the Reformation, and
Paul is one of the greatest exponents of liberty. If
he allowed no man to restrain his liberty, he was
ready to fight to the death for the liberty of his
Gentile converts. He declared that they had great
rights and privileges, but he refused to claim any for
himself. His glory was that he renounced his liberty
that he might serve others. The paradox is that
man has to give up liberty to be really free; but, if
he hates the sacrifice, he is only exchanging one servitude for another.

For liberty in the Pauline sense has often to be
voluntarily surrendered for the sake of others. It
is too often assumed to be rather the right to dictate
to others, for their own good it may be, but generally whether they like it or not. The danger of all

Protestantism is an unloving spirit. The very word 'protest' has an unpleasing sound, since it implies dislike. The attitude of protest is that of men who have a grievance: and, whether they are right or wrong, their mood cannot possibly be loving. Now love is essential to real freedom. The man who loves his country, his family, his God, never feels the burthen of a loss of freedom for their sake. In a word, true freedom must be inspired by love, otherwise all restraint is a form of slavery. Protestantism, to carry its work to perfection, must cease to protest by condemning all which is not in accord with its principles, and never attempting to see good on the other side. When it does this, it may hope to make mankind ready to make those sacrifices for others by which 'the perfect law of liberty' is fulfilled.

LIBERTY AND LAW

By Zechariah Chafee, Jr.

SINCE most laws involve a restriction of some kind of liberty, I shall limit myself to one sort, freedom of thought and of its expression. The problems in this narrower field will sufficiently illustrate the principles which should apply in the application of law to other forms of liberty. I hope that nobody will be disappointed if I go over a good deal of familiar ground. At this day there are no new principles of freedom of speech. All the essentials have been said many times, but the trouble is that people pay very little attention to them.

I

Because of our constitutional form of government we are too apt to approach legal problems by considerations of phraseology. We attach too much significance to the presence of certain words in a fundamental document. It is far from my intention to belittle the influence on the minds both of those who enforce law and of the citizens at large, which comes from the noble language of our bills of rights. They make it possible for us, when liberty is in danger, to strengthen our appeal to reason and common-sense by calling into play the associations which attach to the constitutions that were framed with so much thought by the founders of our government. Nevertheless, we cannot afford to forget that the guarantees of liberty in the bills of rights do not of themselves operate to preserve liberty. They are brought actively into our lives by the intervention of human beings in ways which must be determined by specific legal rules. Dicey in his "Law of the Constitution" has shown that in England, where there are no constitutional guarantees at all, good legal machinery has made possible a large measure of liberty, while the eloquent language of the French Declaration of The Rights of Man in 1791 was followed by some of the worst deprivations of liberty in modern history because of the lack of efficient remedies which a citizen could invoke for his protection.

This point may be illustrated by the fate of some of our own constitutional rights. The right not to be imprisoned illegally is rarely violated because our statutes provide with much detail, developed through centuries, the remedy of the writ of *habeas corpus,* by which an imprisoned person can have the legality of his detention investigated by a court with great speed. On the other hand, the constitutional right to bear arms is practically meaningless because there is no method provided by law for asserting it. The constitutional immunity from unlawful searches and seizures is very important, as anybody can testify who has been forced to submit to the humiliating experience of a search of his person, but numerous

American judicial opinions in recent years show that this right has been repeatedly disregarded by officials who are zealous to enforce the criminal law. In England such violations are rarer. The reason is plain. Both countries provide in theory the same remedy for protecting the right, a civil action for damages against the officials who carry out the unlawful search or seizure. In England, however, this machinery works because juries have brought in heavy verdicts against the officials, and they in turn have become law-abiding, whereas I do not recall any case in this country where substantial damages have been given. In the United States courts the judges have without legislation provided a different remedy, the exclusion of the evidence which has been unlawfully obtained, but state officials are subject to no such practical check. Again, consider the divergent strength of the same right under different circumstances. The various constitutions declare that no one shall be compelled to incriminate himself. In the courtroom this right is effectively protected, because judges have developed specific rules limiting the duty of a man to take the stand or to testify when this might result in his condemnation for what he says. Possibly he receives too much protection, but there is no doubt that the legal machinery secures his liberty. Contrast the same right in the stage between arrest and trial. The accused is frequently subjected to the "third degree," consisting of prolonged questioning by relays of police officials and deprivation of sleep, perhaps of food. The legal machinery does exclude a confession thus obtained, but does not prevent the officials from following up clues furnished by the confession, so that these violations of the right continue. We need to consider new machinery, for instance, the presence of a lawyer or a public defender at all interviews between the accused and the police. These instances show that the constitutional definition of a given liberty is less important than the legal machinery which determines the scope of the liberty in a particular case, that is, which demarcates the line between permissible and forbidden governmental action and which forces the government not to cross that line.

Consequently it is essential, in discussing any situation where freedom of speech or some other form of liberty is involved, to examine the existing legal machinery and if this is unsatisfactory to canvass the merits of possible alternatives. Three aspects of such machinery at least are important: (1) its nature; (2) the persons who constitute it, for we have no mechanical devices or litmus paper for detecting unpermissible speech and writings but must always rely on human beings; (3) the speed and expense with which the line is drawn.

First, the nature of the machinery, which is extremely varied. Often, it operates in at least two stages, the initial power of restricting liberty and an independent check on abuses of the initial power. Under our constitutional system, for instance, the initial stage of arrest under a sedition statute is followed by intermediate stages of indictment, jury trial, sentence, culminating in the independent check of a determination by the Supreme Court of the

United States as to the possible unconstitutionality of the statute. As already indicated, we have focussed our attention too exclusively on this type of check, which is peculiar to this country. Other types have already been suggested, such as a civil action for damages against the official, or the exclusion of evidence illegally obtained. Where the initial stage consists of a determination by an administrative official, who refuses to license a play or to admit a book to the mails, the check may be furnished by a review of his decision in the courts.

Secondly, the persons who compose the legal machinery. Whenever we authorize a particular restriction on liberty we ought not to forget that we are entrusting to fallible human beings a power over the minds of others. Benjamin Franklin stated the problem in saying that the desirability of stamping out evil thoughts is obvious, but the question remains whether any human being is good and wise enough to exercise it. In some situations the evil is so serious that we must take this risk of abuses in the limitation of liberty. For instance, the modern tendency is to limit liberty of action in all sorts of ways through administrative boards, which compel parents to vaccinate their children and send them to school, inspect food offered for sale, license street musicians, or order rotten tenements torn down, and similar limitations on freedom of discussion may be necessary, but the risk of human error ought to be weighed in each case and even when run it ought to be minimized as far as possible through the selection of persons who by training, habits, social background, are less liable to act mistakenly or unjustly. For example, our building inspectors ought to have some architectural training, and the censorship of plays will vary enormously, accordingly as it is exercised by a police official who has devoted years to the suppression of burglars and the regulation of motor traffic, or by a student of literature whose familiarity with the *Oedipus Rex* of Sophocles and the *Hippolytus* of Euripides may affect his apprehensions of social corruption when he is confronted with incest on the stage in O'Neill's *Desire Under the Elms*.

Thirdly, the speed and expense with which the legal machinery operates, that is, the rapidity and cheapness with which initial abuses are checked by a subsequent independent decision. The effectiveness of *habeas corpus* is due in large measure to the summary fashion in which the writ may be at once obtained from any judge. On the other hand, while an erroneous injunction against peaceful persuasion by strikers may be corrected by an appeal to a higher court, the time which intervenes is often so long that it amounts practically to no check at all. Thus in the Tri-City case the Supreme Court of the United States lopped off certain clauses of the injunction seven years after it was granted whereas the strike had probably ended within a few months, so that an appeal was not worth waiting for. Similarly, the severe sentence imposed on Rose Pastor Stokes under the Espionage Act was not reversed until after the war was over, so that though wrong it maintained its deterrent effect on other pacifists until the question had become academic. In like manner the process of carrying appeals from convictions or injunctions through the state courts and perhaps to Washington may be so expensive that no use will be made of it. When the determination of the scope of liberty is of immediate importance, a slow and costly review is equal to no review, and the initial stage becomes of vastly greater importance as to both methods and personnel.

II

These questions of legal machinery will constantly recur in my subsequent consideration of my subject, but I now turn to a different problem, the meaning of freedom of speech. The United States Constitution prohibits Congress from abridging this right but fails to define it, and this is also true of the state constitutions although these sometimes are a bit more specific and declare that there is liability for its abuse, leaving open, however, the question of what is an abuse. This reticence on the part of the founders has doubtless permitted restrictions on discussion which they did not intend, but on the whole I consider it fortunate since it avoided a permanent crystallization of the ideas of the late eighteenth century and imposing on each generation the responsibility of reformulating afresh the conception of freedom. At different times in the past it has had very different meanings, and these I now consider, both because they affect the meaning today and be-

cause they illustrate the kinds of limitations on
liberty which are proposed and the methods for protecting it.

We can roughly block out four stages in the development of Anglo-American law, with which alone
I plan to deal.

First, until late in the seventeenth century there
was complete control over discussion by the government, chiefly through the censorship of publication.
This was exercised at first by the Crown and then
taken over by the Long Parliament, an example of
the persistency of legal machinery through changes
of political rule which may be paralleled in the con-
tinuance of the Russian Czarist censorship by the
Soviets. The opposition to this censorship is forever associated with the name of John Milton.
Despite his *Areopagitica,* however, this form of control lasted until after the Revolution of 1688, and
the method of its abolition in 1695 is very significant.
The House of Commons in stating the reasons for
terminating the censorship asserted no broad principle like the French Declaration of Rights, that the
"free communication of thoughts and opinions was
one of the most valuable of the rights of man."
They devoted themselves to the bad features of the
existing legal machinery. To quote Macaulay:

"The Licensing Act is condemned, not as a thing essentially evil, but on account of the petty grievances, the exac-
tions, the jobs, the commercial restrictions, the domiciliary
visits, which were incidental to it. It is pronounced mischievous because it enables the Company of Stationers to
extort money from publishers, because it empowers the agents

of the government to search houses under the authority of
general warrants, because it confines the foreign book trade
to the port of London; because it detains valuable packages
of books at the Custom House till the pages are mildewed.
The Commons complain that the amount of the fee which
the licenser may demand is not fixed.   They complain that
it is made penal in an officer of the Customs to open a box
of books from abroad, except in the presence of one of the
censors of the press.   How, it is very sensibly asked, is the
officer to know that there are books in the box till he has
opened it?   Such are the arguments which did what Milton's
Areopagitica failed to do."

With the termination of the censorship began the
second stage which lasted for about a hundred years
until late in the eighteenth century. The publication
of books was so free that Continental writers like
Voltaire printed in England, and newspapers sprang
up in abundance.   However, the government attempted to control sharp political criticism of its
methods by prosecutions in the courts for seditious
libel, convictions being followed by severe sentences.
Famous cases were those of Zenger in New York,
and of Wilkes and the Junius letters in England.
In as much as the judges were appointees of the
Crown and natural supporters of the existing
political system while the juries were drawn from
the commercial classes who suffered from misgov-
ernment and corruption, the result of a prosecution
depended much on the question whether the main
issues should be decided by the jury who would acquit
or the judge who would convict.   The courts permitted the jury to find whether or not the defendant
was responsible for the book or newspaper by writing, printing, or publishing it, but kept for the judge

the decision whether or not the book, etc., was seditious. Moreover, the truth of the charges made by Junius or other writers against the King's ministers was not allowed to be an issue at all, because of the doctrine that prevailed in criminal cases, "the greater the truth the greater the libel." Conservatives like Blackstone supported these drastic limitations on political discussion by saying that freedom of speech meant only the absence of restraint before publication and did not affect prosecutions after publication, so that in their opinion complete liberty had been secured with the disappearance of the censorship. Their opponents, the liberals on both sides of the Atlantic, recognized that a censor who passed on all material that came from the press was more objectionable than an occasional prosecution before a judge who was not so liable to be arbitrary in his standards; but they preferred even more the decision of twelve men drawn at random from the community and thus applying its views of the type of discussion desired by citizens. In this struggle the leadership was taken by Thomas Erskine, who was counsel for the defense in many of these cases. Eventually the liberals were victorious. Charles James Fox's Libel Act (1792) gave the jury the power to determine whether the publication was seditious or defamatory, and later legislation made truth a defense. It has been argued that the contemporaneous free speech guarantees in our constitutions were intended to effect the same reform, but the courts here continued to take the old position until specific constitutional or statutory provisions gave the juries power over all aspects of the prosecutions. The solidity of the new procedure is shown by the Sedition Act of 1798 designed to punish attacks on the federal administration, which with all its sweeping provisions made truth a defense and gave the jury control of all the issues.

The third period covering the nineteenth century was probably the freest of modern times. Old penalties for heterodox opinions were gradually removed and there was almost no new legislation against them. Although Mr. Leon Whipple in his "Story of Civil Liberty in the United States" has collected many instances of the violation of liberty before 1900, these are mostly acts by mobs or of officials, police, and soldiers, done under old laws or no laws at all. Except the statutes against Mormon polygamy, I recall no new statutes against minorities and in this case behavior was involved rather than opinions. Not only were there few prosecutions, but also immigrants with strange views for which they had suffered in Europe were given asylum and welcome in England and the United States, and socialistic communities were established in our midst and even permitted without legal interference to pursue experiments in relations between the sexes. In short, the prevailing doctrine of *laissez faire* was extended to the field of discussion. The outstanding representative of the liberty of the time was John Stuart Mill.

Unfortunately, his arguments did not become deeply ingrained in popular consciousness in this country. Freedom of speech was a cherished tradition but remained without specific content. Perhaps

the very freedom from interference allowed the
philosophical and political principles which underlay
the constitutional guarantees to be forgotten for
lack of constant assertion and examination of them.
Consequently, these guarantees proved of slight use
against the growing tendency to resort to governmental action for the limitation of individual liberty
in the field of discussion as well as in other departments of life. It seems odd to link together the legal
restrictions on business and wealth enacted by collectivists at the opening of the twentieth century and
the sedition laws enacted against collectivists since
the war. Yet I think the antagonistic factions in a
bitter political and economic struggle are both
moved by the same impulse, entirely alien to the principles of Benthamite individualism, namely, an increasing insistence on interests of the community and
on their protection by the state.

This new tendency became articulate in proposing
restrictions on free discussion in the late eighties.
The Haymarket bomb may serve to mark the
turning-point of toleration for extremists, and after
the assassination of McKinley the new spirit
emerged into legislation with the New York Criminal Anarchy Act of 1902 and the federal statute of
1903 excluding anarchists from our shores. More
serious suppressions were forecast in industrial dis-
putes, for instance, the prohibition of street meetings
in San Diego in 1912, so that the Espionage Act and
the sedition laws after the war did not come out of
a clear sky. Nineteen hundred and seventeen certainly found us in a fourth period, when the scope

of freedom of speech once more became a burning issue.

On the one side were those who insisted that liberty of discussion had not been violated. Just as Blackstone defended the suppressions of his time by saying that freedom of speech was preserved years before when the censorship had been abolished, so the conservatives today insist that it was made sufficiently secure a century ago when juries were given control of sedition prosecutions. Thus Professor Corwin of Princeton writes (30 Yale L. J. 55):

"The cause of freedom of speech and press is largely in the custody of legislative majorities and of juries, which, so far as there is evidence to show, is just where the framers of the Constitution intended it to be."

And Mr. Day Kimball says (33 Harv. L. Rev. 448):

"Of whatever lapses our 'twelve good men and true' may have been guilty on specific occasions, they are too typical a feature of our legal system, are too ingrained in its structure to be condemned without mature reflection. They are drawn from the people. Their opinion may be considered representative of public opinion in general. And that public opinion in this matter should rule is in full accord with the spirit of our government."

On the other side are those who maintain that freedom of speech means more than the abolition of the censorship and the right to trial by jury, that the fear of severe sentences may kill open discussion though there is no previous restraint, and that while juries will safeguard the criticism of the government by spokesmen of views popular among the electorate they are far less likely to acquit men who hold unpopular opinions, which nevertheless for the public good ought to be allowed expression. Therefore, they want the reviewing power of the Supreme Court to become effective legal machinery for the protection of freedom. They urge that the Constitution to be vital must be interpreted to impose limits on legislation against speech, beyond which statutes become invalid and juries must not be permitted to convict. Such vague descriptions of this limit as the statement that "liberty" does not mean "license" are meaningless, for "license" is merely a name for what one dislikes. In this fourth period, which is still existing, the struggle is for a reformulation of the definition of freedom of speech which shall make it possible to restrain the government from interfering with valuable discussion by prosecutions or by other methods. According to the participants in this endeavor, the Constitution does more than embody the Blackstonian prohibition of previous restraint and Fox's Libel Act; these are but types of legal machinery to secure a principle, and it is that principle which is affirmed by the Constitution. I have spoken of Milton and Erskine and Mill as leaders in the previous three periods. In the fourth, I should add to these names that of Oliver Wendell Holmes.

What is the principle thus embodied in the Constitution?

In the process of reformulation it is plain that freedom of speech, despite the unqualified language of the First Amendment, cannot be regarded as an absolute right.   Indeed, as I have stated elsewhere, we do not get far by talking about rights, for liberty is denied in the name of the right to national self-existence and so on.   It is like the old problem of the irresistible force meeting the immovable body. As in so many legal situations it is helpful to fall back upon Von Jhering's theory of interests, namely the various human desires or claims to legal protection, which necessarily conflict with each other so that it is impossible to satisfy all of these claims, at least in their entirety.   We must allot a weight to each according to its social value and then balance them against one another in order to determine how far each can receive legal expression.   For our purposes, it is immaterial whether we define a right as a claim or interest which is given legal protection, or as the legal method of protecting the human interest, though there is a great dispute about this.   So treated, a free speech situation is a conflict between the interest of the community in national safety from external or internal violence, or in morality, etc., on one side; and on the other side an individual interest in talking or writing coupled with what is too often overlooked, an interest of the community in the discovery and dissemination of truth.   In my book "Freedom of Speech," I emphasized the need for sound opinions, but in the light of Mr. Walter Lippmann's writings still greater importance attaches to the ascertainment and spread of the actual facts.

The nature of this social interest in truth has been set forth so eloquently by Milton, Mill, Bagehot, and

Mr. Justice Holmes that I shall not venture to state it myself, but shall add to their well-known formulations this thoughtful passage by Professor Merriam (Am. Journal of Sociology, July, 1921):

"Society is dissolving every moment, and the question is, How shall the reconstruction of authority in the minds and lives of men be made? In the past largely by the authoritarian process, by taboo, superstition, ignorance, and force. In our day this is still largely true, perhaps, but there is also an increasing process in which authority is maintained by recreating appreciation of and agreement with the values that are transmitted, with allowance for shifting values and attitudes and interests. That order of things, whether social, economic, or political, is now most secure which constantly recreates the loyalty and obedience of its members, which constantly redevelops the sources of its interest and power from interest and reflection. That order is weakest which must largely depend upon authority and force with suppression of discussion and reason and criticism."

The meaning of constitutional freedom of speech has not crystallized at the termination of any of the historical stages just outlined. The spirit Merriam presents motivated each phase of the struggle, and the specific victories won represented only the obtaining of machinery considered essential at the time to achieve this continuing purpose, whose great and permanent significance is triumphantly proclaimed in the opening clauses of our federal Bill of Rights.

The process of balancing which I have outlined is in no way novel to our law, and closely resembles the principles on which the due process clauses of the Fourteenth Amendment must be applied in situations involving liberty of action. As interpreted by the

Supreme Court, it invalidates arbitrary legislation, that is, statutes which do not aim at an object which the Court considers within reasonable possibility. The police power, through which the state may secure the safety, health, and welfare of its citizens, must be balanced against liberty of action, liberty to sell, to employ labor, to engage in useful occupations. It may be that such liberty has been excessively emphasized by the decisions, but at least they should serve as precedents for a similar wide protection for freedom of speech.

It makes an enormous difference how we approach a free speech situation. If we begin by considering the interests threatened by open discussion, such as safety from invasion or from communistic violence, or the maintenance of youthful morality against corrupting circulars, books, and plays, we soon become so alarmed by the dangers which our minds picture that we have little thought left to devote to the importance of freedom for the discovery and spread of truth. Such has been the mental state of most of our legislatures and of the majority of the Supreme Court of the United States. On the other hand, if we begin by considering the great value of this social interest in truth, then when we turn to the risks of freedom they may not seem so serious, especially when we remember the forces—police, army, public opinion—which will be at the disposal of the state if discussion should chance to give rise to evil acts. Not that we should ignore or minimize the true extent of such dangers, but when we have carefully considered, *first,* the value of open discussion, and *secondly,* the risks, then we must lean just as far as we possibly can in the direction of free speech.

Such substantially was the interpretation given the First Amendment by Justice Holmes, speaking for a unanimous court in Schenck *v.* United States, 249 U. S. 47:

> "The question in every case is whether the words used are used in such circumstances and are of such a nature as to create a clear and present danger that they will bring about the substantive evils that Congress has a right to prevent."

This "clear and present danger" test has since been declared by Justice Sanford not to be a constitutional limit on legislation but merely a rule for interpreting the language of the Espionage Act, but it is to be hoped that his view will not prevail, because this test is the best which has yet been authoritatively laid down.

While the First Amendment limits only Congress, "liberty" under the Fourteenth Amendment has been interpreted in cases under the New York Anarchy Act and the California and Kansas Syndicalism, Acts to include liberty of speech. While thus far the majority of Supreme Court simply say that such liberty is protected again "unreasonable and arbitrary" sedition laws and convictions, without defining these words, Holmes and Brandeis insist that the "clear and present danger" test should apply in delimiting the permissible scope of state action as well as federal.

III

It is now time to turn to another matter and consider briefly the numerous points at which liberty of discussion is subject to restriction by law, and the existing or appropriate legal machinery for demarcating the limits of liberty, keeping always in mind the principles already set forth.

1. Criminal prosecutions where a jury is involved. These may be brought for sedition, indecency, blasphemy (a topic which would seem to be forbidden by the "clear and present danger" test and which is apparently obsolete outside of Massachusetts and Maine), and libels so outrageous as to make probable breaches of the peace. In Washington, libels on the dead are included, a deterrent to historians. In these prosecutions, the human machinery includes the legislature which enacts a sedition law, and legislators have of late years become curiously subject to an epidemic, borrowing laws from other states without regard to local conditions; then the prosecuting attorney, who starts proceedings, and whose powers are very much greater than is generally realized— in the war the federal district attorneys differed widely in their employment of the Espionage Act and some unification from Washington was necessary; then the jury, whose method of selection is material, and the trial judge who is elected and so risks being sensitive to waves of popular indignation, or is appointed on the recommendation of the Department of Justice, which also may aid in speeding or retard-

ing his promotion; finally as a check, the appellate court. Under our system this check is imperfect, for unlike the English Court of Criminal Appeals it cannot reduce unduly long sentences if the conviction itself was proper, so that the personality of the trial judge, who fixes sentences, is very important.

2. Prosecutions without a jury for minor offenses, e.g., language liable to cause a breach of the peace—a convenient catchall to hold soap-box orators. The sale of indecent books and periodicals may be so tried in some jurisdictions. Here the trial judge, who has entire control, has been selected to deal with drunkards, traffic violators, etc., and naturally has had little experience with issues of free speech. Furthermore, these police judges are more independent of one another than Superior or Supreme Court judges, so that we get odd incidents like the acquittal of Mr. Mencken for selling a copy of the "American Mercury" in Boston, and the conviction of a newsdealer for selling the same number in Cambridge. Some method of unification is necessary as in the cases of the federal district attorneys during the war, and it would be better if freedom of the press were taken out of the hands of police judges and placed in the jury trial courts. True, there is in all cases an appeal for a jury trial after a conviction in the police court, but this check is not sufficient because the penalties are too small to make it worth while to incur the expense.

3. Control of assemblages under municipal ordi-

nances. The police have a very wide power to stop agitators for such vague offenses as obstructing traffic, sauntering and loitering, picketing, carrying placards, distributing handbills, parading without a license. The initial stage is in their hands, so that the superintendent of police really determines the limits of expression of opinion in the streets. Theoretically, a later stage is provided in the courts, but practically such a check on the police is useless since it operates long after the day when the street demonstration would have been effective. Consequently, if the superintendent decides to stop a demonstration, he can go ahead even though the courts may later overrule him. The additional check of a suit against the arresting official for damages is worthless because juries will not bring in a substantial verdict.

Another method of restriction on open-air agitation is to require a permit from the mayor or some other official for speakers in a street or park, which may be arbitrarily refused. He then constitutes the entire legal machinery. In England in Hyde Park no such permit is necessary; the Government must close the whole park to the public or else allow a speaker to proceed until he violates some law. In France the speaker must send a notice to the authorities and automatically gets a receipt which serves as his permit; the police are thus warned to be on hand in whatever numbers are thought needful to stop unlawful acts.

Indoor agitation is usually less restricted, because it does not interfere with the general use of public

areas. On the other hand, listeners are more liable
to be excited in a crowded room than in the open air.
Sometimes meetings on a distasteful subject are
virtually forbidden in advance by the threat to revoke
the license of the hall for narrow stairways, insufficient lighting, etc., if the meeting be held.

4. Control of theaters, moving pictures, and the
local sale of books and periodicals. Beside actual
prosecutions, other methods may be employed. The
simplest is a definite censorship, which exists in London for plays, in New York for motion-pictures, but
nowhere in Anglo-American law for books. However, notification in advance from the police that
prosecutions will follow if a play be produced or a
certain novel be sold often has the same deterrent
effect as a censorship. To the producer or bookseller such notification is preferable to a prosecution
without warning, which may involve him in serious
loss. Consequently, we have found booksellers in
Boston co-operating with the Watch and Ward
Society and the police to draw up a blacklist of books.
Notification that a theater license will be revoked if a
play is continued is another form of practical censorship. Convenient as such machinery is, it must be
carefully considered. The personality and training
of the officials or private persons who blacklist books
and plays become decisive. A jury trial brings in
the man from the street, and an experienced trial
judge is less likely to act from arbitrary prepos-
sessions than a censor, who may get into this unattractive occupation because of a morbid desire to

keep himself and other people from going to the devil.

The practical problem is very puzzling. Most of us would recognize that there is a limit for pornographic literature, especially when sold to the young, and that even a play may become dubious when they twitch the nymph's last garment off. In New York, it has been attempted to combine the advantages of prior warning and of a jury by having the trial take place at the start of the run. If an adverse decision were not followed by any penalty to the producer except the stoppage of the play, the plan might give adequate protection to morals without an undue sacrifice of dramatic freedom. If, however, the penalty is a season's padlocking of the theater, this is so severe that no producer can afford to take the risk of carrying a case to trial. Consequently, the right to a jury remains nugatory, and the fate of the play is entirely in the hands of the officials, who can stop it merely by threatening to begin proceedings. In Boston a bill has been introduced to have supposedly indecent books investigated in advance by a judge sitting in equity, and booksellers would not be prosecuted unless they sold after a judicial finding of indecency. This again would give advance warning and take control away from the police superintendents, although the decision would be made by a legally trained judge, not a jury. No solution as yet offered is entirely satisfactory.

5. Civil actions for libel and slander. These protect the reputation of the plaintiff rather than a social

interest. Here we have a possible deterrent on speech by heavy damages which might be very serious if abused, but the issues are decided by a jury which represents community opinion on what is defamatory—juries are retained for this purpose in England though generally abandoned in civil cases—and there is a check by the appellate court. Expressions of opinion by a writer on public matters, like the merits of a book or play, are protected though erroneous if bona fide, and truth is a defense if proved—sometimes a difficult task even if it actually exists. In England juries are more ready to give substantial damages than in this country, and this greater sensitiveness to the value of reputation may be the indication of a more civilized community.

6. Contempt proceedings before a judge for violation of an injunction against supposedly intimidating or boycotting speech or for criticism of the court. Injunctions have been extensively used, not only against strikers but also to break up the I. W. W. The effect of lack of speed of appeal, which makes a single equity judge virtually the final arbiter of the fate of the strike, has not been sufficiently appreciated. Provisions are much needed for a rapid review of his rulings on questions of law. Even the theoretical working of the machinery is not satisfactory, and Professor Eugene Wambaugh has suggested three changes: (1) The judge who issues the injunction should not try the question whether it is violated, since he may naturally be somewhat prejudiced, but should send this issue to another judge.

(2) There should be an appeal on the facts and not merely on law as at present. (3) There should be some limit on the penalty which may be imposed. No matter how high it is, there ought to be some limit. Now, the severity of the judge is absolutely uncontrolled except by his own discretion. There is also need for investigation of the power exercised by some judges to punish adverse criticisms of their rulings as contempt of court even after the case is closed and there is no longer the slightest danger of interference with the proper conduct of the litigation.

7. Administrative proceedings by the federal government. These are especially important in the post-office, which has great power to limit the liberty of the press. It can exclude publications from the mail altogether, or it can deprive a newspaper or magazine of its second-class postal rates, thereby virtually driving it out of business. The courts refuse to review the departmental finding that a book is obscene, a business circular fraudulent, or the circulation of a newspaper falsely stated, so long as this finding is supported by some evidence, no matter how insufficient. Thus there is a very inadequate check on the legal machinery of the post-office. When we examine the nature of this machinery, we find that there is no satisfactory hearing. Moreover, the publisher receives no warning before his book or periodical is definitely excluded from the mails. Unlike the old-time censors, the Postmaster General will not give a ruling in advance of publication. Thus the publisher loses the advantages of a censorship, which

at least gave warning before the imposition of penalties, and gets all its disadvantages. It is difficult to tell who are the officials who make the actual decisions, and there is no indication that the government requires them to be educationally qualified for their delicate task. The requisite of speed is conspicuously lacking, for even the limited review in the courts comes much too late for the publisher to mail out the forbidden issue of his periodical on time. It is true that the post-office has performed a valuable service in stamping out the commercialized exploitation of the young by vicious advertisements, but beyond this its powers over speech are very questionable. Certainly the fitness of its machinery should be fully investigated by the President and Congress.

The control of the Bureau of Immigration over the admission of aliens into the United States depends, not only on the usual social interests in public safety and order, but also on the interest of the nation in the character of its population. A policy of drastic restriction has resulted, under which neither Mazzini nor Marx would probably be admitted to the United States today. There is practically no judicial check. Even on the issue of citizenship the departmental ruling is final, and a native American can be forever barred without a day in court, so long as there is some evidence against him. The administrative machinery is adapted to the numerous questions of racial origin, health, sanity, and earning power, which have to be decided rapidly. The officials are chosen for determining such questions rather than for their ability to discriminate between

various types of radical European thought.   Even if
the national interest in the character of our population justifies the exclusion of heterodox aliens who
would not dwell comfortably in our midst, it does
not apply to temporary visitors who propose to exchange ideas with us for a few months and then depart.   Yet the same hostile policy is exercised toward
these, and the nation which welcomed Kossuth is
afraid to admit Karolyi.

The deportation from the United States of aliens
who have already made a home here is a much more
serious restriction on liberty, but is subject to a
similar administrative power with slightly more restrictions.   It is an interesting question whether the
decrease of immigration under our recent quota laws
will diminish the desire to deport radical aliens as
they become a proportionately small element in the
population; or whether the feeling against them will
grow stronger as the rest of our inhabitants acquire
approximate homogeneity in political, social, and
economic outlooks.

Liberty of thought may also be restricted by the
discretionary power of judges to refuse naturaliza-
tion to radicals and pacifists, and by the denaturaliza-
tion of such persons on the technical ground that they
originally obtained their citizenship without loyalty
to the United States.

8. Governmental control of education.   In the
public schools the social interest in the spread of
truth may be restricted by the natural desire of the
community to determine the purposes for which it

will spend its own money. The legal machinery is
ordinarily operated by school officials with very little
check by the courts. Usually the only check is an
appeal from the official immediately in charge to
some higher educational board. The nature of the
machinery for the selection and promotion of
teachers raises difficult problems, such as security of
tenure, adequate hearings before dismissal, and the
disqualification of teachers for heterodox views,
either expressly through a licensing system such as
formerly existed in New York under the influence of
the Lusk Committee, or indirectly through the necessarily wide powers of officials to find that a teacher
is inefficient, when occasionally the real objection
to him may be heresy. The personnel of the officials
who control freedom of thought in the schools is fortunately better adapted for the investigation of such
issues than in other departments of the government.
Here the officials are or should be chosen for their
fitness to understand mental questions. If they fail
to deal wisely with liberty it is probably because they
are not well qualified to have charge of education at
all. On the contrary, a police superintendent or an
immigration official may conduct his ordinary tasks
admirably and yet have no capacity to discriminate
between thoroughly vicious ideas and those which
should have a chance to be heard.

The arrangement of the curriculum and the selection of text-books could best be performed by the
teachers themselves, but financial reasons often
bring these questions under official control. It seems
doubtful whether men who are selected for their

ability to regulate expenditures are also qualified to determine the probable validity of the evolutionary hypothesis or the accuracy of historical discussions of the American Revolution.

In private schools the liberty of teaching is greater, for the state cannot base its interference on its control of its own funds, but only upon the general interest of the community in the training of the young. This reason has been held by the Supreme Court not to justify the total abolition of private schools by legislation. Some governmental regulation of their curriculum will be permitted for the sake of public safety, but teaching a foreign language is not dangerous enough to be constitutionally prohibited. The Lusk Committee sought to bring private schools under strict state control through a system of licenses, but the statute was repealed before its validity was finally adjudicated in the litigation brought by the Rand School. If public school teaching is to be rigorously restricted by officials, the need for free private schools is all the greater. Somebody should be able to experiment. In so far as such schools are regulated, the powers and training of the public officials who supervise them becomes a matter of great importance.

9. Control by the government of its own officers. The earliest form of freedom of speech secured by the English Parliament was the immunity of its members from responsibility to the King or in the courts for what they said in debates. Our constitutions give a similar protection to American legislators. They

are accountable only to the body to which they belong. This notable right does not, however, insure
complete liberty of thought in legislatures. Whether
properly or not, the legislative powers of exclusion
and expulsion are sometimes exercised against a
member because of his heterodox views. The exclusion of Victor Berger from Congress and of the
five Socialists from the New York Assembly showed
that legislatures are no more likely than courts to in-
vestigate men's opinions in an enlightened and impartial spirit. In discussing these two cases I have argued
in my book on "Freedom of Speech" that Senator
Knox was right in maintaining that the constitutional
right of a legislative body "to judge of the qualifications of its own members" means only the qualifications specifically listed in the Constitution, and does
not permit the body to add new requisites at its own
discretion. Consequently, a United States Senator
who is elected without fraud or bribery or violation
of state and federal law and who conforms to the
constitutional requirements as to age, citizenship,
and residence, should in my opinion be seated. This
view seems contrary to the recent action of the Senate
in excluding Smith and Vare for large campaign expenditures. Little as I like the election methods of
these two men, if the Senate can create an extra-
constitutional requirement of fitness for them, it is
also entitled to impose its own standards of loyalty
and orthodoxy in the future upon men whose views,
however unacceptable, have been approved by the
majority of the voters in the state which elected
them.

The responsibility of government employees for adverse criticism of their superiors is a difficult question, which deserves more discussion than it has received. The advantages of thoroughgoing loyalty in a military or a civilian subordinate officer are obvious, and most people feel that if such a person is dissatisfied with the conduct of affairs he should resign before having his say. Still, not every officer can afford to throw up his job, and the result of an enforced silence within the service may be that inefficiency or corruption on the part of men higher up will continue unchecked because honest persons who know the facts do not dare to tell them to the public. Certainly, if subordinate officials must address all their adverse criticisms to their superiors, great care should be taken to provide adequate machinery by which such a criticism shall receive adequate attention, shall not be suppressed by the very superior against whom it is directed, and shall not be a cause for dismissal of the critic or loss of promotion.

Space does not permit comment on other topics affecting liberty of discussion, such as the law of copyrights, deprivations of the constitutional right to petition Congress, unreasonable searches and seizures, the liability of lawyers to be disbarred after they have defended extreme radicals, the relation of liberty of the press to the legal position of large news agencies like the Associated Press, and the governmental regulation of radio broadcasting stations so as to promote or discourage the opportunity for all kinds of political parties to present their respective views to the public. The foregoing survey of the various types of legal machinery affecting the scope of liberty is far from complete, but it may at least have suggested some of the problems and difficulties involved.

The actual conflicts are not so acute now as they were a few years ago. Yet I do not think we have become more tolerant. We are simply more indifferent and less frightened. We no longer listen attentively to bed-time stories. Yet excitement is bound to come again and the time of tranquillity should be used to overhaul and improve the numerous kinds of legal machinery. Nor should we be content with adjusting the negative forces which restrain liberty. We should also consider the development of positive forces which will encourage it and remove the sluggishness of thought into which we all easily lapse even without any prohibitions upon opinion. We cannot afford to neglect methods for obtaining livelier oral discussion and places available for it, and for encouraging fuller presentation of all sides of international and industrial controversies in the press and over the radio.

The experiences of suppression in the past decade have been destructive of any passive confidence that liberty will go on of its own accord. Its price still remains eternal vigilance. Freedom requires much tiresome labor over the technicalities with which I have dealt, for it cannot be maintained by eloquent expositions alone. Yet in the end such expositions furnish the main strength of liberty. A people gets

sooner or later as much freedom as it wants.
This want is not created by us lawyers but by the
prophets who influence the minds of legislators and
administrators, and of the public to whom members
of the government react with extreme sensitiveness.
The best safeguard against repetition of the errors
of 1917 lies in the ferment in the thoughts of the
young and of those who do not let themselves grow
old.   The persecutions have not been wholly without
a gain.   They have made us look to the neglected
defenses of liberty.   Despite sedition laws, adverse
judicial decisions, deportations—

> "Yet freedom, yet, thy banner torn but flying
> Streams like the thunderstorm against the wind."

PERSONAL LIBERTY

By Clarence Darrow

M Y subject is personal liberty. As applied to
the United States it is pretty much like talking about the snakes in Ireland. There is none. It
is probably not necessary to enlarge on it to any
great extent. Of course liberty is a thing that is loved
by people who haven't it and those who have it never
think anything about it. The last thing anyone
thinks of is to protect liberty unless it is something
they are especially interested in. All poor people
believe in liberty. Its home is in the mountains, the
deserts and the waste places where no one can get
money. In rich countries, lands where the soil is
fertile and the natural resources great and men turn
to producing things from the soil and from the
earth, liberty can not survive. It never has and I am
inclined to think that it never will. There may be a
succession of liberty and tyranny but as an ideal it
can not survive. Liberty always produces property
where men are free and more or less happy; that is,
as happy as intelligent people can be in this world
and still be poor. For most men are not intelligent,
but a country where there is opportunity and chance
and liberty soon gets rich. Give a people hope and
courage and a chance by soil and climate and other

natural resources and the country grows rich and then always loses its freedom. Liberty produces wealth and then wealth destroys liberty. That is the way it goes over the same eternal circle forever. I am inclined to think that liberty can not live long in any rich country.

Now of course in discussing liberty one is talking more or less about an idea. To define what is liberty and what is not liberty is not an easy thing to do. Most of us think there must be some general rules that people must be forced to obey if they won't obey them without force. To one who takes that attitude the question of what bearing liberty should have on the problems of the State is always a question of doubt. The world is made up for the most part of morons and natural tyrants, sure of themselves, strong in their own opinions, never doubting anything. I can hardly conceive of a world of that sort without believing that any scheme which contemplates the absolute right of every individual, sane or insane, vicious or kindly, to go his own way without any restraint is an impossible idea. I can conceive of no such system that could be practical in this world, and as I can't conceive of any other world I can't conceive of its being practical anywhere. So I think for any practical purpose one must admit that any system that is organized always has and always will forbid certain things, and still every person for himself has a natural yearning to do as he pleases. Freedom simply means the power to carry out your own emotions.

Nobody nowadays believes in any such doctrine

as free will; that is, nobody whose intelligence is worth talking about. The most that intellectual men claim for freedom of individual conduct is that one may be free to choose to do the things that he wants to do. Wanting to do it isn't a matter of intellect at all; it is a matter of emotion, and every desire comes from something back of it and nobody has the power of creating his own desires in a world like ours, and in an organism like a human being, which is most likely like every organism. Back of every act is something else, and back of that something else, and all life is a series of sequences, one following the other, and when we know the sequences that precede it we know the next step, and it comes. If there were any way of choosing there would be absolute chaos in all the affairs of the universe and men. Liberty only means having the chance to do what you want to do. Of course if you're ill, or too poor, or too rich, or in jail, you don't have a chance to do the thing you want to do; so liberty means the greatest opportunity to do the things you're inclined to do. Your desires and inclinations come from a long line or series of events which generally have the relation of cause and effect. All that has gone before constitutes cause for the next movement, and so on, and the life of the individual like the life of the universe is simply a series of sequences; so liberty doesn't mean fixing up your own desires or your own hopes, or your own minds, commonly called will, which of course isn't will in any such sense as theologians and other unintelligent people use the word. All there is to will is a state of mind, and that means a state of mind before action. It is the way you feel before you do something. It is not a faculty. It is not a physical thing. You can see the nose on your face but you can't see the will. Doctors can find the stomach but not the will. It is only a state of mind which comes from what has gone before. Will means little except wish or desire. That is all it means. It does not mean that one can be a lawyer, a doctor or a preacher or a sewer-digger, as he sees fit. It means that whatever he is he still has a desire to do certain things and a person is as free as he can be if he is able to do what he wants to do. There may be all sorts of things to prevent it but a person is only free in the sense that he may be able to carry out those wishes and desires. All people in this world are always anxious to do something. They always have a will to take some new step, and they are very impatient with anybody who interferes with their will to take that step. They are never interested in the will of anybody else. They never think of trying to harmonize their inclinations with those of other people. I don't know whether they can or not. They can, in a way, but their will and desire is the same anyhow. So everybody believes in liberty for himself and very few care enough about the principle involved to have any care for giving it to other people. So organized society is full of conflict. It always has been and doubtless always will be filled with all sorts of conflicts.

If a man were on a desert island, it has often been said, he would be free to do anything his will told

him that he could do, but that wouldn't be much, because he would lack companionship. We have to
adjust ourselves to society and do the best we can
to get society to adjust itself to us and get along with
as few bumps as we possibly can. Free people go
back into slavery, and people in slavery often get
freedom. We always find, as I have said, that the
yearning and desire for freedom comes from the
poor. The rich have it anyway and as a principle
they care nothing about it. This can be pretty well
illustrated today by our own history.

Take the history preceding the Revolution. The
Revolution in this country was not brought about by
people who were looking for religious freedom. The
immigration from Europe wasn't for that; it was to
get a living. People had a poor chance there and
they thought they would get a better chance here—
the everlasting urge to go west where there is more
room, or go in some other direction or place where
there is more room. They had no idea whatever of
religious freedom; that is, the founders of this
country. They brought with them practically the
same ideas and the same institutions they had when
they left home, but they did want land, and they did
want wealth, and they did want more freedom than
a poor man can get, for poverty is one of the things
that prevents freedom. They settled this country
and then grew impatient at being controlled by a
country which was three thousand miles away as it
is today, but that meant three months away or more,
then, and it meant all kinds of hardships and all sorts
of inconveniences. They naturally grew impatient at

all of this and little by little they pried themselves away from England. They wrote the Declaration of Independence, which is a very radical document. A good many men were sent to jail in the late war because they believed in the Declaration of Independence and talked it, and they are still under the Espionage Act in many of the States. The writers of the Declaration of Independence believed that all men were created equal, which of course isn't true in any sense. They declared governments were instituted to serve men, which perhaps should be true, but it is not, and that governments derived their just power from the consent of the governed, which is an impossibility. Nobody ever consented to be governed. To be governed means the absence of consent. The two words are as utterly inconsistent as sweet and sour. Men may consent to pool their issues but not to be governed. When it comes to being governed consent means to be controlled either by the State or the strongest power or in some other way. The Declaration said all people had the right to alter their government when they saw fit or abolish it if they saw fit, and it said a good many other things.

The word "right" does not mean anything. People talk a great deal about rights but the word means nothing. The legal definition of a right is much better than any other definition, which is not often the case. But in law there is no such thing as a right unless you have a remedy. The word right means nothing unless you have a way to get it. It has a technical meaning, but this is only theory, and it really has no meaning.

But while the founders of the country were intelligent and ambitious they were very oratorical and used language loosely and said the people had the right to abolish their government if they wanted to. You can not talk that way today. You might have rights if you could get them, but not otherwise.

Nobody can conceive of a right without a remedy, and in this the law is a philosophical theory. But the war was fought after the Declaration of Independence was written. The Declaration was written by a gang of rebels. The leaders would have been hanged if they had failed, which is the fate of all rebels who fail. The people were enthused with dreams. They were going to own a great fertile area where everybody could be rich and therefore happy, and they were very radical. It was a very radical thing indeed to say that governments were instituted among men for the benefit of the governed, or that men could only be governed by their own consent, and had a right to change the government when they wanted to, or abolish it when they saw fit. It was all right then because they had no government, so why shouldn't they say it. They were talking to the other fellow; it was a very different proposition. But they won the war, and seven or eight years later they met in a convention to write a Constitution, which everybody says is a miracle. It is common for politicians who call themselves statesmen to say the Constitution is an inspired document.

Anybody who wants to understand the difference
that the attitude of a people makes in the writing of
a document ought to read the Declaration of
Independence and the Constitution. They are as
unlike as any two documents can be. Of course when
the people came to write the Constitution they were
then masters of the country; they weren't talking
about giving away somebody else's property; now it
was their own. They weren't talking about gaining
rights; they had them. Then the question was, what
were they going to do with them? So they made the
Constitution, which was largely the work of lawyers,
of course (which made it impossible, to start with),
and they provided a government for Democracy
which is the least democratic form of government I
know of in any part of the civilized world. Perhaps
there is no other government in the world that comes
as near to being an aristocracy or a monarchy as the
United States, with two possible exceptions; one is
Italy and the other is Russia. For of course while
the English have a king, and free America feels very
sorry for them because they have a king, he has no
power whatever. The King just instructs the people
in table manners. He has no power to do anything.
Norway and Sweden are the same way. Italy was
the same way until Mussolini came in; they had a
king without power, and were ruled entirely by
parliament. There was probably only one European
power that had a semblance of Autocracy before
the late war; that was Germany; and, possibly,
Austria. But, while countries still retained the
name of king, the people had slowly taken away their

power until there was none left, and the President of
the United States was the only real king either in
Europe or America.   Compare his power to the
power of any modern king anywhere.   First, the
President can veto any law that Congress may pass,
no matter what it is, and before any law can be passed
both branches of Congress must act, and not only
act but they must act at the same session, and then
the President has the right to veto it if it is passed.
The authority of our government was divided in
such a way that the President was elected for four
years and the senators for six and the members of
Congress for two, so they never had a chance to
make a clean sweep at any one time.   No matter
what might be the rising tide it could not overthrow
the government, because all these bodies were elected
at different times and generally on entirely different
issues, and to make it doubly safe there was a
Supreme Court which had the power to set aside
anything that Congress might do and they were appointed for life, so they were safe; and of course a
Democracy could not be made in any such way.   I
would guess there isn't any government in the world
that's as impossible to change as the United States.
If one just thinks for a minute what it requires to
pass the simplest law.   We must have a Senate and
a President and a Congress, all elected for different
terms.   If the President doesn't approve of a law it
takes two-thirds of both houses to overrule his veto.
No king has ever had such power in the modern
world.   If everything goes smoothly with the three
branches then there is the Supreme Court in session

forever; old men, unimaginative, satisfied, not desiring change. It is only the young that want change.
It takes daring and adventure to want it.   All
of these things must be accomplished before you can
get any lawful change of any importance in the
United States.   You might get some unimportant
thing like woman suffrage or income tax or some
moral reform, which isn't so moral as it is fanatical,
but nothing important; and then if you were ever to
want to change the Constitution, that is out of the
question almost, excepting for some moral or
immaterial thing.   You might change it on a sentiment involving religion, or on a sentiment involving
something allied to it like prohibition.   You might
change it that way but on an important matter affecting the government and the rights of the people, you
couldn't do it.   See what it involves.   Before
you can change the Constitution you must have the
President and the Senate and Congress; all of them
must agree to it, not two, but all, and all at the same
time.   If you get a law through the Senate in one
session and Congress does not pass it you have to
begin all over again.   The next time the Senate might
pass it and Congress might not.   Then you might
get it through both houses and after that of course
the President has to take care of it.   So if you want
to get a new Constitution you must get Congress and
the Senate and the President all at once to pass it, and
if you can't get the President to approve it you must
get two-thirds of both branches to pass it over his
veto and then submit it to the people.   It is submitted
to the various states and three-fourths of them must

agree to it; three-fourths of all the states, including such states as Arizona, New Mexico, Georgia and Mississippi, etc., etc.; three-fourths of all of them. Now it is plain that it would be impossible to get three-fourths of them to agree to a constitutional change that would affect important interests. They succeeded in getting prohibition through under great strain and stress and it is a law today. What would be required to get it out? You talk about this country being ruled by the majority; and the prohibitionist is very strong in his talk about the right of the majority to rule. He doesn't care about the majority; he's interested in prohibition; with him it's a religious issue. A small fraction of the population in the United States located in the states that are naturally for prohibition can forever prevent the people from changing the Constitution. About 10,000,000 out of 120,000,000, in a quarter of the states, Arizona, New Mexico, Utah, Kansas, North and South Carolina, Alabama and Mississippi, a mere handful can prevent the change. The K. K. K. have more power than all the rest of the people put together on that question. It is utterly impossible to make an important change in the Constitution of the United States. Even this scheme was fashioned up in the name of Democracy but the people who did it knew perfectly well what they wanted to do. They wanted to make change impossible. They fought for Democracy under the Declaration of Independence but when they got control they wanted to do what everybody else does, make it safe; and so they fixed a government that couldn't be changed.

Compare this to England. The Supreme Court of the United States can set aside any law passed by Congress and sustained by the President on the ground that it is contrary to the Constitution of the United States. When you say contrary to the Constitution you mean contrary to their interpretation of the Constitution. Nobody else might think it was but the Supreme Court says so. It can set aside any law, no matter what it is about. Compare this with England. There is no power in England anywhere to set aside an act of Parliament. Nobody would think of doing it; when the people decide a thing that is the law. They decide it by a majority. There is no king or prime minister to veto it. No prime minister has any such power, and there is no Supreme Court that can declare it unconstitutional. When Parliament acts that is the end of it, and when the Court interprets it they interpret that law and can't possibly set it aside. Yet we think we have a democracy and England a monarchy. All written constitutions must inevitably result in tyranny, in time, because peoples' ideas change in a hundred years, if they have any. England has what is known as an unwritten constitution consisting of Magna Carta and the Bill of Rights, but these have no power against an act of Parliament. Parliament can override all of them. In the absence of an act of Parliament they have power, but none as against an act of Parliament. In England questions are put up directly to the people and every time the people manifest sufficient strength to want something changed and evidence a lack of confidence in the administration they call a new election and go to the people again for instructions. This is about as simple a democracy as we can conceive of. Although there might be things better there surely can be things worse, as we have shown. So when it comes to power to make our own laws and preserve our own liberties or enlarge them, we haven't any. We're governed by laws, such as they are, and most everybody says it is wicked to disobey the law, that is, everybody that wants it enforced says so; also some other people who don't know any better say it is wicked. A great many of the people in legislative bodies are crooks and most of them are ignorant and care nothing about the rights of the people; they're only interested in their jobs and not the rights of the people, and when they make a law, even if you know they're paid to make it, you must obey it. That is the doctrine they're preaching so strenuously today, which nobody believes but which those who believe in tyranny insist on. So it is plain enough that the prospect of getting any more freedom into the law in the United States isn't very promising.

Of course in times of great crises, like wars, you can put over almost anything. People then are patriotic, and often too patriotic. They haven't any sense left at such times and everybody is a hundred per cent American. Of course nobody knows what that means except that it sounds good. It means that whatever the ruling forces want to have go through should go through, and especially it means keeping people quiet and uncomplaining. In times of great wars it is easy to put these things through. War always creates super-patriotism. All men shout for their own country which can do no wrong when they go in, and they come out as extreme patriots. War brings about all sorts of reactions, like tyranny. Nearly every state in this union passed a horrible law after the war; these statutes were written in the same office and prepared by the same people; they forbade criticism of the government and its laws in every state of the Union. And then professional patriots like the "keyhole" men of America go around protesting against ideas. They are ignorant, of course, but as bigoted as ignorant, and they work in secret in colleges and schools in the name of patriotism. We have passed any amount of laws, and some of the most impossible and reactionary that can be conceived of, since the war. We are more and more losing our freedom. We are more and more losing any power to do the things we want to do. Liberty of speech has been proscribed in every possible way. You can't criticize the government. You can't publish a book which a man who is seventy-five years old thinks is obscene or the W. C. T. U. does not openly approve of. You can't do that without going to jail. You can't even get a drink to drown your sorrows, supposedly. And then of course we talk about the increase of crime. It takes two things to make crime. It takes some conduct on the part of a citizen. It takes some law forbidding the conduct. If there wasn't any law there wouldn't be any crime. I used to take a drink without committing any crime. When I take a drink now, who is guilty of the crime, I, or the law? Nobody inquires for a moment how these "crimes" come about. We talk about an increase of crime when we never think about an increase of law. You must bump up against the law before you can commit a crime. Just as a fellow who in the good old days was a little bit soused bumped into a lamp-post. If you put up twice as many lamp-posts he would bump into twice as many. It is a perfectly simple proposition. They put people in jail today for violation of a law which never was a law until very recently and which probably is not believed in by over one-half of the people.

There are such organizations as the Lord's Day Alliance, a set of crape hangers who want to make it wicked to smile on Sunday. Can you vision all the legislative bodies of the United States passing criminal statutes against enjoying yourself on Sunday because, if you haven't any other place to go, you might possibly go to church and they need the money? With the Comstocks, the Anti-Saloon League, the W. C. T. U., the "keyhole" men and all the rest of them, liberty has been pretty well abolished. Still people don't mind so long as they get money; but some of them don't even get money out of it. Of course if you can get money you can buy a fair degree of liberty. If you have power you can more or less do as you please, but if you haven't, try and see. So far as legal liberty is concerned, if it hasn't gone, it is going. It is surely on its way, and nobody mourns over it. There are a hundred men who will vote for a new law where one man will vote to repeal an old one, and there is not a law so bad on the statute books today that you can't get a committee of estimable people to keep it there, a committee of solemn-visaged men and unattractive women who make it impossible to repeal a law. The only way to get rid of bad laws is to let them die from lack of use; to forget all about them. That is the way they got rid of the laws against witchcraft and the old blue laws of New England. In Boston they once had to come to New York to go to a theater, not on Sunday, but on week days, and on Sunday they had to go to church because there wasn't any other place to go, for a long while. The preachers wouldn't allow people to either work or play on Sunday; nobody but a preacher could be allowed to make a living on Sunday. In a large number of the states nobody is permitted to go to an entertainment on Sunday. Of course the churches are kept open, but you could hardly consider that an entertainment, and the law doesn't so construe it. There are some fairly broad questions that ought to govern in passing a law. There are people who can tell you just where the line is to be drawn between the rights of citizens and states; I can't. The single taxers can, but they are about the only ones I know of. They classify everything, put everything in its place. There isn't anybody who can really tell where to draw the line, which I am willing to confess must be drawn somewhere, for I can't imagine that organized society ever will permit anybody to wander too far from the beaten path. There will probably always be laws against murder, robbery, burglary and obtaining property under false pretenses, although nobody knows what this last one means.

It would be construed by the courts to mean such things as the old thimble-rigging game, but the courts would never say that it meant fooling others so they may sell something that people don't want for more than it is worth. However, in a small way, you can't obtain money under false pretenses; in a big way you can. That shows the difference between having power and not having power. There will always be some laws. Where shall we draw the line? The tendency today is to increase the powers of the state, and when I say the state I mean the state and the Federal Government. Those who founded this government of ours never meant the Federal Government to have any power except as to foreign affairs. States were sovereign. In this way they sought to preserve local self-government and have such government as the people of the community wanted. We haven't much in common with the South. We haven't much in common with the desert country in the West. We have different sorts of population in different parts of the country and the laws should be made to fit different parts of the country, and for that reason we preserved local self-government in the Constitution. But it has been well-nigh destroyed.

The Federal Government interfered in giving suffrage to women, which was not its affair. It seems that all men, no matter how well intentioned they are, always are willing to override every principle if they want to get something. They interfered with prohibition, the whole government utterly ignoring most of the big centers of population and most of the large cities. They let Arizona govern New York.

They won't take a drink out there if they know it, what they want is water because they haven't any. Under our modern system Arizona governs New York utterly regardless of that principle of representative government on which this country was founded, and in my mind this destroys individual freedom. We have been doing this so long that when anybody has a new fad he wants a constitutional amendment.

The W. C. T. U. are trying to get a uniform divorce law. They are composed of women, well, from middle-age up, who've got over being venturesome. They are not so interested in getting free from their husbands as they are afraid of their husbands getting free from them, and so they want the conservative element to rule that situation so that some of the states which have seven or eight grounds of divorce will have to conform to such legislation as New York now has. Of course New Yorkers would have more than one ground except for their religious feeling which they ought to get over by this time. There ought to be enough different religions here to overbalance the Catholics and the Episcopalians in their antiquated views on divorce but somehow they are not in the legislature, and so New York is as archaic as any state in the Union, except South Carolina, where they have no divorce laws. The only way people can get rid of husbands or wives there is to kill them. But, barring New York and a few of the Southern States, to which we don't look for intelligence, there are a good many grounds for divorce. There are a good many grounds, anyhow, but there are also a good many recognized by the statutes; and here comes the W. C. T. U. and the X. Y. Z., etc., and the Lord's Day Alliance and demand to put divorce in the hands of the federal government. They care nothing about liberty. They don't know the word or its meaning. They are simply interested in putting over their own ideas, and in making everybody else do the way they do and say what they say and think what they think, if anything; and they appeal to the people with poor logic and impossible cases to show the great evils of different states having different grounds of divorce. Bosh is about all they can say. Of course, while New York has not the intelligence to create more statutory grounds for divorce, her citizens do go to Reno, and they are not so far away from France; but that only is open to the wealthy ones, who are the only people who count anyway; it doesn't give any relief or mean anything to the poor.

The discussion of the line between the state and the individual of course is always important. A man will say to me, "Well, you would forbid murder. If you would, why not forbid taking a drink?" I can reply, "Why not forbid eating something that I don't like? For instance, chicken; I never eat it; I don't see how any sensible person could." But just because I don't eat it ought it to be a criminal offense for others to eat it? We have to settle that, if we can, by certain broad principles.

All men want freedom; they yearn for it; that is, they yearn for the power to do the thing they want to do. When it affects an individual personally he ought to have it. If I choose to drink myself into the grave, what of it? Whose business is it? You might say that a man's wife is affected by it. Well, she can leave him. If it troubles the W. C. T. U. they can help her leave him. Of course everybody who takes a drink doesn't beat his wife; some of them are afraid to. I have known people who drink and still buy shoes for their children. I have known people who ran automobiles to sell their homes to pay for them, which to my mind is more foolish than to drink. You could ask one thousand people and no two of them would agree on the best way to spend $10,000. Some would buy gas for automobiles and some would spend it for alcohol. Some would buy more alcohol and less gasoline, and some others would buy more gasoline and less alcohol. Why should the government bother about it?

There is a difference between criminal statutes and civil statutes. There's a difference between teaching a person or laboring with him to show him he's on the wrong track and passing a law to put him back on the other track. There is a wide difference. No people can get along together unless they have a large degree of tolerance for each others' opinions. The Protestant seems to feel that everybody should agree with him and would send the Catholics to jail because they don't agree with him. The Catholics would like to send the Protestants to jail for not agreeing with them, and every other religion is the same. But why, if a Catholic or Protestant believes that his soul is the only one that can go to Heaven,—why bother about mine? His soul is safe.

Why should he bother about mine when I don't bother about it myself? I'm like Omar Khayyám. I say "take the cash and let the credit go." If the other fellow wants to live on credit I'll take cash, but it isn't up to me to bother him; if he wants to live that way all right, he probably enjoys it; I wouldn't. There is a difference between criminal statutes and civil statutes as there is a difference between preaching and passing a law. I hardly think people object to being talked to about religion or politics or anything else if one does not talk too long, as most preachers do. If they're in your house they can leave you, and if you're in their house you can go away. There's a difference between preaching and law. Everybody ought to be willing that everybody else should preach to him as long as he pleases but not send him to jail. There is a difference between criminal and civil statutes, but I am not going to tell you just where the line is to be drawn on criminal statutes. The line will never stay fixed. The theory of the criminal law is that the thing done is wicked and that men have a consciousness of sin when they do it. The theory is that nobody can kill another without having a consciousness that he has done wrong; that nobody can commit a burglary without having a consciousness that he has done wrong. Because the basis of all the criminal statutes is the idea of right and wrong and the consciousness of right and wrong; that you've done evil and know you've done evil and have the power to resist doing evil. That's the basis of all of them. Yet a criminal statute ought only to forbid some act that almost everybody felt was wrong,

not a majority, not 40 per cent, not 75 per cent.
We assume that a large majority of the people will
live in a way to let the other people live. They will
not do anything anti-social. Not one of 50,000 will
kill anybody. If it is put to a vote to punish murder
probably not one in ten thousand would vote against
it, and if it is put to a vote as to whether to punish
burglary not one in a thousand would vote against
it. Almost everybody would say, "Yes, that is an evil
in itself and one of the things which should be forbidden." An overwhelming majority is against it.
But when we find 25 per cent of the people who
believe the thing forbidden isn't a harmful thing in
any way, like religion or food or drink, it is not a
proper subject for a criminal statute. No bare majority should have the power to send anyone to
jail and no criminal statute will last under such
circumstances. It must have back of it the public
opinion which almost universally approves of the
law. Unless this is back of it, the law will fail, no
matter whether it is left on the statute books or not.
You can't get one-half of the people to put the other
half in jail. Somebody has to work.

The only rule that I believe at all feasible is that no
criminal statutes should be passed except as an overwhelming majority of the people believe that the act
carries with it a consciousness of guilt in those who
commit the act. If three-quarters of them thought
the act was wrong it is not a matter to be forbidden
by criminal statute. I never had any feeling of sin
when I took a drink. Once in a while I had other feel-
ings but not of sin. I never had a consciousness of guilt

in taking a drink; very few people have, even prohibitionists. They wouldn't have been able to pass this law if they hadn't allowed the farmers to make cider and let nature do the rest. When no such law can be enforced with any feeling of tolerance no one should ask for it. Of course we've had all kinds of criminal statutes in the past. It used to be punishable by death for anybody to be a Christian. We don't need this law now for there aren't any. But once the Christian religion used to be a capital offense, punishable in all sorts of horrible ways, and when Christianity became supreme they made it an offense to be anything but a Catholic, and when Protestantism became supreme in England they made it an offense to be a Catholic; you couldn't be anything but a Protestant. So there you are. They made everything an offense. Whenever too large a bunch of people feel a certain way we are bound to have tyranny and all sorts of force. The rule I have in mind is that no conduct ought to be forbidden by criminal statute unless the overwhelming majority of the people believe that conduct is evil in itself. I can't imagine people voting one in a thousand against passing a law to prevent murder or robbery. But as to a law like prohibition, the way the people deal with it is by disregarding the law. When that is done to any large extent it shows that the particular act should not be the subject of criminal statute.

FREEDOM OF SPEECH, CONSCIENCE AND THE PRESS

By Silas Bent

SINCE the World War, when the United States conscripted human life, gagged its press and threw conscientious objectors into prison, there has been a widespread denial of the democratic dogma that liberty and equality are the bases of this government. The denial has taken executive, legislative, judicial and spontaneous popular forms. Individualism has been severely restricted in the process, and certain liberties which are commonly regarded as fundamental have been circumscribed.

Merely to enumerate the forms in which this denial has manifested itself gives an effect almost bizarre: Americanization programs, prohibition, the limitation of immigration, the open shop movement (or "American plan" for the closed shop against unionized labor), the rise of the Ku Klux Klan, the outburst of Fundamentalism and enactment of anti-evolution laws, the spread of military training in our schools and colleges, the establishment of the spy system in industry, and a series of Supreme Court decisions striking at the freedom of political opinion.

Varied as they are, all these manifestations are distinctly modern. Under a feudal autocracy there would have been no occasion for them. The form of government which limited to a few, favored by birth, privileges, opportunity and distinction, had no need of the regimentations sought in each of these encroachments. The democratic process meant that greater and greater numbers arrogated to themselves a share in privilege, opportunity and distinction. But the democratic revolution was born a twin of the industrial revolution. Representative government came by its inches alongside certain vested interests. The feudal baron has been replaced by the captain of industry, an agricultural economy by a mechanistic economy, the serf by the "wage slave." In the United States this change has been more marked than elsewhere. The New World has given birth to a new culture, a new civilization, quite different from the Old World civilization. And since the World War our industrial order has intrenched itself more deeply than is manifest even from the encroachments on individual freedom already enumerated.

The new civilization generated its own religion, and its most devout communicant, occupying the White House, was surrounded with its presbyters and minnesingers. From the first the faith of Calvin Coolidge was a faith that prosperity was a sort of morality. "Life," he said, "is made up of the successful and worthy." In the person of his Secretary of the Treasury, the third richest man in the United States, was exemplified the success and worth he had in mind. They shared a mystical devotion to the magic of material well-being. And Herbert Hoover,

Secretary of Commerce, wrote: "Intellectual, moral and spiritual products are not the products of poverty. Upon the structure of material progress as a base we are erecting a structure of idealism that would be impossible without the material foundation."

These men voiced a prevailing faith in the dollar as the substance of things hoped for. Politically, the faith was expressed in the axiom that the greatest good of the greatest number was a thriving Big Business; parties which had once divided on the tariff and the trusts, particularly the "Money Trust," became indistinguishable. Everywhere there was a glowing conviction that whatever a mechanized industrial order has cost in limiting personality and standardizing the individual, had been more than compensated by an automobile, a bathtub and a radio set for every home.

No one denied the immense gains which this country had made on the material salient, but there was a tendency to deny the retrogression on another part of the American battlefront. There was an acceptance of property-holding as a test of self-government; the test that every man should be master as well of his own conscience and his own mind was ignored. The question whether men should be free to do the different, distinctive and difficult thing was forgotten in doing the common, conventional and convenient thing. Privilege and opportunity were restricted to the few; and thus by an ironic indirection "representative" government arrived at the conditions of feudal autocracy.

It was still the fashion, nevertheless, to speak of the first ten amendments to the Constitution as our Bill of Rights, and to assume casually that freedom of conscience and expression were natural rights, which each of us brought into the world, like eyes and ears; but more precious far, because while we might lose and might even dispense with sight and hearing, these others were imperishable and inalienable. Of course there is no such thing as a "natural" right. We have only such rights as we can enforce. And the tendency of everyone is to give to freedom lip service rather than an active allegiance. We accept the theory of toleration and personal liberty but balk at their practice. Not many minds have the capacity to tolerate opinions which they regard as unenlightened. If freedom of speech and religious freedom mean anything, they mean freedom to criticize any other man's religion. The spectacle of a Heflin, delivering himself of stupid and bigoted tirades against the Roman Catholic Church, was as trying, doubtless, to Protestants as to Catholics. The Senator enjoyed legal immunities by reason of his office, but that should not be permitted to obscure the fact that he was putting into practice a fundamental principle of personal freedom. The incident served very well to illustrate the drastic mental discipline which the practice of liberty entails.

Thus the theory that, though all the world save one man agree in opinion, yet this one must be permitted free expression, suffers in its application. The majority rules. Theodore Roosevelt, regarded in his day as a great progressive and liberal, said: "The anarchist is the enemy of humanity, the enemy of all mankind, and his is a deeper degree of criminality than any other." This majority attitude has found expression since the war in the enactment by nearly all our legislatures of statutes making "criminal syndicalism" and kindred political theories a felony, and in noteworthy cases the Supreme Court has upheld these laws. So far as the active propagation of anarchic ideas is concerned, the Declaration of Independence and the Bill of Rights have gone by the board. This government and its courts do not care to demonstrate their righteousness and strength by the toleration of non-conformist ideas.

Undoubtedly repressed opinion has explosive and inflammatory qualities. The pretension of infallibility which must accompany any active silencing of expression can seldom be maintained against the forces which the suppression generates. Society gains in sanity, health and security by suffering each man to speak his mind freely, to follow his own feeling, tastes, sentiment, to plan his life as best he can according to his own notion, rather than by coercing him into a life approved by his fellows. One might suppose that for its own safety society would set up a system of education which would inculcate tolerance and independence, rather than a system which would tend to reproduce itself.

Mr. Justice Holmes, in a dissenting opinion from one of the Supreme Court decisions I have mentioned, spoke earnestly for a "free trade in ideas," and set as a test of truth its "power to get itself ac-

cepted in the open market." That is the only test
to which it need be subjected. The copy-book maxim
that "truth, crushed to earth, will rise again" is an
optimistic overstatement. Truth perishes when persecuted and oppressed. And the approximation to
it is so rare, so likely to be lost in the fogs of error
around it, so indiscriminate in its choice of a ditch-
digger rather than a Cabinet member for spokesman,
that society gambles with its own future when it
takes a chance of suppressing it. Yet the individual
who believes he is voicing a new eternal truth is
eternally in conflict with society. It is of the very
nature of society to fear and distrust the new. What
all of us want most is security; and in the presence
of new ideas, new opinions, new faiths, we feel in-
secure. This is one of the paradoxes of a situation
replete with conflict and contradiction.

In the emergency of war, the attempt of the individual to set himself or his opinion against his society
and his government is always decisively lost. The
Constitution guarantees to him freedom of speech
and religious freedom; the Constitution guarantees
to his Government the right to adopt any means
necessary to successful prosecution of war. Thus
there come into conflict two indubitable and sweeping constitutional guarantees, one of which must
suffer eclipse. It is the individual guarantee which is
defeated. During the World War there were about
181,000 draft evaders, and fewer than four thousand who, scorning to evade conscription, refused on
conscientious grounds to fight. These few were
found in a body of nearly three millions drafted, and

the disposition made of them, in round figures, was as follows: thirteen hundred accepted non-combatant service, twelve hundred were furloughed to agriculture, ninety-nine were sent with Friends' reconstruction units to France, four hundred and fifty were sent to prison by court martial, and the others were still in military camps when the Armistice was signed.

Of these objectors, some for religious reasons, some on philosophic grounds, nine-tenths were native born. There were many negro objectors, but only on religious grounds. Although members of a race oppressed and persecuted and socially ostracized, north and south in the United States, not one negro, so far as I can find, refused to fight on the ground that this was a white man's war. White and black, the objectors acted on the ground that it is not the primary duty of any man to defend his country, that his first allegiance is to his own conscience and his own integrity. They acted on Thoreau's statement: "Must the citizen even for a moment, or in the least degree, resign his conscience to the legislator? Why has every man a conscience, then? I think that we should be men first, and subjects afterwards. It is not desirable to cultivate a respect for law, so much as for the right."

To these men right conduct could not be exemplified in mass murder; they declared they could not bear arms and keep house with themselves. This conscience they opposed to the holy fervor of a nation engaged in a war, as it thought, to end war and to make the world safe for democracy. Some of the political prisoners were not released until during

President Harding's administration, long after all other English-speaking countries had freed such offenders, and the fact is a stain upon American liberalism. In the clear light of later years it is not difficult to determine the moral and legal status of these objectors; but that conclusion cannot be regarded as offering any guarantee of justice to their fellows in any future war.

Freedom of the press is but an extension of the freedom of individual speech. The two are inseparable; they stand or fall together. Together they were put on trial when the government undertook the prosecution of certain newspapers, in a test case based on the income tax law conferring the right of publicity. An earlier statute had forbidden that returns should be made public, and had not been repealed. The newspapers based their defense on the fact that the income tax lists could be placed in post-offices, and that any man, after inspecting them, was free to discuss their contents; therefore, since the freedom of the individual was not restricted in this regard, the freedom of the press could not be. On that ground the privilege of publication was upheld. The larger issue, as to whether Congress, ignoring the First Amendment to the Constitution, could penalize newspaper men at its will, was not decided, and the amendment thus remained without clarification. The amendment reads:

Congress shall make no law respecting the establishment of religion, or prohibiting the free exercise thereof; or abridging the freedom of speech or of the press; or the right of the people peaceably to assemble and petition the Government for a redress of grievances.

The government's brief in the income tax case, prepared by James M. Beck, then Solicitor General, was probably the most illiberal utterance regarding the press which has ever had the sanction of this republic in time of peace. Mr. Beck's argument, baldly stated, was that, since the First Amendment guaranteed only that freedom should not be abridged, it guaranteed only such privileges as the press enjoyed in 1787, when the Constitution (not the amendment) was ratified; that the English common law defined those privileges; and that in England at that time the publication of a book or paper without the consent of censors constituted a crime.

This may have been good hard-boiled constitutional law. Mr. Beck's subsequent effort to evade the Constitution and get into Congress as a Representative from Pennsylvania, although living in Washington, indicated his hard-boiled viewpoint. His brief may have been good constitutionalism; for twice after the amendment was adopted the press of the United States was put under a rigid censorship. The first time came only seven years after the amendment, and took the form of the Sedition Act, which made it a felony for a newspaper to criticize a governing official. The second came during the World War when, after only one branch of Congress had passed a Censorship Act, an unofficial censor was set up, and the press required to bow to his will. By that arrangement the newspapers in this country were much more strictly circumscribed than in any other English-speaking country.

It is interesting to compare the attitude of the public in these two emergencies. In 1798 the American people regarded the press as their palladium, and in wrath at the Federalists, for their arrogance in passing the Sedition Act, forever wrecked that great party. During the World War censorship there was scarcely a murmur of disapproval.

Nor was there a murmur of protest when, on more recent occasions, President Coolidge enounced as his policy virtually the policy of the Sedition Act. "We have lived to hear the strange doctrine," William Ellery Channing once exclaimed, "that to expose the measures of rulers is treason." The doctrine is not strange to Mr. Coolidge. He tried it out first in one of his anonymous semi-weekly statements to the press, then amplified it in a formal address to the United Press Associations, and then repeated it at the dedication of the National Press Club in Washington.

At no time after entering the White House did Mr. Coolidge manifest the slightest disposition to taffy the newspapers. He would pretend to be pitching hay for the photographers, or put on a ten-gallon cowboy hat and chaps, but for reporters and Washington correspondents he apparently felt a sort of contempt. He made more and more rigid and humiliating the conditions under which the correspondents, in their semi-weekly "conferences," were permitted to spread abroad, as the opinions of their papers, his opinions of current events. He refused to have a transcript made of what was said, or to permit correspondents to have a stenographer present. He thus reserved the power to repudiate any official sanction for the stories they printed; and he refused to permit correspondents to print questions they had put to him, unless he chose to answer them. It was not surprising, therefore, to find him denying the editorial right to criticize his foreign policy, and demanding that the press keep its mouth shut unless it wished to voice acquiescence in his program. At the National Press Club dedication he even went so far as to say:

Whenever any of the press of our country undertake to exert their influence on behalf of foreign interests, the candor of the situation would be greatly increased if their foreign connections were publicly disclosed.

It was apparent that the President had gone much further than he should, and that he must have been misled by malicious slander; for, whatever the shortcomings of the American newspaper, it cannot be accused of secret and corrupt foreign interests. A few newspapers, notably the New York *World*, treated the canard as what it was, "an insinuation which directs suspicion against every newspaper which happens to differ with the politics of the State Department"; and reminded Mr. Coolidge that no reputable journal would resort to such methods in attacking his Cabinet. The New York *Times* gently complained: "Doubtless the President would not wish to countenance that slander in its more vulgar form, but the words which he used will unfortunately

lead some credulous people to believe it." The
Herald Tribune urged him to be as "discriminating"
in his criticism as he wanted the newspapers to be.
The Birmingham *News* asked for more light.
"What can Mr. Coolidge have in mind?" it queried
innocently. The Terre Haute *Tribune* said that
most newspapers placed the President's strictures
"among their cardinal principles." Many others accepted it as a needed admonition. William Ran-
dolph Hearst, as usual the Peter Pan of the press,
averred with a straight face that what Mr. Coolidge
had in mind was decorations by foreign governments, and announced virtuously that he had forbidden his staff to accept them.

Such was the reaction to slander of a great and
free journalism. The legal grounds were obvious on
which the press could have demanded the President's
impeachment. His oath of office binds him to "preserve, protect and defend the Constitution of the
United States," which guarantees freedom to the
press. In this and other speeches he had sought
arrogantly to abridge that freedom, he had denied
the right of criticism, and he had tried to under-
mine public confidence in newspapers.

That the press made no demand for impeachment
was not alone due to its notorious lack of courage.
It was due also to the mortifying realization that the
President had the public with him. The demand
would have aroused a roar of wrath, not at Calvin
Coolidge but at the newspapers. The public recognized and sympathized with the bases of his "strange
doctrine." The newspaper editor, although legally

and morally in the right, dared not, on account of his own record, challenge the slander vigorously.

What was it that had happened to the American newspaper? Why was it that, although its public avenged encroachment on its liberty in 1798 by wrecking a political party, its public stood by in silent approval in the presence of an encroachment in 1928?

For half a century after the Constitution was adopted, news was printed in the American press only for its political effect. That was the sole formula. Newspapers sold at six cents a copy, and they were edited for the educated, well-to-do class, which was the ruling class. A penny press was established in the middle thirties of the nineteenth century to meet the needs of those who could not pay six cents for their papers, to respond to the new emphasis on popular rights which Andrew Jackson's administration brought forth, and to supply tidings of its invisible environment to an audience which, though literate and intensely alive to its need for greater political privileges, was not educated to the standards of the six-cent papers. Editorially, the penny press met this need by crusading for popular rights. But in its news, it practically discarded the political stereotype which had dominated the newspapers theretofore, and began printing for the first time stories of illicit sex relations, the hazards of the race track and prize ring, the filth of the police courts, crime, violence, suspense, romance and conflict. In the selection and presentation of its news

the penny press betrayed its constituency; and that
betrayal has now crystallized into a journalistic convention. The news patterns cut nearly a century ago,
and based on primitive passions, unconscious hun-
gers, now dominate the whole American press.

If you will pause to reflect what a wide area of
news is excluded from the press by its enslavement
to these ancient stereotypes, you will realize why it is
that your daily newspaper has a sameness day after
day, despite the fresh material poured into its molds;
and you will realize why it has become stupid. The
newspaper now has at its very fingertips an entire
world, every day more complexly organized, every
day more moving and intellectually exciting; and yet
year after year the press continues to spit forth
papers which are vapid, flat and only *emotionally*
exciting. Our jaded nerves refuse presently to respond to the old repeated stimulus; after glancing at
the headlines we cast aside the paper with a sense
of frustration and disgust.

These stereotypes, operating impartially on domestic and on foreign news, aroused the President's
ire only in the foreign field. There the patterns of
conflict and controversy had their way. The press
printed only such news as appealed to savage passions, to fear and envy and hatred. The Geneva
Naval Conference was reported in such fashion as
to leave but one total effect on the newspaper reader:
the impression that the next war would be between
Great Britain and the United States. For three
years the press republished intermittently the lie that
British naval guns had been elevated, and then, when

an official correction was made, ignored it because
its effect was pacific and friendly. It gloated over
an Associated Press dispatch from Nicaragua de-
claring that the official seal of the Sandino government pictured a rebel beheading an American marine.
The kind of news which would promote international
good feeling and maintain world harmony could not
be made to fit into those old stereotypes. Harmony
wouldn't make a headline. Only the kind of foreign
news which aroused controversy and anger and
terror was welcome to the press; and the newspaper
reader, realizing this, silently applauded the rebuke
Mr. Coolidge administered.

That was not all the newspaper reader realized.
He perceived also that the press, limiting its own
freedom through its bondage to these patterns, was
by the same token invading his personal freedom.
He saw that the daily paper's devotion to triangular
love affairs, private scandals, the ballyhoo of bathing
beauties, prize fighters and stunt aviators, the recru-
descence "in real life" of Cinderella, Bluebeard and
prince-and-peasant folk stories, meant a freedom to
take and publish his picture without his consent, in-
vade his home and set reportorial spies upon him.
He noted that the freedom of the press meant the
freedom of the Philadelphia *Public Ledger* to ignore
the Republican primary scandals of 1926, until a
reporter went into the state from Washington and
forced recognition of them; meant the freedom of
the New York *Times* to ignore the Teapot Dome
scandal, until a Senate "smelling committee" happened to force it on public attention; meant the free-

dom of the Hearst press to print a series of for-
geries as Mexican State documents, in the hope of
engendering ill-feeling between this country and a
friendly neighbor; that this was done with impunity
from prosecution or even a verbal rebuke from the
Senate Committee which proved the papers for-
geries. This was the freedom of the press as the
newspaper reader saw it, smarting meanwhile under
its gadfly questions in regard to his private affairs
and revolted at its persistent attention to the trivial
and the erotic.

It must not be supposed that these stereotypes
managed to solidify their hold on American journalism without manifesting any merit. They have just
one merit. They sell newspapers. Whether other
patterns, putting a premium on news having solid
worth and interesting informational value, might
also sell papers, is a question the American press has
not yet attempted to answer. It is true that there
are newspapers which give space to important tidings of the world and thus throw a sop to the
Cerberus of more mature intelligence; but these
newspapers print even more news about crime and
scandal than their more frivolous competitors. At
least one generalization is provably true: That the
old patterns dominate the whole press of the United
States, with perhaps three or four exceptions of
small circulation; and another generalization is provably true: that saving such exceptions as the Boston
Evening Transcript, for example, there is no quali-
tative difference between American newspapers—

there is only a quantitative difference. The only difference is in the amount of space devoted to different stereotypes.

The mere selling value of these patterns could not avail to maintain them if the press were not as a whole pretty thoroughly commercialized. The process by which this has been accomplished can be set down very briefly. When the penny press made its appearance, Morse was tinkering with the device which was to be the "magnetic" telegraph. The invention of the rotary press in the forties, the laying of the transatlantic cable in the fifties, the substitution of cheap pulpwood for rags in paper making in the sixties, the installation of the typewriter and the invention of the telephone, as well as a cheap method of reproducing photographs, in the seventies, and mechanical type-setting in the eighties, assured the mass production of cheap and ephemeral papers. The press kept step precisely with the forward march of industry; and when, in the nineties, a demand was made for faster and wider distribution of commodities through advertising in the modern manner, the press was able to satisfy the demand. Advertising came to supply more than half its revenue, then more than two-thirds, then more than three-fourths. In 1927 the daily newspapers had a gross turnover of one billion, one hundred million dollars; and of this eight hundred and fifty millions came from advertisements.

Thus the advertiser assumed paramount importance, and the reader of the newspaper became merely the victim of his exploitation. The advertiser demanded mass circulation, at whatever cost, and the newspaper owner met the demand by a more complete enslavement to the old stereotypes. More, he became, in addition to a distributor of thrills, a mountebank and a clown. He dispensed counsel to the lovelorn, advice to the socially incompetent and comic strips to the mentally deficient. More and more pictures were printed to ease whatever slight strain the newspaper might impose upon a fourteen-year-old intelligence, and the invasion of personal privacy knew no bounds.

Vaudeville and motion pictures enjoy no special constitutional guarantee. Entertainment and thrills afford no basis for a privileged status in the economy of this republic. The daily newspaper, manufactured on the same basis and for the same motive as toy balloons, confers on its publisher no better title to a favored status than other manufacturers enjoy. The publisher was recreant to the trust behind his guarantee. He ignored or disavowed the obligation of the charter under which he functioned. He pretended still, when it suited his purposes and his purse, to act as a censor of the government, an agent of enlightenment and a protector of popular rights, but the record was against him. He had sold out. He had sold himself, his press and the public whose voice the press pretended to be.

In the circumstances, it is not surprising to hear a great deal of talk about censorship. Since the newspaper owner has sold himself into bondage, has sold his birthright for a mess of advertising, and is no longer the master of a free press, why not make his bondage definite and certain by the sort of Federal supervision which will protect the newspaper-reading public's last vestiges of freedom? Questions of this sort are not sporadic and occasional. They permeate the mind of a whole people, disgusted with the press and distrustful of its motives. Only a leader is lacking to convert this attitude into an aggressive movement.

There is good reason to doubt whether the arguments for a censorship are any less convincing than the arguments against it. A greedy, cynical and lawless press can oppose to the realities of the situation only abstractions and a philosophical creed. On the basis of present fact the newspaper has nothing to say for itself; it can only plead that censorship has led always in the past to tyranny, and that the tyranny it begot was always worse than the evil which was intended to be remedied. Yet this argument starts from the premise that we have an uncensored press —a premise obviously false.

For the press is not only limited from within, through its enslavement to rigid news patterns, its standardization of news and features, its timorous surrender of any forthright unpopular expression; it is limited also, and in the most serious way, from without. Not only has the President encroached on its liberties; the Postmaster General exercises a severe censorship after publication, and the Supreme Court decision in the case of the Philadelphia *Tageblatt* appeared to make this censorship as sweeping in peace as in war. In one state at least there was censorship of news about divorce, and the press had not even the spunk to test the statute in the courts. There were innumerable examples of executive interference with the freedom of printing, sometimes by fiat, sometimes by civil and criminal suits; and from the bench more than one judge used the club of contempt proceedings, refusing to admit truth as a defense.

Against these encroachments the press could cite only an extra-constitutional "privilege of publication," extending to executive acts and public utterances, and built up within the last half century. The bench was more tolerant of criticism when applied to the executive or legislative arms than when applied to itself. But such liberties as were thus conferred on newspapers were seldom put to the uses contemplated in its charter of freedom; its liberties were employed oftener for scurrilities than for the actual exposure of malfeasance in office. Its record in this regard was too thin and insubstantial to answer the grave charges brought against it.

Undoubtedly an overt Federal censorship, in the hands of an irresponsible and bigoted bureau, would prove disastrous. If censorship cannot be averted, it should be restricted to the worst stereotypes of news, such as are employed ruthlessly to deprave public taste in stories of crime and scandal, and to endanger our national peace in foreign news. Unless the press mends its ways, it should prepare itself for such supervision, and may count itself lucky if it is no worse. Only a public realization that censorship stultifies alike those who exercise it, those against whom it is directed, and those who are its indirect victims, can prevent drastic measures.

The assumption that there should be liberty of speech, conscience and press is new. At the most one can count its age at not more than a century and a half, a brief span in the recorded history of humankind. We have no assurance that the assumption is more than a passing fad. If we examine the ground gained and the ground lost since the beginnings of this republic, the score is none too encouraging; and if we audit the balance sheet for the last ten years, we find more items in red ink than on the credit side. The state of freedom is parlous in this land of the free.

POLITICAL LIBERTY

By Max Eastman

I DON'T know why the New School For Social Research has raised up this old-fashioned question of freedom. I suppose that this course of lectures is something in the nature of a memorial ceremony. When we get freedom safely and honorably buried, I trust we are going out from this place in a brave and optimistic spirit, to see if there is any other beautiful thing in the world we can fall in love with.

Freedom lived a great life in America. I imagine there have been few times in history when the common man was more independent of dictation from the state than he was in the early history of this country—especially before they began to protect his liberties with the Constitution of the United States. "All men were created free and equal," "Life, liberty and the pursuit of happiness," "Give me liberty or give me death," those were the thoughts in men's minds in those days. And even after they nailed down the twelve articles of the Constitution, the spirit of liberty survived to a degree that is now difficult to imagine. Difficult to imagine a President of the United States casually remarking, as Thomas Jefferson did, that "A little rebellion now

and then is a good thing—pray God we may never
be twenty years without a rebellion!"   Can you
imagine Calvin Coolidge pausing for a moment in
his arduous task of preventing the embattled farmers
of Nicaragua from shooting into the profits of the
United Fruit Company, pausing to say a few
kind words for rebellion?   All the time that
Thomas Jefferson used to spend loving liberty, Cal
Coolidge spends worrying about prosperity—about
efficiency.   You might describe the entire ideological
history of this country as a gradual extirpation from
the public mind of the ideal of liberty, and all that
is associated with it—the liberty-complex, as we say
now—and its replacement by the complex of national
efficiency.

You can realize how far this process has gone, if
you will remember that in the year 1805 an American citizen by the name of Joseph Dennie was
arrested and indicted for sedition.   He was described
as "a factious and seditious person of wicked mind
and unquiet and turbulent disposition."   (How much
better English they wrote in those days, too!)   And
among the principal charges against him was this:
that he had written and published statements "intending to condemn the principle of revolution."
Just think of that—indicted for sedition in the
United States of America—and moreover, if you
will believe it, in the city of Philadelphia,—for condemning the principle of revolution!   That is how
things really were in those days.

A good deal of that spirit survived until the Civil
War.   It still lived in the mind of Abraham Lincoln,

who asserted, you remember, the "revolutionary right" of a people to overthrow their government if they don't like it. And it lived again with a pale academical flicker in the mind that Woodrow Wilson had before he went to war. I remember clipping with considerable gratification from the pages of the *New Republic* the following passage from Woodrow Wilson's pre-war writings:

"We have forgotten the very principles of our origin, if we have forgotten how to object, how to resist, how to agitate, how to pull down and build up, even to the extent of revolutionary practices if it be necessary. . . ."

About two years after he made this remark and I clipped it from the *New Republic* with such happy gratification, Woodrow Wilson was spending the funds of the United States government in a peculiarly obstinate effort to send me and my political friends to the penitentiary, not for indulging in revolutionary practices but for making semi-revolutionary remarks.

Our entry into the World War marked the final and complete eradication of the liberty complex from the mind of the American people, its replacement by the complex of national efficiency. Since that date anybody who raises a serious question about the "principles of origin" of the American republic is regarded as un-American. Anybody who touches on the more fundamental rights of Anglo-Saxon citizens as they were laid down in Magna Charta is regarded as quixotic. Anybody who breathes a word of the right of revolution is criminally insane—or criminally syndicalist, which amounts to the same thing. You can't read the Declaration of Independence to a body of striking workers without getting arrested for inciting them to riot. A man's house is no longer his castle, except in the sense that if he is going to protect it against unlawful entry from the state's agents he has got to have a moat, a portcullis and a body of men-at-arms in the cellar. He has got to have either that or a large roll of bills in the bank. And just who are these dry-agents who transgress so conscientiously and so profitably all the fundamental rights of Anglo-Saxons that were laid down, as was thought, for all time in the Great Charter of King John? What motive in our body politic do they represent? From what new principle or dominating interest in the public mind do they derive the sanction for these irresponsible invasions of a domain heretofore presided over by an individual intelligence? From the ideal of national efficiency. From that goal, and that purpose of life, and from no other source.

Sacco and Vanzetti were burned to death without a judicial trial—that is the plain truth of the matter, for they were condemned with an obscene epithet before the consideration of the evidence by the judge who tried them—they were burned to death without trial within two miles of Bunker Hill for talking to the people of Massachusetts in extreme language about liberty. But that is not all their crime. You can talk in extreme language about liberty, if you choose the time and place and the audience. But they talked to the working people, and they talked about *industrial* liberty. Such talk holds a menace to the smooth operation of the machinery of our economic life. It holds a menace to our national efficiency. That is why they were burned to death with the consent of the vast majority of the population of Massachusetts. And such old-fashioned New Englanders as Edna St. Vincent Millay, who stood up in Boston Common and attempted to say a word in favor of the old ideals—of liberty and equal justice—were arrested for what? For *loitering!* There you have in a single picture the whole change of trend and color, and of the basic intention of the public mind of America in its short century and a half of life. We have abandoned our first love, human liberty, and we are in love with industrial efficiency and the business prosperity of the nation.

It is interesting to understand the causes of this. Virgil said that a man is happy who understands the causes of things. And I don't think he meant merely because that understanding gives him power to change them. He meant that it is fun. It gives us a feeling of superiority to things to understand them. This feeling of superiority is about the only consolation left for those who used to love liberty, and who now mourn her loss. They can write books about the rise of American civilization, and explain just why it is that American civilization has fallen so low, and that gives them a kind of spiritual elevation over the tragical facts, which are nothing more imposing after all than just plain economics or ways of doing business.

I don't intend to go into the economic explanation of the decline of American civilization. It is enough to remind you of it.　But in so far as it was a decline and disappearance of liberty, I should like to make in the process a distinction which I consider significant.　In the first place we ought not to talk about liberty, but about liberties.　And then we ought to divide these liberties which are gradually but so obviously disappearing with the growth of our machine civilization into two classes.　First, those liberties whose disappearance is an inevitable consequence of the growing complexity of the industrial machine, and its increasingly social or cooperative mode of operation.　The relation between what one person or one group is doing, and what another person or group is doing, becomes continually more close and more complicated in this machine age.　And thus it follows by an almost mathematical necessity that the liberties of each individual and each group grow less.　All society is coming to be more and more like a big business house or factory.　And to the extent that this is true all society has to be run on schedule and by a boss.　A great number of liberties are thus automatically and irremediably lost.

For instance, I have to wait until a man in a blue uniform with brass buttons up and down his belly holds up his hand and beckons to me, before I can walk across the street in my own home town.　That doesn't accord very well with the phraseology of the Declaration of Independence either.　But I don't believe even the most fanatical lover of liberty would feel inclined to revolt against the tyranny of the traffic policeman.　Not on Forty-second Street.　He would only make it absolutely certain that he was going to die under the wheels of a truck or a taxi-cab—whereas if he obeys the policeman he has at least one chance in ten of surviving. I believe that if all our lost liberties were gathered together and tabulated, we should find that an astonishingly large number belong in the same class with these liberties we have lost to the traffic policeman. They are lost because they are absolutely incompatible with a modern machine civilization. We must either kiss these liberties a gallant good-bye, or break the machines. There is no other choice.

But there is another class of liberties that are dead or dying, not because they are incompatible with the machine and factory system, but because they are incompatible with the wage system. There are re-straints and regimentations which arise, not from the social or cooperative way in which our industrial machines are operated, but from the anti-social and un-cooperative way in which they are owned. It is fairly easy to explain to any sound-minded men that if a group of people are going to cooperate in producing something, there must be one boss and the rest must submit themselves to his orders. But when it comes to dividing up what they have produced, it is not so easy to make them see that a very small group, composed mainly of those who were standing on the side-lines cheering and encouraging the work, should take the lion's share, and that the vast majority of those who were actually doing the work should content themselves with the mean, cheap and contemptible handful of crumbs which we describe as a "living wage."

There are a good many things, such as insurance
and the distribution of stock-holdings, which mitigate the rigor of this wage system or class system of
producing wealth. But they are superficial. Five
per cent of the people own 65 per cent of the
wealth and 65 per cent of the people own little
or nothing but the hands with which they work. The
wealth is increasing all the time, and the *proportion*
which goes to the toiling masses is not increasing.
And yet these masses are becoming more and more
educated, more and more thoughtful of their
interests, more and more aware of the economic
situation as a whole. And besides that there are
always a lot of us disreputable agitators going
around telling them how bad it is, and there always
will be. It is quite obvious that for the successful
and efficient operation of such a system, the liberties
of these masses and of the agitators who go among
them must be pretty closely cropped down and killed.
To put it in short language: the working classes
must be kept in order.

I do not pretend that these two necessities of our
economic system exhaust the causes of the disappearance of liberty and the ideal of liberty from America.
There are other causes. America is suppressing the
free expression of sex, because she is for the first time
confronting in her conscious mind the realities of
sexual life, and she is frightened by them. That accounts for the absurdities of the movie censorship,
the padlocking of New York's most intelligent
theaters, and the rigid prohibition of love-stories in
Boston. In these respects we are actually becoming

more free, and that is the reason why the censorship is so absurdly and, in fact, pathologically exaggerated. Boston is an hysterical old maid going into convulsions at the mere literary reminder of the existence of her own bare skin. These convulsions will soon pass off, and we shall find that the process marked by this hysteria has been wholly a process of liberation. In fact, I think we are on the verge of a revival of faith in nature, a revival of the straightforward, affirmative living of life as we were made to live it, such as characterized the Elizabethan era. We are not exactly on the verge of it, but we are approaching it. This country is going to have its youth, you may be sure of that. And when grown-up people wake up and find out that they were old all the time that they ought to have been young, and then start in to make up for it, you might as well clear away the furniture and get out. That is what is going to happen in America.

A similar thing is going to happen, and is happening, in my judgment, in the sphere of religious opinion. The back provinces are passing laws against the theory of evolution, not because they are becoming more orthodox and intolerant than they were, but because they are just beginning to hear about evolution. They are just waking up to the fact that some people honestly believe that monkeys played a serious and even a passionate part in the creation of man. They would have passed these same laws any time in the last hundred and fifty years, if they had had any cause to dream that anybody had such a reverent thought about monkeys. The fact that these laws are being passed is the first streak of the dawn of an age of enlightenment. Just as the burning at the stake of Giordano Bruno was a sign and signal for the great rebirth of knowledge and the pagan faith in life that we call the Renaissance—so in its more modern and more ludicrous way, the monkey trial in Tennessee was a sign of the rapid and victorious march of science and free thought over these medieval United States. Of that I feel quite sure. And I think it would be wiser to worry about what we are going to put in the emotional place of orthodox religion when it is all gone than to worry lest these ridiculous and pitiful provincial resistance-hysterias are going to stop the victorious march of science.

We are going to have free thought about God and the earth and the universe in these states. It is an inevitable consequence of our prosperity and our mechanical achievements. And we are going to have free art and poetry too, freedom in love and in the experience of life for those who have wealth enough to attain it. All the signs point that way—and these exaggerated repressions which are almost as futile as they are exaggerated, point that way most of all.

But we are not going to have freedom to act in ways that throw out of gear the gigantic social and industrial machine upon which our civilization is founded. In that respect we are going to be more and more regimented and repressed as time goes on. That is why I say that the problem of liberty, so far as it is a real and deep and tragic problem, is merely this problem of how a group of free people can constitute a factory and operate a machine. And the answer is, that if you take freedom in any very extreme or realistic sense, they can't. We have lost half of our liberties to the imperious demands of the belt and the traveling crane, and we can't do anything about that.

The other half we have lost to the way these instruments are owned, and it does seem as though we might do something about that. It is neither humane nor practical for a comparatively small class of people to own all this precious machinery, as well as the earth under it, and to enjoy the profits of the general toil at the expense of the rest. It entails a continual repression at home and a continual search for new markets and consequent preparation for imperialist wars abroad. In these wars and preparation for wars whatever little remnants of liberty we might have left, are lost. Therefore the problem of reviving liberty or saving what little of it we can, reduces itself to the problem of getting rid of the wage system, or the class system, of owning our vast social and industrial machine and distributing its profits. It does seem as though if we put our minds to it, and our muscles, we might be able to accomplish that supremely wise and beautiful task.

The task is gigantic, however. It is certainly a far greater task than the rearing up of this mythical city of towers into the sky. And we know that such tasks are not accomplished by magicians or ministers of the gospel. They are not accomplished by conjuring or by prayer. They are accomplished by scientific men, who have studied the materials and the laws of mechanics, and devised, in close and most realistic contact with hard facts, a careful and systematic and realistic and reliable method of procedure—a method of procedure which we call scientific, in order to distinguish it from the method of the magician and the priest.   It is fairly obvious, then, that if we are really and seriously intending to produce a class-free civilization, we must turn to these same sort of men.   We must turn to science.   This has been obvious now for almost a hundred years, and the two great doctrines as to how this new and free society might be produced have both laid claim to the title of science.   The doctrine of Karl Marx is called scientific socialism, and the anarchist doctrine lives largely by its boast of being more scientific than Marxism.   I do not think either of these doctrines is scientific in the sense that an engineer is scientific who plans and constructs a skyscraper. Quite the contrary, I think that anarchism belongs in the same general category with the belief in magic, and I think that Marxism, in its orthodox form, is a relic of religious belief.

A scientific method for creating a free society would consist of three distinguishable parts: an outline or ground plan of the society to be created; an examination and analysis of the existing society; and a plan of action for arriving at the goal outlined upon the basis of the existing facts.   That is the general form taken by any practical scientific enterprise.   Now, magic differs from science in that the magician concentrates his mind almost exclusively upon the goal to be attained and pays very little attention to the existing facts or the laws of their behavior. In his effort to change or control the world, he ignores almost entirely the unchangeable or uncontrollable element in it. The scientist, on the other hand, not only pays attention to existing facts, but he spends most of his time ascertaining their exact character and defining them. His effort to change and control the world is based upon and guided by a definition of what is unchangeable or uncontrollable in it. Thus, for example, the alchemists of the Middle Ages attempted by every sort of random device to convert various substances into gold, but they did not examine the interior structure of these substances or the laws of their behavior. The science of chemistry was born when Robert Boyle turned his attention exclusively to determining that interior structure and those laws. But the original purpose was in principle only postponed; the science of chemistry may yet succeed, it seems, in converting other substances into gold.

Revolutionary anarchism, as a method for creating a free society, is very closely akin to alchemy as a method for producing the noble metals. It has the same happy way of ignoring the stubbornness of the existing facts. Its method consists of "holding the thought" of a free society, and then taking any kind of drastic and extreme rebel action which might be supposed to "call up" that free society. I remember reading in Russia an account of the trial of the famous socialist revolutionary, Vera Figner. In a statement which she made to the court, she explained herself and her organization with these simple words:

"Our plan was by the systematic annihilation of Governors-General to annihilate the office of Governor-General."

However much you may admire the bold simplicity of that formula, you can hardly describe it as scientific method. And the same thing may be said for the slightly more elaborate formulas of Kropotkin and the other anarchists and anarchistic leaders. They remind you rather of the asseverations of Christian Scientists and Yogis and New Thought Healers, the element of faith prevails so greatly over the element of fact. The relation of anarchists to a real science of progress towards liberty is in fact the same as that of amateur healers, the survivors of wizardry, to the science of medicine. They survive by refusing to acknowledge, or concentrate their attention upon, the unchangeable or uncontrollable elements in the given facts, to formulate these elements in "laws," and thus arrive at a systematic procedure by which the given facts can be actually and not only imaginatively changed or controlled. The method of revolutionary anarchism, speaking broadly and yet with technical accuracy, is to conjure up the free society by the magical act of revolution.

The other great scheme or system proposed, during the nineteenth century, for creating a free society, was Marxism, or, as it was more commonly described in this country, scientific socialism. It is my main contention in my book called "Marx and Lenin," that Marxism—in its intellectual form at most, its orthodox form—is not a scientific hypothesis but a very ingenious and peculiar system of religious belief. It is not easy to prove this thesis, which flies in the face of the passionate convictions of most of my colleagues and political friends. About all I can do here is to advertise my book—which is, of course, the main thing. It is just being published in this country by Albert and Charles Boni, and if you really want to know what I think about all these things I am talking about, that is where you will find it.

I will try, however, if your attention is not already tired, to give you a hint of what I mean about Marxian socialism being a religion. In primitive culture it is possible to distinguish two quite different kinds of thinking—animistic thinking, in which one tries to adjust oneself to the external world as to a person and the ordinary practical thinking by which the daily arts of life are carried on. Animistic thinking consists essentially in trying, by some sort of hokuspokus, to transfer your own wishes into the external world and so get them realized. Practical thinking recognizes that your wishes are in your own breast, and tries to realize them by operating upon the external world as an impersonal and indifferent material. Religion grows out of the animistic attitude towards reality. Science grows out of a practical attitude. And philosophy, insofar as philosophy is anything more than a generalization of science, occupies itself with an attempt to defend the animistic attitude in the face of the advancing success and general recognition of the scientific attitude.

That, at least, is what Hegel's philosophy occupied itself with. And Karl Marx was educated as a Hegelian. He was educated in the animistic attitude to the objective world. He believed up to the age of twenty-five that the world is not matter but spirit, and that the spirit of the world is engaged in a process of development or evolution which is akin to the impulses of idealistic men. He believed that true wisdom consists of finding out the purposes of that World Spirit and then cooperating with Him. Let me read you a passage which will illustrate the intellectual attitude of Marx and Engels up to their twenty-fifth and twenty-third year respectively:

"And that faith in the omnipotence of the idea, in the victory of eternal truth, that firm certainty that it will never waver, never depart from its path, though the whole world turn against it—there you have the foundation of the real positive philosophy, the philosophy of universal history. Just that is the supreme revelation, the revelation of man to man, in which every negation of the critic becomes an affirmation. That everlasting struggle and movement of peoples and heroes, above which in the eternal world soars the Idea, only to swoop down into the thick of the fight and become the actual self-conscious soul—there you have the source of every salvation and redemption, there the kingdom in which every one of us ought to struggle and be active at his post. . . ."

In this animistic attitude, Marx and Engels developed their intellectual powers, and formed their habits of thought. Their thinking consisted, up to the age of about twenty-five and twenty-three respectively, in imputing their own aspirations to the World Spirit, and then proceeding fervently to cooperate with that spirit. At twenty-five Marx fell under the influence of the materialist, Ludwig Feuer-

bach, and experienced an enormous emotional change
—a conversion to the belief that the world is not
spirit but matter, and that spirit is something that
exists only inside a man's head. It was after this
change, that Marx set out to write the science of
socialism. His science therefore starts off with the
uncompromising assertion that the world is material,
and there is no spirit in it. He bases all his thinking upon this assertion, and he calls his entire philosophical system "Dialectic Materialism" and he has
been cursed for a hundred years as their arch enemy
by those who believe in a spiritual world.

The fact remains, however, that Marx's writing
and all his thinking was still, in the essence of the
matter, animistic. It still consisted of persuading
himself that the external world was doing what he
wanted it to do, and that his task was to cooperate
with it. Let me read you a short passage in which
I summarize this fact:

"Marx did not examine this material world, as an arti-
san examines the materials of his trade, in order to determine by what means he could make something else out of it.
He examined it as the priest examines the ideal world, in
order to see if he could not find in it, or failing that, trans-
plant into it his own creative aspiration. Marxism in its
intellectual form was not a step from utopian to scientific
socialism—from impractical evangelical talk about a better
society, to a practical plan, based upon a study of the existing society, for producing a better one. Marxism was a
step from utopian socialism to a socialistic religion—a scheme
for convincing the believer that the universe itself is producing a better society, and that he has only to fall in properly with the general movement of this universe.

" 'We explained,' " says Marx, in describing his own
innovation, " 'that it is not a question of putting through

some utopian system, but of taking a conscious part in the process of social transformation which is going on before our very eyes.' "

That was Marx's conception of a scientific undertaking.

Plekhanov has a passage in which he describes the mental process by which Marx became a "scientific socialist."

"A disciple of Hegel," he says, "remaining true to the method of his teacher, could become a socialist only in case a scientific investigation of the contemporary economic structure brought him to the conclusion that its inner lawful development leads to the birth of the socialist order."

In other words, if you wish to create a socialist order, there is only one way to go about it, and that is to persuade yourself that the inner law of the objective world is creating it for you. If this attitude is remote from prayer, it is remote in the direction of its primitive origins. Dialectic Materialism rests its hope in the very sticks and stones, instead of in a spirit that is supposed to reside behind them. Otherwise it is not different from any other animistic philosophy. And whatever may have been the case with Marx, it is certain that many of his followers derive from this philosophy a support not unlike that derived by the pious from their God.

"If in spite of all the violence of its enemies," writes Rosa Luxemburg, "the contemporary workers' movement marches triumphantly forward with its head high, that is due above all to its tranquil understanding of the ordered objective historic development, its understanding of the fact that 'capitalist production creates with the necessity of a natural process its own negation—namely, the expropriation of the expropriators, the socialist revolution.' In this understanding the workers' movement sees the firm guarantee of its ultimate victory, and from this source it derives not only its zeal, but its patience, not only strength for action, but also courageous restraint and endurance."

It is not difficult to recognize in those lines the essential features of a religious psychology.

You will understand very much better what has happened and what is happening in Russia, if you remember this one fact: that the Bolsheviks are not purely scientific people with a plan or working-hypothesis as to how they can produce a free society. They are religious people with a complicated system of belief—a belief that the material world is itself automatically producing a free society, by a certain kind of evolutionary process which they describe as "dialectic," and that they are merely links or agents in the process.

Now Lenin, I hasten to add, was not a very devotedly religious man. He was known all through his life as an incorrigible heretic of Marxism. He was denounced and excommunicated by all the great priests of the Marxian church—German and Russian alike. And his heresy consisted essentially of a refusal to take this proposition about the dialectic evolution of the material world towards communism, and the historic necessity of the proletarian revolution, seriously. He refused to take it seriously *enough* so that it might interfere with his practical work. So far as achieving the proletarian revolution goes, he took the position of a practical scientific engineer, who does not rely in the least de-

gree upon the destinies or necessities inherent in the
material with which he worked. He did not regard
himself, as orthodox Marxists do, as "bringing to
the working-classes a consciousness of their destiny."
He regarded himself as doing something by means
of and in company with the working classes, and he
regarded his own conscious thinking as an essential
element in getting it done.

Nevertheless Lenin thought that he believed in
the Marxian religion. And insofar as concerns any
problem which was not immediate and practical, any
problem which he could push off into the remote
future, he did believe in it. Now according to the
Marxian religion the problem of political liberty *is*
pushed off into the remote future. The Marxian
believes that history is going to produce a free
society, by first producing a proletarian dictatorship
which shall expropriate the capitalists, undertake the
collective ownership of the industrial machine, and
thus reduce everybody to the level of the proletariat.
This will be accomplished during a "transition
period" in which there will be a very rigid and violent
suppression of liberties as heretofore conceived. But
as soon as that process is accomplished, the entire
institution of the state will "die away," and we shall
have not only liberty, but complete anarchy—each
fulfilling his appropriate task without any force or
violence—each working according to his abilities and
each receiving according to his needs, and all of
them living happily ever after. That is the Marxian
view of the problem of political liberty—the famous
theory of the "dying away of the state."   I think

there is a solid practical science mixed up in the Marxian religion, which we ought to and will preserve.   Indeed I think the practical science of engineering with class forces which Lenin inherited from the Marxian system, is one of the greatest, if not the greatest, discovery of the nineteenth century. But as for this theory of the dying away of the state, I think it is purely and simply a religious myth, a legend, entirely comparable to the legend of the second coming of Christ.

It is amusing to note that while the communists theoretically believe in the dying away of the state after the proletarian revolution, their one practical boast at the present time is that proletarian Russia has the most stable government anywhere in the world today.   Most of them have actually forgotten all about that legend of the dying away of the state under socialism.   At least most of the followers of Stalin have.

Stalin boasts that he is actually building socialism in one country.   He is not merely holding fast the dictatorship while awaiting the development of world revolution.   Therefore it is legitimate to ask of Stalin that he show us some preliminary signs or first faint glimpses of the dying away of the state.   Instead of that he is showing us a tyranny growing daily more and more similar to the tyranny of the czar.

As a first step towards building socialism in one country, Stalin directed his secret police to arrest a half a hundred of the oldest, most intelligent and most devoted of those who had given their lives to the struggle for socialism, and shipped them off to Siberia and Afghanistan under police guard, giving them a salary of thirty rubles, that is fifteen dollars, a month, and no work to do. I am told that some of them have arrived in exactly the same place of exile where they lived so long ago in their young manhood under the czar. Their followers meanwhile have been arrested by hundreds and locked up in jail among common criminals without the privileges of political prisoners. That is the condition of affairs with regard to the dying away of the state in Soviet Russia at the present moment.

I fear I have contributed little besides reinforced and carefully demonstrated gloom to this memorial meeting in honor of political freedom. Others have told you that freedom is dead, and I have added that the sciences by which she is supposed to be revived at some happy day in the future are not entirely scientific. The extreme ideal of liberty is incompatible with a machine age, and the thing for extreme idealists to do, as I said at the beginning, is to go out and find some other beautiful thing in the world to fall in love with. The thing I would advise them to fall in love with is the justice and bold wisdom of a change in the manner in which the machines are owned. That is not quite so glorious-sounding a thing as freedom, but it has the advantage of being relevant to the situation we are in. It has this further advantage that there *is* a scientific method for achieving it. And finally it is the sole method by which we can win back and protect and establish those liberties which are *not* inherently incompatible with a machine civilization. In struggling towards this end, I am afraid we are going to have to get rid of our liberty complex altogether, and quite frankly recognize that the political problem in these days is resolving itself into a choice between two kinds of state authority— the authority which rests upon the support of the wage-working masses, and the authority which rests upon the support of an owning class. I would at least earnestly advise all liberals and libertarians to pause from time to time in their struggle to revive freedom or awaken again the spirit of freedom which has sunk into the earth—to pause and ask themselves the question: What decision will you make in case history ignores your efforts altogether, and presents you with this inexorable alternative—Lenin or Mussolini?

Under Mussolini the constraint inherent in the machine system is multiplied by the restraint inherent in the class system, and we have a tyranny not only absolute in the present, but holding no hope for the future. Under the dictatorship of the proletariat— or, to be more accurate, of a party of the proletariat—we have still the constraint inherent in the machine system, but we have the reasonable hope that the constraint inherent in the wage system can be progressively removed.

That is all I can say for political liberty as an institution. But I would like to add that those who love freedom with a hard and daring force will have a great deal of freedom, no matter which way the world goes. Those who love liberty will take

liberties with any system. Those who love freedom will "make free." There will be rebels
in the millennium. Christ on his Throne will never
be twenty years without a rebellion. A *bund* composed of the intellectuals, the vagrant, and the criminally insane will raise the torch of revolt against the
Brotherhood of Man. And eternal vigilance, combined with a certain foxiness in finding out the small
cracks in the system, will always be the price of
liberty.

FREEDOM IN THE FINE ARTS

By Robert Morss Lovett

THE subject assigned me in this course is, I believe, the most difficult of all the problems of freedom. It is difficult both in the matter of laying down principles and in prescribing rules for their application, difficult in law and in administration. This difficulty arises primarily from the fact that in considering the censorship of art in terms of morals we are obliged to deal with matters belonging to different categories. If we could premise at the outset that these things were of the same kind, that the aim of art was to do good to people in an ethical sense, either to enforce the mores of existing society or to criticize established customs in the interests of progress, there would still be difficulties; but we should be dealing with commensurate quantities, in terms of the same class. Questions of freedom of opinion and speech on social matters are of this sort. They tend to resolve themselves into a consideration of social welfare from the point of view of social organization, stability and progress. But the censorship of art involves an aesthetic as well as a moral element, and a whole range of values which appeal to the individual as worth while in themselves, not as means but as ends, not as machinery of life but as

183

life itself.   This is the peculiarity of aesthetic as contrasted with social values.   It is owing to this fact that the class which feels most strongly their appeal, and is especially devoted to their conservation and replenishment, is constantly in battle *à l'outrance* with a class which is not sensitive to them, and which would even suppress them in the interest of social conformity, or morality, or convenience.

As a mode of practical approach, let us divide the subject into its elements, the three groups who are concerned—the censors, the censored, and the public on whose account the censorship is undertaken.   The first includes governmental agencies, official censors, like His Majesty's reader of plays, the police, the post-office, etc., as well as chartered institutions, churches, libraries, institutes, salons, Watch and Ward societies and the like.   At the outset, it may be thought that their case for censorship falls to the ground, for history has never shown a body of men capable of exercising censorship with an authority that has stood the test of time, or even, except for brief intervals, of exercising it effectively at all.   On the other hand, this same history is full of ridiculous and humiliating errors and failures on the part of civil, ecclesiastical or ethical authorities.   There is either a congenital incapacity in human nature to deal with aesthetic matters according to a code representing political, social or ethical interests, or else there has been singular ill luck in choosing the human instruments appointed to the task.

Sir Edmund Gosse finds the first instance of cen-

sorship in the Christian Era offered by the Council
of Carthage in the Fourth Century, which forbade
Christians to read pagan books.   Exactly the same
prohibition was enacted by the Emperor Julian,
felicitously known as the Apostate, but for a different
reason.   He proposed to starve out Christian culture, and his edict forced the Christians to provide
for the studies of the trivium and quadrivium out
of the Scriptures.   Without pausing over the Coun-
cils of Toulouse and Trent, the Inquisition and the
Indices, for a historical example of censorship let us
take the British censorship of plays, an institution
which assumes its modern form with Sir Robert
Walpole's Licensing Act of 1737, by which plays for
presentation were required to be submitted for
license to the Lord Chamberlain.   This measure was
inspired by Walpole's fear of political criticism
rather than love of morality.   It had the immediate
effect of depriving the English stage of Henry Fielding, whom Mr. Shaw thinks the greatest dramatist
since Shakespeare, and transferring his genius to the
novel.   Obviously if Fielding was a dangerous character, this action increased his power for harm.
More people read novels than see plays, and through
more generations.   Accordingly, whatever was accomplished for the benefit of contemporaries by the
suppression of Fielding the playwright was enormously at the expense of posterity.   Another curious
circumstance connected with this establishment of the
censorship of the drama reminds us of the ill-luck
which has attended that institution in respect to its

personnel. For the Lord Chamberlain, too busy to
attend to the matter, was allowed to appoint a
Licenser of Plays at £400 *per annum,* and he in
turn a deputy at £200, and for this latter office a
certain Odell was selected, the Manager of the
Goodman's Fields Theatre, which was precisely the
playhouse most under criticism on moral grounds.

The censorship of plays continued its activities
through the 18th century. It vetoed Brooke's
Gustavus Vasa, because of some "strokes of liberty,"
and *Edward and Eleanora* because of reflections on
the royal family. Both were at once published as
books and sold largely as the result of the favorable
advertising which they had received. Another event
has been pointed out as an example of the curious
unforeseen and unpredictable results of the interference of the state in the diocese of the artist. One
of the legitimate reasons for censorship in the theater
has always been the danger of impairing relations
with a friendly power. A company of French actors
which appeared in London in 1777 was hissed and
booed off the stage in the presence of the French
Ambassador, by an audience which claimed to be
irritated by the suppression of English plays. I am
inclined to think, however, that the favorable attitude
of the French Government toward the revolting
colonies of North America may have had something
to do with it.

When theaters producing legitimate drama in
London were restricted by patent to two or three,
there was a certain propriety in the licensing of plays,

and when this restriction was removed in 1843, a favorable opportunity occurred for abolishing the censor. Since this opportunity was passed up, the censorship has remained an object of exasperation tempered by derision. In 1878 the censor refused to license Augier's play *Les Lionnes Pauvres* on the ground that though it was "profoundly moral in its ultimate purpose . . . if presented to an English audience it would give much offence!" In 1896, at a time of great tension between Great Britain and Germany over the Kaiser's telegram to President Kruger congratulating him on his escape from Doctor Jameson, the censor did nothing to prevent the theaters from introducing into plays songs celebrating Jameson's raid and damning the Kaiser. A little later he closed the Mikado, which was then old stuff. I believe the Japanese ambassador himself was responsible for its resumption.

In 1892 and again in 1909, committees of inquiry were appointed by Parliament, and both occasions were field days for dramatic authors. In 1892, the Examiner of Plays was a certain Pigott. At this time, it will be remembered, a few actors and critics —Miss Janet Achurch, Miss Elizabeth Robins, William Archer, Bernard Shaw—were trying to put Ibsen over on the English stage against a ferocious clamor from conventional critics, led by Mr. Clement Scott, who found in Mr. Pigott a somewhat uncertain ally. Pigott said, "I have studied Ibsen pretty carefully and all the characters of Ibsen's plays appear to me to be morally deranged." When he was charged with inconsistency in licensing some of these plays, he defended his action on the ground that he thought them too foolish to do any harm.

The inquiry of 1909 was much more searching, and initiated the discussion which has lasted until today. I do not flatter myself that this evening's exercises will put an end to it. By that time what Mr. Henry Arthur Jones describes as the Renaissance of the English drama was in full swing, and one sign of it was the supplanting of Mr. Pinero and Mr. Jones himself by Bernard Shaw, Granville Barker, Israel Zangwill and others. Some of these had fallen under the ban. Mr. Shaw's *Mrs. Warren's Profession* and more recently *The Shewing Up of Blanco Posnett* had been held up, Mr. Barker's *Waste*, Mr. Zangwill's *The New Religion*, Mr. Eden Phillpott's *The Secret Woman*, Mr. Garnett's *Breaking Point*, Mr. Lawrence Housman's *Bethlehem*, as well as Maeterlinck's *Monna Vanna*.

The examiners of plays were two, Mr. Brookfield, who was himself the author of a successful but scabrous farce entitled "Dear Old Charlie," and Mr. Redford, who was originally a bank manager and had eased himself into his licensing job as a friend of a former licenser by relieving him as *locum tenens* when the latter was away on vacation. When asked about his standards, he said that he tried always to take "the official view," which meant, among other things, that the deity and other scriptural persons must not be mentioned on the stage. Mr. Redford fell back on the classic argument that if it was wrong to have a censor, the offence was mitigated by his being such a little one. In fourteen years he had read 7,000 plays, of which he had rejected only thirty, and of these only five were English. In short, Messrs. Redford and Brookfield were perfect illustrations of the fallacy in censorship through the fallibility of human means, which Milton had pointed out long before in the *Areopagitica*.

Another reason, whereby to make it plain that this Order will miss the end it seeks, consider by the quality which ought to be in every licenser. It cannot be denied but that he who is made judge to sit upon the birth or death of books, whether they may be wafted into this world or not, had need to be a man above the common measure, both studious, learned and judicious; there may be also no mean mistakes in the censure of what is passable or not; which is also no mean injury. If he be of such worth as behooves him, there cannot be a more tedious and unpleasing journey-work, a greater loss of time levied upon his head, than to be made the perpetual reader of unchosen books and pamphlets, ofttimes huge volumes. . . . Seeing, therefore, those who now possess the employment, by all evident signs wish themselves well rid of it, and that no man of worth, none that is not a plain unthrift of his own hours is ever likely to succeed them, except he mean to put himself to the salary of a press corrector, we may easily foresee what kind of licensers we are to expect hereafter, either ignorant, imperious, and remiss, or basely pecuniary.

The outcome of the inquiry was a report for which Mr. Herbert Samuel was chiefly responsible, which declared that:

"In view of the danger that the official control over plays before their production may hinder the question of a great and serious national drama . . . we conclude that the licensing authority . . . should not have the power to impose a veto on the production, but may suspend the performance of unlicensed plays which appear to be of an improper character."

The kinds of impropriety are: (1) Indecency; (2) Offensive Personalities; (3) Representing invidiously persons living or recently dead; (4) Irreverence in religious matters; (5) Conducing to vice or crime; (6) Impairing relations with a friendly power; (7) Causing a breach of the peace. I suppose that if it be admitted that any restrictions are to be put upon the stage by public officers, this list is as good as could be devised. Its very terms are an argument in favor of such restriction. The report, it will be noted, would remove the licenser as an authority of last resort. Mr. Robert Harcourt introduced a bill which went farther, and transferred all licensing powers from the Lord Chamberlain to the London County Council. The effect of this would have been to abolish the censorship and hand the matter over to the courts, as is the case in the United States, a condition of freedom which was frequently referred to with admiration during the progress of the hearings. We in this country have had an opportunity to see the workings of this arrangement, and note the same crass ineptitude and stupid inconsistency as have characterized the operations of the censorship in England.

The theatrical situation of America is more and more controlled in New York, as that of Great Britain in London. What passes the police power in New York will generally pass elsewhere; the sup-

pression of a play in its tryout in New Haven, or
Harrisburg, or Baltimore, is sometimes good advertising for it in New York, but its suppression there
ends its career, for no play can succeed in the provinces without a New York run.   The New York
police have to their credit the suppression, among
others, of Hauptmann's lovely *Hannele,* of Bernard
Shaw's *Mrs. Warren's Profession,* and lately, among
a number of other plays, *The God of Vengeance* by
Sholom Asch.   Last year, *The Captive* was withdrawn to avoid being stopped.   It is needless to remind this audience of the number of plays which,
year by year, are allowed in spite of a deliberate
pandering to what are called the baser instincts.   In
general, the only ground of suppression is serious
presentation of sexual problems.   Such plays of
social criticism as *Professional,* or *Spread Eagle,* get
by, though with something of a spasm.   An exception to this statement is afforded by *The Racket* by
Mr. Bartlett Cormack, which ran successfully in
New York, and would in the natural course of things
have gone to Chicago.   But the scene of the play
is Chicago, and the action turns on the political
alliance of the State's Attorney's Office with criminal
gangs, and the murder of an Assistant State's
Attorney, which is covered up with the pregnant
phrase: "He knew too much."   Now a year ago in
Cook county occurred a murder of such an official,
which a grand jury of eminent citizens investigated
under the guidance of State's Attorney Robert E.
Crowe, with no more definite report than commenda-

tion of the Chicago Crimes Commission and condemnation of the Volstead Act. Mr. Crowe was interested in Mr. Cormack's play to the extent of having a stenographer take it down from the actors' lips, and Mr. Cormack informs me that he understands that the Shuberts, and doubtless other theater owners, have been warned not to bring the play to Chicago.

The question of censorship, supposing it to exist at all, by a single responsible person, or by the police and magistrates amid their other duties, is a crucial one. Lord Chesterfield in opposing Walpole's original act exclaimed: "If poets and players are to be restrained, let them be restrained as other subjects are by the known laws of their country; if they offend, let them be tried as every Englishman ought to be by God and their country. Let us not subject them to the arbitrary will and pleasure of a single man." But the case is not entirely simple. Censorship as an institution usually does away with the rough justice of the police. Licensing may act as protection, as well as prohibition. Above all, it may be a means of education, especially if public opinion should call the censor to account for his behavior more frequently. This is doubtless what Bernard Shaw had in mind when he assured the Committee that "the stupidest censor is the least mischievous." Police censorship is not largely productive of educational values. The best that can be said for it is that it is part of our present civilization. Until we agree with Mr. Shaw that the criminal instincts of the population, let alone to do their worst, will not result in as great mischief as is occasioned by the effort to control them by police and courts, we shall have to accept the occasional slugging of a play as we do of a citizen by the police in the performance of their duties. Slugging and third degree methods are usually upheld by judges in the interest of the prestige of guardians of public order.

The official censorship of literature in general involves most of the same considerations as censorship of the drama. Obviously there is a difference. A play may raise in more immediate form the question of public morals and public order than a book. What you read has not the same effect upon you as what you hear or see as one among many. The herd instinct is always a menace. The censorship of books and magazines does not call for special functionaries, except in time of war. It takes place through the post-office and through the courts; and its exercise affords the same spectacle of inconsistency and ineptitude. Under our national law, the post-office authorities occasionally send to jail people who are too active in limiting the birth rate, and occasionally withhold mailing privileges from matter that is pronounced obscene. This, of course, amounts in many cases to suppression. Apparently the inspectors take, like Mr. Redford, "the official view." For example, certain words,—vulgar they may be and offensive to many of good taste, but not inciting to physical or mental insurrection—are sufficient reason for barring reading matter from the mails, a practice

copied from the censor of Naples under King
Bomba, who marked for destruction all books con-
taining references to God, the devil, or the Virgin
Mary, and let the rest pass. Occasionally, the police
and the courts take a hand. Mr. Lawrence's *The
Rainbow* was barred in England, as were Mr.
Dreiser's *The Genius,* Mr. Cabell's *Jurgen* and Mr.
Joyce's *Ulysses* in this country. The futility of this
proceeding is evident when it is considered that these
books, except the last named, are all now in general
circulation. Indeed it may be stated that since the
prohibition of the circulation of the Bible broke
down, no official authority, civil or ecclesiastical, has
had the power to keep from the public books which
the public has made up its mind to read, and its
desire is usually whetted by the attempt.

Before leaving the subject of the censors, a word
should be said of the volunteers who exercise a kind
of espionage and are often the *agents provocateurs*
of official action. Most of the prosecutions in New
York have been instigated by the Society for the Suppression of Vice and its agents, Anthony Comstock
and Mr. John S. Sumner; in Boston by the Watch
and Ward Society. But in every small city or town
there are usually individuals of this kind of public
spirit who make themselves felt by library boards
and local booksellers. The trouble with such voluntary censorship is that it is rarely disinterested. In
the case of societies supported by the dues of mem-
bership, the paid officials must manifest activity and
secure convictions to justify their existence. In the

case of churches and individuals, usually some special interest or prejudice determines their action rather than a broad view of the field. To give a personal instance, I once served on a committee of reference to pass on recommendations of the censors of moving pictures in Chicago. On one occasion we witnessed an elaborate production called *Truth,* which was the object of the pursuit of a hero who in his first incarnation is a Romanist monk, and in the second an Episcopal rector. We all voted to pass the film except one member, a Roman Catholic priest, who objected violently. It was not that *Truth* was fair, naked and unashamed, only that there was represented a scene of harmless revelry among the monks which he contended tended to bring religion into disrepute. If the happy gathering had taken place in the second part, among the hero's Episcopal associates, there would have been no objection. Altogether, the influence of special interests, moral, ecclesiastical or social, on the restriction of the freedom of the artist, as on the freedom of the scientist, is usually productive of confusion of standards and injustice in their application. When any such special interest gains control, the result is suicidal. The censorship of the Abbe Mutet in the reign of Charles X, of France, put Le Sage, Beaumarchais, Chateaubriand and even Fénélon's *Télémaque* on the forbidden list, and was a cause of the Three Days of July. As Rémy de Gourmont remarked, "When morality triumphs nasty things happen."

If I have given so much time to the censors, it is

because they have taken to themselves a dispropor-
tionate share of the subject. To the artists and what
they want, as Sir Edmund Gosse remarks, no one
pays much attention. It will be remarked that of
the several classes of artists, writers only have come
in for any large share of the attention of the censors.
It is true that now and then a painting or a piece of
statuary, as in the case of Mr. MacMonnies' Bac-
chante, falls under the ban of a puritan Boston, but
some concession in the matter of the figleaf is usually
sufficient to avoid trouble. The reason for the com-
parative immunity of the other arts from the restrictions placed on literature is clearly due to the fact
that they are protected, both from general practice
and general appreciation, by technical processes difficult to master. Writing is the democratic medium
of expression, protected by no esoteric technique
and finding through the printing press an unlimited
means of circulation. It is especially since the appearance of realism as a creed and method that
literature has been persecuted as an art. *Madame
Bovary* was the first challenging achievement of
modern naturalism, and its priority in art was signal-
ized by priority in persecution. Its arraignment was
a *cause celèbre* in France. It once gave a judge the
opportunity to illustrate unforgettably the difficulty
of which I spoke at the outset of evaluating art in
terms of morality. "The question is," said this Dog-
berry, "did Madame Bovary love her husband or did
she try to love him?" The struggle for the right of
the literary artist to picture the world as he sees it

has had its martyrs. Ernest Vizetelly was imprisoned in England for translating and publishing Zola's great novels. Theodore Dreiser for many years was deprived of fame as the result of a treacherous suppression by his publisher, and later of his rewards by official action.

It may be contended that the proper way to free any art from the interference of unqualified and improperly interested persons is for the practitioners of it to organize as a guild and set up their own censorship responsible to the public as well as to themselves. In this way, it might be thought, the dignity of art might be recognized; irrelevant considerations banned by the consensus of authority of the guild; and the principle maintained that aesthetic things must be aesthetically discerned. A moment's reflection will convince anyone that censorship by artists is the worst sort of censorship of art. Such internal control exercises a far more depressing restriction upon the arts than the most rigid external censorship. The safety valve in the case of the latter is that it is illogical in theory and stupid in practice. There have been musical guilds, and their adverse influence is depicted in *Die Meistersinger* and *Feuersnot*. If these guilds had prevailed, we should have had no Wagner, no Strauss, no Schoenberg, no Stravinsky. There have been salons of painting and sculpture. The operation of a jury is described in a striking scene in Zola's *L'Oeuvre*. If the salons had prevailed, we should have had no Pre-Raphaelites, no Impressionists, no post-Impressionists, no

Monet, no Cézanne, no Matisse, no Gauguin. The greatest thing that the salons have done for art is to furnish stimulus for the secessions. And the same may perhaps be said of the leading attempt at the organization of literature, the French Academy. John Stuart Mill, whose social outlook no one will question, has declared in his book *On Liberty,* that individuality is the most precious thing in the world. In the arts, surely this individuality is more than elsewhere essential. Freedom to create and joy in his work are fundamental elements in the artist's career. Whatever may be said for censorship of art by social authority for social reasons for the artist it is unmitigatedly an evil. And a society which cares for art will make large concessions and adjustments to avoid it. It will put the burden of proof squarely on the Comstocks and Sumners, the Watchers and Warders, when they pass beyond considerations of decency that are as elementary as the loin cloth. It will take to heart the words of Mr. Auerbach in his defence of Theodore Dreiser's *The Genius*—"Do we wish to destroy a pen such as his because it is not the pen of an exhorter? Are we entitled to expect much of him if we relegate him to a desk with some official of the Society for the Suppression of Vice looking over his shoulder to tell him what he may and what he may not write?"

To be considered in connection with the artist's case is that of his bankers and brokers, the business interests which handle his product, especially the producers, publishers and booksellers. We should not be surprised to find the point of view of these last radically different from that of the artist. What business wants immediately is profits, and ultimately security; and where business is well conducted the latter takes precedence. Of course, there are producers and publishers, art dealers and musical publishers, whose point of view is very near to that of the artist, who regard art first and business second. This is the case most often with the middle men of the esoteric arts, but even there the individuality of the artist has to make head against the conservatism of the directors of art institutes and orchestras. But in general, business seeks standardization. In the hearings on the dramatic censorship in Great Britain, the producers were in general in favor of the censor, and the more mechanical his rules, the better they liked it. Give them a deep black line and they will hew to it. The publishers began to look with envy at the theatrical censor, and a committee of them headed by John Murray (whose house published and still publishes Byron's *Don Juan* and *Cain*) approached Parliament to ask that a similar official be appointed to supervise their business. In England the circulation of books is largely determined by the great circulating libraries—Mudie's, Smith's, etc. Their orders are likely to make or break the fortunes of any writer of fiction. They can make their own conditions, and almost any publisher will refuse a book which he is sure the libraries will not accept. Some years ago, the libraries came together and announced their joint refusal to place in circulation "any book which by reason of the personally scandalous, libellous, immoral, *or otherwise disagreeable* nature of its contents is in our opinion likely to prove offensive to any considerable section of our subscribers." A joint committee was formed to report secretly on books under three heads—"Satisfactory," "Doubtful," "Objectionable." Publishers were required to submit books to this committee a week before publication. They did not, I believe, object; but the active Authors' Club did. In the long run, however, no one can tell big business how to conduct itself. The circulation of books is a business and the library, no more than the department store, can afford to stock its shelves with unsalable goods. The remedy will come, if ever, when the public decides that it does not want its reading matter selected for it by majority vote, or literature reduced to the level of the dullest reader. The eccentricities of business censorship were brought to light in 1905 when the *Times* established a library which was to outdo the others in speed of service in respect to new books. Here business conservatism showed its hand plainly. A subscriber asking for Henry James' *Italian Hours* was gravely informed that the book was not sent because "it was not likely to promote the library's reputation as circulators of wholesome literature." Obviously, the library had a quarrel with the publisher as to the price of the book, and exactly this was confessed when it refused to circulate De Morgan's "It Never Can Happen Again," because it cost too much.

In the United States, such agreements among pub-

lishers or circulators are forbidden by the Sherman
Law. In Boston,[1] however, the retail booksellers,

[1] A list of the books now proscribed in Boston was compiled the other day by the "New York Times" and runs as follows:

Dark Laughter,
    by Sherwood Anderson
The Wayward Man,
    by St. John Ervine
High Winds, by Arthur Train
Blue Voyage, by Conrad Aiken
The Irishman,
    by St. John Ervine
What I Believe,
    by Bertrand Russell
Circus Parade, by Jim Tully
The American Caravan
Move Over, by E. Pettit
Oil, by Upton Sinclair
From Man to Man,
    by Olive Schreiner
Mosquitoes,
    by William Faulkner
Pilgrims, by Edith Mannin
Horizon, by Robert Corse
The Sorrows of Elsie,
    by Andre Savignon
Nigger Heaven,
    by Carl Vechten
Power, by Leon Feuchtwanger
Twilight, by Count Keyserling
Black April, by Julia Peterkin
The American Tragedy,
    by Theodore Dreiser
The World of William Clissold,
    by H. G. Wells
Wine, Women and War
Manhattan Transfer,
    by John Dos Passos
The Fruit of Eden, by Gerard
Count Bruga, by Ben Hecht
Kink, by Brock
Red Pavilion, by John Gunther
Ariane, by Claude Anet
The Captive, by Bourdet
Crazy Pavements,
    by Beverly Nichols
Young Men in Love,
    by Michael Arlen

On Such a Night,
    by Babette Deutsch
The Starling, by Doris Leslie
Pretty Creatures,
    by William Gerhardi
The Madonna of the Sleeping
    Car, by Dekobra
Dream's End, by Thorne Smith
Tomok the Sculptor,
    by Eden Phillpotts
The Plastic Age,
    by Percy Marks
The Hard Boiled Virgin,
    by F. Newman
The Rebel Bird, by D. Patrick
The Butcher Shop,
    by J. Devening
The Ancient Hunger,
    by E. Greenberg
Antennae, by Herbert Footner
The Marriage Bed,
    by E. Roscoe
The Beadle, by P. Smith
As It Was, by H. T.
Elmer Gantry,
    by Sinclair Lewis
Doomsday,
    by Warwick Deeping
The Sun Also Rises,
    by Ernest Hemingway
Blended Kings,
    by Kessel & Iswolsky
Spread Circles, by Ward
Little Pitchers, by I. Glenn
Master of the Microbe,
    by Service
Evelyn Grainger,
    by C. F. Hummel
Cleopatra's Diary,
    by Thompson
The Allinghams,
    by May Sinclair

weary of sudden incursions of the Watch and Ward
Society, joined with it in a committee consisting of
one bookseller, two Watchers and Warders, three
physicians and one lawyer to pass on doubtful books.
This arrangement seems to be working well for the
booksellers, but what shall we say of the civilization
of a city where Mr. Upton Sinclair's *Oil* and Miss
Pauline Smith's *The Beadle* are banned?

The most conspicuous case of censorship by agreement between the police, the volunteer guardians of
public morals, and the business interests is that of the
moving picture films through a national board. This
need not delay us. It should be remembered that the
moving picture was a business before it was an art.
The exploitation of the public, especially of youth,
by moving pictures is so clear and present a danger,
and the loss to art through curbing the tendencies
toward lubricity on the part of promoters so doubtful and at best so small, that it must be admitted that
here can be made out the best case for censorship; and thanks to the consolidation of business interests and the dominating personality of Mr. Will
Hays, it is effective within its limits. The producers
cheerfully cut their films according to local regulation. Of course, there are amusing discrepancies
between what is passed and what is not. I remember when I was on the board of local censorship in
Chicago, I saw in the chamber of horrors a very
clean exciting film of the Wild West, in which the
hero, a sort of Billy the Kid, aided by a charming
cow girl, robbed a bank and made a get-away. "Why
stop this?" I asked. "I'll have no film that shows

the degradation of American womanhood," replied
the second deputy chief of police. "But how do you
bring this one in?" "Well, it shows a crime, doesn't
it? and crime means degradation, doesn't it?" I
say effective within limits, for there has sprung up a
bootleg trade in movies intended for private production at clubs and stag parties in which everything
goes. The more innocuous and denatured the public
shows, the more vicious and extravagant the private.
It is easy to say that this trade is as criminal as that
in obscene postal cards or whiskey, and a matter entirely for the police. Its apparent growth, however,
suggests that we may soon have on our hands a
second widespread issue of law enforcement. Human
nature has a way of taking its tolls on every bridge.
And it may be questioned whether the public, through
its acquiescence in a régime which tends to become
mechanical, is getting that education necessary for
the advancement of an art which is dependent on
public support.

For after all, it is the public which is the great
factor in the development of healthy art in a democracy. It is the public for which censorship was devised and exists. It may be said that the question
asked by the censor is not what but who? Nobody
thought of closing *The Captive* last year, until the
public took it up. A logical method of censorship
would be to have the public psychoanalyzed, and
individuals licensed as to what they might properly
be allowed to see and hear.

The final questions to be asked are: "Is censorship a benefit to the public? Is it a necessary evil?"

Since it will hardly be contended that restraint is good for the arts, we shall have to answer the first question in the negative, unless indeed we hold with the monks of the Thebaid that art is a temptation, and renunciation of it is virtue. Granting then that art has a right to exist, is it to the advantage of the public that its freedom should be restricted in the interest of morality, or social stability? Even looking at art exclusively from the moral and social point of view, and disregarding aesthetic considerations, the answer is no. For in both fields the play of the imagination as a stimulus to progress is so important, and the service of art as a field of experiment so vital, that their freedom should be as sacred as the freedom of conscience itself. Milton's eloquent plea for books as a test of the ethical life has never been answered:

As, therefore, the state of man now is; what wisdom can there be to choose, what continence to forbear without the knowledge of evil? He that can apprehend and consider vice with all her baits and seeming pleasures, and yet abstain, and yet distinguish, and yet prefer that which is truly better, he is the true wayfaring Christian. I cannot praise a fugitive and cloistered virtue, unexercised and unbreathed, that never sallies out and sees her adversary, but slinks out of the race, where that immortal garland is to be run for, not without dust and heat. Assuredly we bring not innocence into the world; we bring impurity much rather; that which purifies us is trial, and trial is by what is contrary. That virtue, therefore, which is but a youngling in the contemplation of evil, and knows not the utmost that vice promises to her followers, and rejects it, is but a blank virtue, not a pure; her whiteness is but an excremental whiteness; which was the reason why our sage and serious poet Spenser, whom I dare be known to think a better teacher than Scotus or Aquinas, describing true temperance under the person of Guion, brings him in with his palmer through the cave of Mammon, and the bower of earthly bliss, that he might see and know, and yet abstain.

This argument may be applied in the field of social as well as of individual behavior. The idealistic art which has given us the long procession of Utopias, from Plato's *Republic* to Mr. Wells' *Men Like Gods* has unquestionably furnished an inspiration to social experiment; the realistic art which has pictured conditions so remote from these has been a stimulus to the alleviation of human and animal suffering. But the case does not rest here. The highest service of art is in its own field, that of aesthetics, in giving us an activity which has value, not in relation to other values of knowing and conduct, but in its own right as making life worth living to the artist, and furnishing a store of beautiful things which increase the immediate worth of life to all men. In a civilization resting so largely upon the possessive instinct and animated by the incentive toward private ownership, the preservation of this aesthetic element is of immense importance. As Mr. Havelock Ellis says, art teaches us to enjoy things without the necessity of possessing them.

But granting that good art must in the long run be in accord with the standards of conduct and social progress, what shall we say of bad art? Should not the public be protected from that? But who is to assume the role of protector? Here we meet in acute form the difficulties which cast discredit upon censorship from other points of view. The natural

judges of aesthetic interests are the artists themselves, and as I have already undertaken to show,
the artists, by and large, are the worst censors of art.
I think that the argument of Milton must be admitted as valid in the aesthetic as in the moral life.
"As the state of man now is," the only wisdom to
choose and continence to forbear depends on choice,
or a series of choices between good and less good or
bad. And this brings us logically to the conclusion
that if public good is the final objective, the only authority is the public itself. In respect to knowledge
and conduct, there may be absolute wisdom and absolute goodness, but we recognize that science and
ethics in their public functions are practical only in
so far as they become parts of the general background of thought and the accepted behavior of mankind. Similarly aesthetic considerations are socially
valid only when they become a part of public experience. Otherwise art is a matter of decoration and
luxury, representative of leisure and connoisseurship,
of private views and esoteric cults, withdrawn from
participation of the public and of little value to it.
Connoisseurship and criticism are important, of
course, but mainly as instruments of public education,
and institutional methods of censorship may be legiti-
mately defended only on the same ground—they
show the public where it stands. But the censorship of
public opinion is most useful as a means of education
when it is exercised directly and registers an immediate choice which becomes a part of experience and
is subjected to the pragmatic test of action—does it
limit further action and result in a general dis-

harmony of relations, or does it move to its own enrichment by bringing along with itself a release of
further activities in harmony with what we call
progress?

Doubtless to many artists, as well as moralists, it
may sound like dangerous nonsense to talk of entrusting the freedom of art to public opinion. There are
a few considerations which perhaps may mitigate this
verdict and to which I would call your attention in
closing. First, the history of censorship has shown
that the public has an instinct for what is necessary
or delightful and beneficial in the long run. The
long list of artists and works of art which were
originally cursed and banned, only to be later welcomed and blessed is an ever-present reminder of the
capacity of the public mind to change and renew
itself. This is not to say that there has not been
waste and tragedy in the process—the price of intolerance—but the lesson is so clear that it must some
time appeal to intelligence. Second, the education
of the public in purely aesthetic matters is demon-
strably advancing. It is an anomaly, though his-
torically explainable, that our culture should be so
largely literary. Literature is the handmaid of
democracy by virtue of the printing press, and aesthetic considerations are so confused in literature
with the functions of distributing useful knowledge,
of discussing social problems, of persuading people
to action, that the former are hardly to be differentiated. As I said at the outset, freedom of art
becomes confused with freedom of opinion and
propaganda. The advance of the other arts as ele-

ments of culture is slowly clearing up this confusion. To take a homely instance, a few years ago a picture appeared in the window of a store in Chicago, representing a woman hesitating at a bath in cold water, and entitled September Morn. Crowds gathered; it was part of the news of the day; the police interfered; the picture vanished, its title remaining, however, as a term in the popular vocabulary. Now the picture would excite no particular attention. The reason is that the public no longer identifies nudity with lust but with beauty. The process of education may have been advanced by the bathing beaches, but in part, at least, it has been due to a wider acquaintance with plastic art. The police, instead of haling the picture into court, should have directed the curious spectators to the Art Institute, thus enforcing both the moral and the aesthetic lesson. And this process of education is going on wherever we make the fine arts other than literature a part of our culture. In short, the public must become its own censor; the stream of public opinion must cleanse itself in running. Criticism is the natural means of purification. In the meantime, we must look to the courts to protect the public from exploitation in this as in other matters, and such protection will, as in other matters, inevitably result in transient folly and injustice. But the emphasis should be on freedom, not on restriction. The rule which the Supreme Court has laid down in the matter of freedom of speech, that suppression is only legal where there is a *clear and present* danger of results inimical to the public good, will have to serve for a general guide for freedom of art.   But the truth that the difficulties and dangers attendant upon freedom, great as they may seem, are less than those which result from repression is always to be insisted on.   Under freedom, these difficulties and dangers tend to resolve themselves at once.   Under repression, they accumulate, until they can be liquidated only through a crisis.   The only justification of democracy is growth, and the essential condition of growth is freedom.

FREEDOM AND PSYCHOLOGY

By Joseph Jastrow

THE psychological sector of the problem of human freedom is concerned with determinism in the mental life, and specifically with the agencies and mechanisms of determination. In the background of whatever approach and whatever application our interests select, is the fundamental and persistent question: Are we free agents or are we bound, not only hand and foot but nerve and muscle, feeling and thinking, fated by our make-up to folly or wisdom, vice or virtue, mood and outlook, type and temperament and career? Would an omniscient psychologist predict your behavior from an infinitely comprehensive and infinitesimally minute inventory of your psyche, of your mind-stuff units, your emotional atomic composition, your molecular volitional constitution? Though the modern psychologist neither shirks nor sidesteps this formidable problem, he finds in the temper and positions of his science a sufficient warrant to pronounce the older form of the question irrelevant, and congratulates himself upon this dispensation. Modern psychology inevitably includes in its transformation of values a restatement of the problem of freedom.

In the modern scientific setting the question does not appear with the implications appropriate to the interests of other days and other ways of reflection. This applies equally to the source of morality, the nature of the will, and the technique of directing human behavior under a knowledge of all its conditioning factors. The pragmatic problem has shifted its center, appears altogether differently in the light of a new focus under a new horizon. We moralize less and differently, and we neurologize more.

Like so much else, the shift reflects the panoramic sweep of the searchlight of evolution. At closer range it becomes the illumination of the genetic principle. Unquestionably we are very much what we are born to be; but in all respects we become. The simplest formulation of the offices of heredity and environment is that heredity determines what a man is, environment what he does. But the interplay of original nature and acquired behavior is so intricate, so many-sided, so comprehensive, that the principle offers the guidance of a sign-post, rather than that of a map. Or, granted the map, it is no less intricate than the map of life. The course is not determined by the geography, or at all events no more so and no less, in the case of the psychological than of the topographical contours. A map does not tell you where to go; it helps you to plan your route when you know your destination. Much of our planetary environment as of our organic structure we share, and bound we are to our local habitation and our special inheritance, our temperamental allegiance, by whatever name we call it. But within these restrictions we shape our course with such measure of essential freedom as gives each of us a fling at the art of living. Our problem consists in adjusting our possibilities to our limitations. That defines the major orbit of our decisions.

If an architect were told by a plutocratic or an autocratic client to design and build for him an ideal house with *carte blanche* to select site, materials, style, arrangements, furnishings, sparing no expense, recognizing no obstacles, he wouldn't be in extraordinary luck; he wouldn't be able to proceed at all. The problem of building a house consists in adapting site and materials and service and expense and the individual needs and circumstances, each in turn and in part to one inclusive solution. Certainly architect and owner are in that pragmatic sense free, and in that freedom find their problem. Only in case the client were an inveterate and incorrigible philosopher would he persist in harassing the architect with the project of an ideal house; and philosophers—except in their own private Utopias—rarely have unlimited means.

The psychologist in close touch with the realism of affairs appreciates and accepts the limitations of his freedom to construct an ideal man, and to examine his works in order to determine what manner of automaton he may be dealing with. If the psychologist happens to be a convert to that hyper-pragmatic obsession called Behaviorism, he will be as untroubled by this problem as he is by so many others which he dismisses with a majestic assurance exceeded only in its impressiveness by the denials of the Christian Scientist. His form of the Cartesian dogma reads: What you think doesn't exist. A man is only what he does; and being nothing to begin with, you can make of him anything you like. It is then clear that one's fundamental position in psychology includes a position on the matter of freedom and determinism.

The position in psychology which serves as the guiding principle of my approach is naturalistic. Back to nature! is a cry always authentic if rightly interpreted. Yet this is no assured salvation, since we are so prone to envisage nature in our own image. But assuredly the child is authentic nature; primitive man is authentic nature; and nature has written her psychology in every one of our physiological systems, in every branch and twig and stem of our psychic growth. Consequently my leanings are all to the determinism of nature, of biological nature, of human nature, of racial nature, of family nature, of temperamental-type nature, of individual nature, down to the minute variations that are all part of the natural determinism. So in terms of preference or prejudice, my leaning is ever, when in doubt or when, though the algebraic formula is clear the arithmetical values are indeterminate, to give the major values to original bent, the minor ones to nurtural influence; and I am disposed to look everywhere for nature's determinations.

Thus I find myself in the opposite camp on this issue from the behaviorists—meaning the extreme behaviorists—though a naturalistic psychology is in-

timately dependent upon observed behavior for its
content and interpretation. I believe that because
each of us—though by no means all of us equally—
is so much what he is to begin with that we are decidedly hampered (or if we choose comformably,
decidedly aided) in making of ourselves or anyone
else what we will. And practically in the near-by
and far-flung applications, in matters alike trivial
and consequential, this means that we are more dependent on selection than on education, as we draft
men for special service. For it is in this issue, more
decisively than in any other, that the fate of the
problem of psychological determinism lies. We are
certainly less free if what we are is largely determined by original nature than if the major determinism is environmental. But the division between the
two is not one of more or less, but in what spheres
and relations behavior goes back to original nature
rather than to acquired direction.

The more commonly accepted terms for this alternative are heredity and environment; but neither
opposition nor preponderance correctly expresses the
relations involved. It is but a tentative approach
to a correct statement to say that heredity and environment share between them the responsibility for
my psychic assets and liabilities and their expression
in my behavior: that what doesn't belong to the page
devoted to the one in the ledger of my psychic ac-
counting will appear on the page devoted to the
other; and that, in turn, I hold that the more decisive and consequential entries in kind and amount
appear on the pages of heredity. For all of this,

though not wholly false, is as false as true. The more correct view of this relation, this equation in determinism, is that in every typical respect nature offers aid or hindrance, facilitation or resistance, to the efforts of direction that we call training or education, embodied in one or another of the many and variously organized shapings—personal, social, economic, political, traditional, reflectively logical—that we summarize as the environment, including obviously the intellectual, the social-moral as well as the material environment. If then, I were of sufficiently plastic age and ordinary amenability to any desired selection of these influences, and you wished to make a musician of me, you would find in as many phases of my make-up as there are chapters in psychology and more, favorings and obstacles, facilitations and hindrances to your purposes; and these are there by bent of nature, of all the interlocking cumulative natures back of the heredity wedge of which I am at the moment the active, realized point. In a sense you are free to try to make a musician of me, as I am free to try to make a musician of myself or to cooperate with or to thwart your intentions; but your success or mine, or ours jointly, has its very decided limitations,—in this instance so convincingly with the odds against it, that even to make the attempt implies a disregard for the auditory rights of our neighbors.

If you protest or urge that musicians like poets are born and not made, but that this is not the case in most of the applications of such determinism as we are tempted to make, that engineers or lawyers, professors or book-agents, have no fatalistic excuse for their careers, I heartily agree; for the variability of the deterministic equation both algebraically in statement and arithmetically in values of the variables, enters essentially and comprehensively into its composition. There is certainly no initial decree of fate in heredity or environment that dooms anybody to the misfortune of being a professor; and however much we approve Carlyle's savage advice to Miss Martineau's decision on mature reflection to accept the universe: "You'd better," that would be too deplorable an acceptance: and though the universe charitably provides a place for professors, we all agree that this is a man-made and highly artificial concession. Yet one may discover in many a possible candidate some traits favorable and some unfavorable to the making of a professor, and as well of a special variety of professor. This specific inclination or determination applies as well to the "type" and the individual quality of his professoring, his personality as a professor, as to the specific content—mathematical, mechanical, sociological, philosophical—of his *Fach*. It is only because professoring is so amphibious or equivocal a form of behavior that one cannot determine readily its structural or functional favorings or disfavorings, qualifications and disqualifications. But however variable, they are real enough; and we all agree that the uncertain play of complicated circumstance remains most influential in the issue. Yet again, as an aside, it hardly seems likely that "conditioning" has played any part in the issue; that owing to his bringing up, just as that notorious dog salivated whenever the bell rang, the conditioned professor upon hearing the same signal begins to lecture. Unfortunately for the behaviorist's simplification and fortunately for the rest of the world's interests, man isn't that kind of an automaton. Man is not a slave to accidental or intentional conditioning. And if he were, the varieties of conditioning would themselves nullify the behaviorist's assumptions.

Yet in pointing the term "conditioning" to just that functional phase of environmental influence, the behaviorist has added to the cause of clarity. And matching this usage, I employ the term "dispositioning" to indicate the favoring or disfavoring tendency to a specific form of behavior, inherent or latent in the heredity. Equally is this no simple (or composite) dispositioning that by just growing and having its way, results in making each of us, including the professor, what he is. It is still open to any candidate, whether invited or not, and without any idiomatic ambiguity of expression to say: "I do not choose to be a professor,"—and wisely and firmly hold to the decision. But however artificially made or conditioned, and however fearfully and wonderfully made, the making of a professor is based upon real and nature-given traits and tendencies which in pattern run true to form to the typical and representative formula of psychological determinism. A sufficiently astute observer of a mind in the making —at least in fairly clear cases—may discover a professor in the making in time to further or to hinder the disaster. For that epithet for the denouement is not a random shot; it is selected to add the exclusion of its literal meaning as too complex and extraneous a determinism; for the word "disaster" contains an entire theory of fatalistic determinism,—it means: written in the stars. But this fate is written neither in the stars where we have no inclination to look for it, nor in the nervous system where we seek it, in such form as to be capable of prediction. It is written vaguely in nature's script, however hieroglyphic it may be to our imperfect adeptship in that medium of decipherment.

Pragmatically, then, the problem of psychological determinism is that of pursuing with all the refinement of technique available, the course and scope and expression of dispositioning, with correlative attention to the equally important formative forces of conditioning,—but of conditioning not in the technical sense as used by the small company of behaviorists limited and incorporated, but in the liberal sense of environmental influence. What our psychological determinism, both in theory and in practice, means is that by temperament and by training, each of us is disposed or conditioned to be a little dispositional or a little conditionative in our particular scheme of determination, once we have come to a common understanding of its actual and factual basis.

Before leaving this phase of the issue, I may indicate its importance by a momentous example. Dr. Watson has such confidence in the wide and decisive factor of environmental conditioning that he ventures to inform psychiatrists that there is no such condition as mental disorder, that it is indeed a variety of delusion that happens to affect the doctor instead of the patient; that if we were all properly conditioned or brought up in "behavioristic freedom" (note the term) to express ourselves freely without imposed social taboos, all these crowded asylums would become needless and available for the laudable purposes of behavioristic experimentation. He says that when psychiatrists speak to him of hysteria, schizophrenia, manic-depressive psychosis, paranoia, he doesn't know what they are talking about (since behavior is the only accredited reality), and he suspects that they are in the same plight. While this gentle insinuation adds spice to discussion, it helps little to solve the perplexing problems of how minds go wrong, or how they can be made to go right or prevented from going wrong; how much of freedom, how much of determinism there lies in the issue. Our entire program of education and prevention as well as of analysis and treatment will in some measure take its color and its emphasis from the perspective of determinism of mental disorder. The challenge is thus directed to a decisive criterion and is readily accepted. For if there is any field that richly and convincingly illustrates the complete and varied patterns of dispositioning, it is the field of the abnormal. (Both sides agree that marked organic defect and decay produces abnormal behavior). To some Watson's challenge seems an impertinent gesture, to others carries a sufficient refutation of his entire position; that the "psychopathic" evidence alone demonstrates the hopeless futility of so extreme a tenet of behaviorism. For the moment the

point of importance is that the "abnormal" affects
vitally the concept of psychological determinism.

This takes us to the system of psychology that
more than any other stakes its insight to interpret
human behavior upon a minute and detailed determinism, the psychology of the psychiatrist Dr.
Sigmund Freud, who, poles apart from the behavioristic solution, regards psychiatry as not sufficiently
psychological and supplies the correction in the major
principles of psychoanalysis. Yet as students of the
several aspects and theories of psychological determinism, we must proceed discriminatingly to place
correctly the several turns on the highways and by-
ways of the land of Freud. For unfortunately Freud
is a poor system-builder, certainly an unsystematic
map-maker, and we must follow him as independent
surveyors rather than as guided tourists.

The Freudian perspective of determinism appears
in the close-up view, in the minute registration of
expressional features. Not only, he holds, does determinism apply in the rough in matters of mind, it
applies particularly in the bill of particulars. Nothing in psychic expression is accidental, and the so-
called trivial and accidental or incidental is as inte-
gral a part of the deterministic circle of bondage as
the major moments of the mental make-up. In
structural parallel, not only is the general shape of
your head, your coloration and complexion, your
nose or your chin, your father's or your mother's,
or your near and remote ancestry's generally and
compositely, but so is the texture of your hair, the

minute folds and furrows of your skin, the markings and variations of your minute anatomy.

Yet to accept the detailed operation of determinism does not place one definitely in the psychological schools of the day. There is still the commitment to the dispositional detail or the conditional detail. The naturalistic psychologist is on the whole inclined to interpret the natural inheritance in the rough, in a broad triangulation. Though he makes no pretense to know just what a tendency is or how it gets incorporated into the heredity, he finds the evidence favoring that interpretation. He, like all others, is impressed with the minute determinism that brings about the confusing resemblance of identical twins. Thus in revising the views of Galton—the pioneer in the study of natural inheritance—though sympathetic with his conclusions, one may hold that Galton overstated the hereditary factor on the side of its specific trend, of its specialized operation; that when he found so large a proportion of distinguished jurists had sons of the same bent, it is altogether likely that the push of the environment and the pull of family distinction determined the "legal" direction of talents of the sons, with the major influence, so far as the juristical form of the talent goes, environmental. They didn't inherit legal ability any more than a doctor's son inherits medical ability; both inherit the makings of mental ability on the basis of which lawyers or mathematicians, doctors or engineers may be favorably trained for their profession. Freud has been so absorbed in establishing the validity of his own diagnostic procedures, and so little given to the philosophic or general aspects of neurology and psychology that he feels no need to come to terms with this deterministic issue.   He is eclectic and takes what he needs.   As is familiar, he emphasizes a detailed environmental determinism in the individual patterns of behavior, and has no decisive position in regard to dispositional determinism, though he recognizes its play.

Among the neurologists, Dr. Myerson has considered the problem and reaches a significant conclusion.   There is some generic and some specific determinism; it takes extensive statistical experience to establish either.   Does one inherit the tendency to mental disorder or the actual specific variety of one's affliction?   It may be either; in some cases, presumably rather sharply limited, the inheritance is specific.   For the most part in the common varieties of functional impairment, the generic is the rule, with some close relations within the varieties.   This conclusion likewise has important practical bearings. It leaves a large play for preventive and remedial measures; it indicates that the neurotically disposed may be saved from the more serious disqualifications of their inheritance by wise measures applied early and judiciously.   It recognizes a very considerable environmental factor while still regarding the disposition as pivotal.   Dr. Myerson is not a Freudian; he rejects emphatically almost the whole mass of Freud's environmental detailed determinism,—especially the entire "family romance" (a romance it is, but not as Freud means it), and minimizes the play of "fixations," while hospitable to the psychogenic (or of mental origin) source of much abnormal behavior. All this illustrates the varieties of determinism in terms of the influences that by shaping behavior limit that type of freedom that we call free will.

Galton was the father of Eugenics, of the policy of improvement of the human race by favorable selection; and the Eugenicist is thus an hereditarian in emphasis. Eugenics sees the promise of improvement in the support of the environment of stimulation. The naturalistic view—and Dr. Myerson may be placed in that group—leaves distinctive room for both. The sympathetic followers of the general principles of the Freudian doctrine, such as Dr. Hart in England, Dr. Adolf Meyer in this country, emerge as strong advocates of the training possibilities in avoiding and correcting neurotic tendencies. It is not a serious overstatement to say that they regard many varieties of neurosis as bad mental habits. The large program of mental hygiene is similarly oriented.

The Freudian variety of conditioning is typified in the concept of fixation on the one hand, and on the other in the related traumatic shocks and associated episodes. The former are constant, repeated, personal fixations, the latter incidental and episodic, with still others in between in status. Of the first order are the typical father-fixations or mother-images that condition the whole trend of emotional life, and may prevent a young man from marrying,—that is, interfere with such freedom of action in this sphere as he might otherwise have possessed, because he is looking for the counterpart of his mother, or the young woman of her father; while in further conditioning by this family setting, the young man is set against his father as a rival for the mother's affections, and similarly for the daughter with proper modification of the statement. In Freud's original case there is devotion to her father on the part of the hysterical patient, and there is also traced the hysterical symptom of difficulty in swallowing water back to an aversion to a disliked governess in childhood who further disgusted her by letting her pet dog drink from the glass the family used, and there is the episodic hysterical fixation of an incapacitated arm, a persistence of the natural numbness of constriction when while attending her father she fell asleep with her arm over the back of her chair. It is not to discuss the validity of these determinisms, but merely to indicate their type that they are mentioned. For the present reference they may be dismissed as variously irrelevant; and as they are "hysterical," they will not occur except in the hysterically disposed. They seem definitely of an abnormal and thus unusual character, certainly not the type of determination that is representative and formative in human behavior. What is interesting is that they so much resemble the behavioristic conditionings, while yet Dr. Watson regards Dr. Freud and all his works as an elaborate delusion, and predicts that twenty years from now an analyst using Freudian concepts and Freudian terminology will be placed on the same plane as phrenologist;

while, so far as I can ascertain, Dr. Freud doesn't
know that Dr. Watson exists, or if he does, relegates
him to that capacious unconscious where dwell the
completely or incompletely suppressed.

Consequently, I am quite consistent in viewing
both types of environmental conditioning as of
limited range of operation, though each within its
range is real and instructive as part of the deterministic liabilities of human behavior. But for the great
common and significant ranges of behavior, it is far
more characteristic that we are free from Watsonian
conditioning and Freudian fixation, than that some
of us, if so disposed, are occasionally subject to
them. The contrast in the two orders of conditioning is, as is readily observed, that in the behavioristic variety the stimulus is some simple objective one
operating at a lowly level directly on a simple neurological mechanism, while the psycho-analytic variety
derives its motor power and emotional vigor from
its association,—even from symbolic association with
a far more complex high-level cortical experience.

And by the route of that distinction we enter another sector of the deterministic evidence, which may
be called the neurological or more generally organo-
physiological. Here we have "conditioning" only in
the general deterministic sense, and in reality dispositioning; for the determination is from within
the organism and its specific natural physiological
tendencies to response. This field, as the more
familiar, I shall treat in summary. I had the initial
choice of beginning with these mechanisms of dispositioning and proceeding from them to the general

position which they help to frame. Having chosen
to begin with the general aspects, I must dispose
briefly of the former—the supporting data. Our
total mentality and resulting morality, and by consequence our practical freedom of behavior, is accordingly limited by our biological nature and its
setting.

There is one treatment of this problem so distinctive and helpful that I readily follow it,—that of
Professor Givler in his illuminating book: "The
Ethics of Hercules" which presents the problem of
freedom in the light of a scientific physio-psycho-
logical determinism. His presentation has the additional advantage that it points the entire discussion
to the moral or ethical issues. I commend his chapter (Ch. IX) in its entirety and include his five aspects
of the meaning of freedom.

"The first meaning of free action is *action that is
physically possible*. I am not now, I never was, and
I never shall be free (that is, able) to walk backward and forward at the same time or to be in Boston and New York simultaneously. Neither can I,
while kissing Jennie at her fireside, be also kissing
Kate at her doorway a mile from Jennie's house.
On the other hand, the man who is sound of limb,
sensorially acute, and otherwise endowed with natural
capacities can be said to be free to employ these
capacities whenever and wherever the conditions
provide the opportunity."

The second meaning of freedom is the absence
of external restraints. A cliff puts an end to freedom of walking in a straight line; the walker is

stopped or thwarted. Tantalus, Sisyphus and the daughters of Danaus were not free to perform their impossible tasks. They may "have everlastingly *wished* them, but they could not *will* them." But barriers are commonly not so final. Pyramus and Thisbe circumvented the wall that kept them apart; but what barriers are surmountable depends on the nature of the surmounters. It is only to a Hercules that his labors are possible. Third, I am not free to do what I am not trained to do. If you are an engineer and I a writer, I can't do your engineering, nor you my writing, however free to try, and though each of us is not wholly inept in the simpler rudiments of the other's proficiency. Fourth is the freedom of continuous effort or determination; and fifth is the freedom of an expanding activity by which wishes are turned into wills in whatever field opportunity offers.

What this scheme provides is the shifting determinism of native endowment, training, and environmental condition, making freedom an issue of the varying values of the factors of this equation. It is all naturalistic and genetic. When the boy of ten is free to do what was not within his sphere of freedom at five, it is because his organic-functional growth has provided an extension of the capacity to convert wishes into wills (and extended the wishes also); because environmentally through the imposed educational plan of his parents, adjusted in response to his growth, he is given more liberty of action, and *may* as well as *can* now go into the water because he has learned to swim and because this activity is socially sanctioned as a part of his environmental fitness. There is no taboo against it; it may be a part of a cult, or just an open and thus free direction of the thousand-and-one expressions of energy in which behavior consists. Often though organically free, we are environmentally restricted and as much by lack of opportunity as by imposition of social or other restraint. And when environmentally free, we may be physiologically or neurologically bound.

To repeat, this phase of the problem is familiar, and the chief point is to indicate that it likewise received a transformed statement when couched in the terms of a naturalistic psychology. By this route we come to the last which might well have been the first order of determinism, now to be considered in its contributory elements. We are all determined by the organic-functional mechanisms and by our specific status in their terms. The most striking example is that of the glands. We all share in the entire glandular determination; and in addition, your personality and mine are determined by your and my individual glandular balance. Let there be a marked variation from the normal relation, an over- or under-activity of the thyroid (or other gland) in your case or mine, and the practical problem of freedom is no longer the same for you and for me. My over-excitability and your laziness can no longer be regarded as bad habits or the results of indulgence or faulty training, but as symptoms in part of a glandular disposition. Let there be in Adler's sense, an organ inferiority and the personality is again warped, and the crippling whether in heart or lungs or bone or muscle, spreads over to the realms of behavior in which we have our total, markedly our social being. Let there be an organ superiority, great strength, striking beauty, a fine voice, marked skill, an imposing presence, and again are those with and without these gifts of nature differently dispositioned, because differently organically-functionally equipped.

The interest in this type of handicap is not confined to the spread of organic determinism to the field of personality and behavior where the problem of freedom is centered; it invites, and indeed requires, the consideration of the make-up, the determinism of disposition, and that underlies what I have elsewhere considered as the neurological concept of behavior. It's the nervous system that supplies the keynote of disposition. In the large biological vista appears the far older, more elemental, autonomic nervous system, which is the regulating mechanism of the vital functions, including these glandular regulations,—all so closely bound up with the emotions and in turn with their physiological registrations. Here are the deepest sources of our dispositions. But the central nervous system culminating in the marked cerebral development supplies the regulation of that complex behavior in which the problem of freedom is set. It is the peculiar susceptibility to some varieties of stimulation and expression, and the relative insensibility or immunity from others that constitutes my disposition and becomes my dispositional aid or limitation in my freedom of response.

As the naturalistic position in psychology has abandoned as a misguiding fiction the separation of mind and body, the use of the concept of immunity may prove to be more than a fitting analogy. Though we are all environmentally exposed to the same or similar infection, we vary in our susceptibility or immunity: our physio-organic constitution furnishes a realistic pattern for a view of physio-psychic disposition. Disposition is then constitutional. If we select so definite a constitutional-dispositional tendency (presumably organic) as produces the disorder of asthma, we note its central symptom in the disturbed breathing mechanism. Yet modern medicine has discerned specific stimulations—this or that protein or allied irritant—one affecting A's asthmatic tendencies and another B's, and each immune to what the other succumbs to. Yet most of us are unaffected by either, because we have no tendency to asthma, having a normal lung tissue. Just what in addition to the organic factor the nervous factor is in this malady is not clear: but it seems to be operative also. With this we may both compare and contrast the making of a stutterer as a problem in organo-physiological disposition. This means that it takes but a slightly unfavorable environmental conditioning to make a stutterer of X, for he is so strongly disposed to this mal-functioning of the speech mechanism by his marked nervous susceptibility, but it takes considerably more to make a stutterer of Y; and hardly any unfavorable environment would make Z stutter. How differently then are X, Y and Z, free to speak plainly and without embarrassment! Now substitute for stuttering, a disposition to anger upset, fear upset, or to compulsions, obsessions, anxieties, hysterical symptoms, etc., and you have the typical consideration that determines freedom and responsibility and the entire range of practical, including moral and related issues.

Next needs to be added the range of the physio-organic or neurological mechanisms of disposition. Typical and most important are the instincts. However classified, there is a considerable number of human instincts, and every normal individual shares in all of them. But as before, it is the relative dominance or weakness of one or other that shapes the disposition. If we select the submissive as opposed to the aggressive order of instinct, or the sex-instinct, we readily note how my disposition and yours is determined by a dominant or excessive or deficient susceptibility; and consequently I am not as free to follow the normal patterns of behavior as though I were more nearly of the standard nature in these respects. I may be so handicapped that I cannot do what is expected of me by the accepted social code; or I cannot do it so long as my nervous handicap is strong; I can't do it when in the trough of my nervous depression but begin to recover my freedom of behavior as I approach the crest of my condition. And this very fluctuation and such other fluctuations as that I am always far below par in turning my wishes into wills in the early morning, all go back to original disposition, doubtless subject to considerable correction by a wise routine and to aggravation by unwise indulgence.

And similarly one might include and consider the regulation of behavior through sentiments and other institutional products incorporating sentiments,—the family, the church, the law, the social code generally. One might add the formulation of all this in principles and ideals, and the consequent spreading about me of a network of influences, imposing obligations, expectations, taboos, discouragements, prides and shames, all setting objectives to my motives; and yet recognize under all this the variable response to this elaborate environmental stimulation for which (I still maintain) dispositioning is more decisive than conditioning in determining my behavior. Both limit my ideal or hypothetical or formal freedom and set the terms of the actual freedom which I exercise, and ever with varying ease or difficulty.

In passing to the final consideration, we box the compass and make contact with the general considerations with which we set out. It would appear, then, that I am not wholly free to follow my instincts because they come in conflict with established sentiments, and no less any one instinct by reason of the competition of other instincts, to say nothing of more fundamental neurological resistances that interfere with the transformation of impulses, urges, drives, intentions, emotional trends into wills and habits and executions. There is conflict everywhere, and it is thus intelligible why Freud makes conflict the clue to the neurotic or psychopathic situations; equally why he assumes a censor as the mechanism

of that conflict and its settlement; assumes the unconscious to account for its difficulties; assumes a "complex" as the expression of such inner conflict,—all
encroachments on the freedom of behavior as compared with the freer status of those "free" from
these limitations. And since no one is quite free, and
however subordinate his conflicts and resistances, yet
in type they exist and function upon a pattern quite
comparable to that which invites complexes, we all
come under the same comprehensive formulation,
that receives its distinctive and completer values
from the "abnormal."

We are all subject to the same psychology, and
the problem of freedom is itself determined by the
same order of determinisms, which as indicated, the
Freudian further carries out in a detailed system, including a symbolism, that has by no means been accepted by those accepting his major premises. Certainly the man whose intellectual behavior follows
rational conviction is freer than one subject to emotional complexes. But that any and all of our leading beliefs, our affiliations, our views, our positions,
pragmatic, theoretical or idealistic, are but the far-
flung issues of our temperamental dispositions, is a
thesis worth consideration. We hold them by the
issues of the freedom of acceptance, and for all practical purposes that is adequate.

Without and before the appearance of the
Freudian system of determinism, psychologists and
psychiatrists had recognized a form of behavior with
a reversed direction, or psychogenic determinism,—
not, as the glands, affecting behavior from below, but

as an elaborate psychic structure—the complex—
from above. Freud calls it "conversion," by which
an inner conflict results in a bodily pain, an obses-
sional habit, an enforced projection, or transferred
psychic habit, all of which limit freedom of behavior.
The principle of suggestion by which one psychic
mechanism sets off another through similarity of disposition, is similarly founded, while the Freudian
addition is the subconscious play of the mechanism.
Clearly the physiological type of determinism from
below, with which we associate the term mechanical,
is quite differently composed from the psychogenic
(from above) mechanism, which we may briefly call
Freudian. The evidence is conclusive that both
types are real and effective and operate at once to
direct behavior and to limit its freedom of expression.

The statement of the problem of freedom in terms
of modern psychology proceeds by way of a survey
of the determinisms of behavior. The more direct
approach to the core of the argument was by way of
the general positions associated with recent systems,
schools, or positions in psychology. This was supple-
mented by consideration of the supporting detailed
mechanisms from conditioning to dispositioning,
from physical drives and instincts to complexes.
For the problem of psychological freedom derives
from the nature of the urges and mechanisms of behavior from low to high, from simple to adult, at all
stages of development, organization, integration, with
special reference to the limitations which they impose. Behavior is not free in that it is subject to

determinisms, and if it were not it could not exist at all; for it comes into existence in and under these determinisms. That in their sum total they leave large margins of option gives assurance of a practical freedom for all ranges of human purpose. The older formulation loses its pertinence as it is replaced by a psychological equation with algebraic determiners, but whose values and applications are variable with the variations of personality.

We are no longer interested in asking whether there is free will or not, for that forces the question into a distorted alternative; we are interested in obtaining an understanding of the endowments and limitations of human nature, each offsetting the other, and in the elastic boundaries of their configurations providing the arena where a practical freedom proves its worth by converting organized wishes into effective wills.

PHILOSOPHIES OF FREEDOM

By John Dewey

A RECENT book on *Sovereignty* concludes a
survey of various theories on that subject with
the following words: "The career of the notion of
sovereignty illustrates the general characteristics of
political thinking. The various forms of the notion
have been apologies for causes rather than expressions of the disinterested love of knowledge. The
notion has meant many things at different times; and
the attacks upon it have sprung from widely different sources and been directed toward a multiplicity
of goals. The genesis of all political ideas is to be
understood in terms of their utility rather than of
their truth and falsity." [1] Perhaps the same thing
may be said of moral notions; I do not think there
is any doubt that freedom is a word applied to many
things of varied plumage and that it owes much of
its magic to association with a variety of different
causes. It has assumed various forms as needs have
varied; its "utility" has been its service in helping
men deal with many predicaments.

Primary among the needs it has been employed
to meet and the interests it has served to promote

[1] *Sovereignty*, by Paul Ward, p. 167.

236

is the moral. A good deal is assumed in asserting that the center of this moral need and cause is the fact of choice. The desire to dignify choice, to account for its significance in human affairs, to magnify that significance by making it the center of man's moral struggles and achievements has been reflected in the idea of freedom. There is an inexpugnable feeling that choice *is* freedom and that man without choice is a puppet, and that man then has no acts which he can call his very own. Without genuine choice, choice that when expressed in action makes things different from what they otherwise would be, men are but passive vehicles through which external forces operate. This feeling is neither self-explanatory nor self-justificatory. But at least it contributes an element in the statement of the problem of freedom. Choice is one of the things that demands examination.

The theoretical formulation for the justification of choice as the heart of freedom became, however, involved at an early time with other interests; and they rather than the unprejudiced examination of the fact of choice determined the form taken by a widely prevalent philosophy of freedom. Men are given to praise and blame; to reward and punishment. As civilization matured, definite civil agencies were instituted for "trying" men for modes of conduct so that if found guilty they might be punished. The fact of praise and blame, of civil punishment, directed at men on account of their behavior, signifies that they are held liable or are deemed responsible. The fact of punishment called attention, as

men became more inquiring, to the ground of
liability. Unless men were responsible for their acts,
it was unjust to punish them; if they could not help
doing what they did, what was the justice in holding
them responsible for their acts, and blaming and
punishing them? Thus a certain philosophy of the
nature of choice as freedom developed as an
apologia for an essentially legal interest: liability
to punishment. The outcome was the doctrine
known as freedom of will: the notion that a power
called will, lies back of choice as its author, and is
the ground of liability and the essence of freedom.
This will has the power of indifferent choice; that
is, it is equally free to choose one way or another
unmoved by any desire or impulse, just because of
a causal force residing in will itself. So established
did this way of viewing choice become, that it is still
commonly supposed that choice and the arbitrary
freedom of will are one and the same thing.[2]

It is then worth while to pause in our survey while
we examine more closely the nature of choice in relation to this alleged connection with free will, free
here meaning unmotivated choice. Analysis does not
have to probe to the depths to discover two serious
faults in the theory. It is a man, a human being in
the concrete, who is held responsible. If the act does

---

[2] Doubt may be felt as to the assertion that this interpretation
of freedom developed in connection with the legal motif. The historic connecting link is found in the invasion of moral ideas by
legal considerations that grew up in the Roman Empire. The
association was perpetuated by the influence of Roman law and
modes of moral thought, and even more by the incorporation of
the latter in the theology and practices of the Christian Church,
the nurse of morals in Europe.

not proceed from the man, from the human being in his concrete make-up of habits, desires and purposes, why should *he* be held liable and be punished? Will appears as a force outside of the individual person as he actually is, a force which is the real ultimate cause of the act. *Its* freedom to make a choice arbitrarily thus appears no ground for holding the human being as a concrete being responsible for its choice. Whatever else is to be said or left unsaid, choice must have some closer connection with the actual make-up of disposition and character than this philosophy allows.

We may seem then to be in a hopeless dilemma. If the man's nature, original and acquired, makes him do what he does, how does his action differ from that of a stone or tree? Have we not parted with any ground for responsibility? When the question is looked at in the face of facts rather than in a dialectic of concepts it turns out not to have any terrors. Holding men to responsibility may make a decided difference in their *future* behavior; holding a stone or tree to responsibility is a meanlingless performance; it has no consequences; it makes no difference. If we locate the ground of liability in future consequences rather than in antecedent causal conditions, we moreover find ourselves in accord with actual practice. Infants, idiots, the insane, those completely upset, are not held to liability; the reason is that it is absurd—meaningless to do so, for it has no effect on their further actions. A child as he grows older finds responsibilities thrust upon him. This is surely not because freedom of the will has

suddenly been inserted in him, but because his
assumption of them is a necessary factor in his
further growth and movement.

Something has been accomplished, I think, in
transferring the issue from the past to the future,
from antecedents to consequences. Some animals,
dogs and horses, have their future conduct modified
by the way they are treated. We can imagine a
man whose conduct is changed by the way in which
he is treated, so that it becomes different from what
it would have been, and yet like the dog or horse,
the change may be due to purely external manipulation, as external as the strings that move a puppet.
The whole story has not then been told. There
must be some practical participation from within
to make the change that is effected significant in
relation to choice and freedom. From *within*—
that fact rules out the appeal, so facilely made, to
will as a cause. Just what is signified by that participation by the human being himself in a choice
that makes it really a choice?

In answering this question, it is helpful to go,
apparently at least, far afield. Preferential action
in the sense of selective behavior is a universal trait
of all things, atoms and molecules as well as plants,
animals and man. Existences, universally as far as
we can tell, are cold and indifferent in the presence
of some things and react energetically in either a
positive or negative way to other things. These
"preferences" or differential responses of behavior,
are due to their own constitution; they "express"
the nature of the things in question. They mark a

distinctive contribution to what takes place. In other words, while changes in one thing may be described on the basis of changes that take place in other things, the *existence* of things which make certain changes having a certain quality and direction occur cannot be so explained. Selective behavior is the evidence of at least a rudimentary individuality or uniqueness in things. Such preferential action is not exactly what makes choice in the case of human beings. But unless there is involved in choice at least something continuous with the action of other things in nature, we could impute genuine reality to it only by isolating man from nature and thus treating him as in some sense a supra-natural being in the literal sense. Choice is more than just selectivity in behavior but it is also *at least* that.

What is the more which is involved in choice? Again, we may take a circuitous course. As we ascend in the range of complexity from inanimate things to plants, and from plants to animals and from other animals to man, we find an increasing variety of selective responses, due to the influence of life-history, or experiences already undergone. The manifestation of preferences becomes a "function" of an entire history. To understand the action of a fellow-man we have to know something of the *course* of his life. A man is susceptible, sensitive, to a vast variety of conditions and undergoing varied and opposed experiences—as lower animals do not. Consequently a man in the measure of the scope and variety of his past experiences carries in his present capacity for selective response a large set of varied possibilities. That life-history of which his present preference is a function is complex. Hence the possibility of continuing diversification of behavior: in short, the distinctive *educability* of men. This factor taken by itself does not cover all that is included within the change of preference into genuine choice, but it has a bearing on that individual participation and individual contribution that is involved in choice as a mode of freedom. It is a large factor in our strong sense that we are not pushed into action from behind as are inanimate things. For that which is "behind" is so diversified in its variety and so intimately a part of the present self that preference becomes hesitant. Alternative preferences simultaneously manifest themselves.

Choice, in the distinctively human sense, then presents itself as one preference among and out of preferences; not in the sense of one preference already made and stronger than others, but as the formation of a new preference out of a conflict of preferences. If we can say upon what the formation of this new and determinate preference depends, we are close to finding that of which we are in search. Nor does the answer seem far to seek nor hard to find. As observation and foresight develop, there is ability to form signs and symbols that stand for the interaction and movement of things, without involving us in their actual flux. Hence the new by preference may reflect this operation of mind, especially of forecast of the consequences of acting upon the various competing preferences. If we sum up, pending such qualification or such confirmation

as further inquiry may supply, we may say that a
stone has its preferential selections set by a relatively
fixed, a rigidly set, structure and that no anticipation
of the results of acting one way or another enter
into the matter. The reverse is true of human
action. In so far as a variable life-history and intelligent insight and foresight enter into it, choice
signifies a capacity for deliberately changing preferences. The hypothesis that is suggested is that in
these two traits we have before us the essential con-
stituents of choice as freedom: the factor of
individual participation.

Before that idea is further examined, it is, however, desirable to turn to another philosophy of
freedom. For the discussion thus far has turned
about the fact of choice alone. And such an ex-
clusive emphasis may well render some readers impatient. It may seem to set forth an idea of freedom
which is too individual, too "subjective." What has
this affair to do with the freedom for which men have
fought, bled and died: freedom from oppression
and despotism, freedom of institutions and laws?
This question at once brings to mind a philosophy
of freedom which shifts the issue from choice to
action, action in an overt and public sense. This
philosophy is sufficiently well presented for our purposes in the idea of John Locke, the author, one may
say, of the philosophy of Liberalism in its classic
sense. Freedom is *power to act* in accordance with
choice. It is actual ability displayed to carry desire
and purpose into operation, to *execute* choices when
they are made. Experience shows that certain laws

and institutions prevent such operation and execution. This obstruction and interference constitutes what we call oppression, enslavement. Freedom, in fact, the freedom worth fighting for, is secured by abolition of these oppressive measures, tyrannical laws and modes of government. It is liberation, emancipation; the possession and active manifestation of *rights*, the right to self-determination in action. To many minds, the emphasis which has been put upon the formation of choice in connection with freedom will appear an evasion, a trifling with metaphysical futilities in comparison with this form of freedom, a desire for which has caused revolutions, overthrown dynasties, and which as it is attained supplies the measure of human progress in freedom.

Before, however, we examine further into this notion in its relation to the idea of choice already set forth, it will be well to consider another factor which blended with the political *motif* just mentioned in forming the classic philosophy of Liberalism. This other factor is the economic. Even in Locke the development of property, industry and trade played a large part in creating the sense that existing institutions were oppressive, and that they should be altered to give men power to express their choices in action. About a century after Locke wrote this implicit factor became explicit and dominant. In the later eighteenth century, attention shifted from power to execute choice to power to carry *wants* into effect, by means of free—that is, unimpeded—labor and exchange. The test of free institutions was then the relation they bore to the unobstructed play of wants in industry and commerce and to the enjoyment of the fruits of labor. This notion blended with the earlier political idea to form the philosophy of Liberalism so influential in a large part of the nineteenth century. It led to the notion that all positive action of government is oppressive; that its maxim should be Hands Off; and that its action should be limited as far as possible to securing the freedom of behavior of one individual against interference proceeding from the exercise of similar freedom on the part of others; the theory of *laissez-faire* and the limitation of government to legal and police functions.

In the popular mind, the same idea has grown up in a non-economic form, and with the substitution of instincts or impulses for wants. This phase has the same psychological roots as the economic philosophy of freedom, and is a large part of the popular philosophy of "self-expression." In view of this community of intellectual basis and origin, there is irony in the fact that the most ardent adherents of the idea of "self-expression" as freedom in personal and domestic relations are quite often equally ardent opponents of the idea of a like freedom in the region of industry and commerce. In the latter realm, they are quite aware of the extent in which the "self-expression" of a few may impede, although manifested in strict accordance with law, the self-expression of others. The popular idea of personal freedom as consisting in "free" expression of impulses and desire—free in the sense of unrestricted

by law, custom and the inhibitions of social dis-
approvals—suggests the fallacy inhering in the
wider economic concept, suggests it in a more direct
way than can readily be derived from the more
technical economic concept.

Instincts and impulses, however they may be
defined, are part of the "natural" constitution of
man; a statement in which "natural" signifies
"native," original. The theory assigns a certain
intrinsic rightness in this original structure, rightness in the sense of conferring upon them a title to
pass into direct action, except when they directly and
evidently interfere with similar self-manifestation in
others. The idea thus overlooks the part played by
interaction with the surrounding medium, especially
the social, in generating impulses and desires. They
are supposed to inhere in the "nature" of the individual when that is taken in a primal state, uninfluenced by interaction with an environment. The
latter is thus thought of as purely external to an
individual, and as irrelevant to freedom except
when it interferes with the operation of native instincts and impulses. A study of history would reveal that this notion, like its theoretically formu-
lated congeners in economic and political Liberalism, is a "faint rumor" left on the air of morals
and politics by disappearing theological dogmas,
which held that "nature" is thoroughly good as it
comes from the creative hand of God, and that
evil is due to corruption through artificial interference and oppression exercised by external or
"social" conditions.

The point of this statement is that it suggests the essential fallacy in the elaborate political and economic theories of freedom entertained by classic Liberalism. They thought of individuals as endowed with an equipment of fixed and ready-made capacities, the operation of which if unobstructed by external restrictions would be freedom, and a freedom which would almost automatically solve political and economic problems. The difference between the theories is that one thought in terms of natural rights and the other in terms of natural wants as original and fixed. The difference is important with respect to special issues, but it is negligible with respect to the common premise as to the nature of freedom.

The liberalistic movement in each of its phases accomplished much practically. Each was influential in supplying inspiration and direction to reforming endeavors that modified institutions, laws and arrangements that *had* become oppressive. They effected a great and needed work of liberation. What were taken to be "natural" political rights and "natural" demands of human beings (natural being defined as inherent in an original and native fixed structure, moral or psychological) marked in fact the sense of new potentialities that were possessed by rather limited classes because of changes in social life due to a number of causes. On the political side, there was the limited class that found their activities restricted by survivals of feudal institutions; on the economic side, there was the rise of a manufacturing and trading class that found its activities impeded and thwarted by the fact that these same institutions worked to protect property-interests connected with land at the expense of property-interests growing out of business and commerce. Since the members of the two classes were largely identical, and since they represented the new moving forces, while their opponents represented interests vested and instituted in a past that knew nothing of these forces, political and economic liberalism fused as time went on, and in their fusion performed a necessary work of emancipation.

But the course of historic events has sufficiently proved that they emancipated the *classes* whose special interests they represented rather than human beings impartially. In fact, as the newly emancipated forces gained momentum, they actually imposed new burdens and subjected to new modes of oppression the mass of individuals who did not have a privileged economic status. It is impossible to justify this statement by an adequate assemblage of evidence. Fortunately it is not necessary to attempt the citation of relevant facts. Practically every one admits that there is a new social problem, one that everywhere affects the issues of politics and law; and that this problem, whether we call it the relation of capital to labor, or individualism versus socialism, or the emancipation of wage-earners, has an economic basis. The facts here are sufficient evidence that the ideals and hopes of the earlier liberal school have been frustrated by events; the universal emancipation and the universal harmony of interests they assumed are flagrantly contradicted by the course of events. The common criticism is that the liberal school was too "individualistic"; it would be equally pertinent to say that it was not "individualistic" enough. Its philosophy was such that it assisted the emancipation of individuals having a privileged antecedent status, but promoted no general liberation of all individuals.

The real objection to classic Liberalism does not hinge then upon concepts of "individual" and "society."

The real fallacy lies in the notion that individuals have such a native or original endowment of rights, powers and wants that all that is required on the side of institutions and laws is to eliminate the obstructions they offer to the "free" play of the natural equipment of individuals. The removal of obstructions did not have a liberating effect upon such individuals as were antecedently possessed of the means, intellectual and economic, to take advantage of the changed social conditions. But it left all others at the mercy of the new social conditions brought about by the freed powers of those advantageously situated. The notion that men are equally free to act if only the same legal arrangements apply equally to all—irrespective of differences in education, in command of capital, and that control of the social environment which is furnished by the institution of property—is a pure absurdity, as facts have demonstrated. Since actual, that is, effective, rights and demands are products of interactions, and are not found in the original and isolated constitution of human nature, whether moral or psychological,

mere elimination of obstructions is not enough.
The latter merely liberates force and ability as
that happens to be distributed by past accidents of
history. This "free" action operates disastrously
as far as the many are concerned. The only possible conclusion, both intellectually and practically,
is that the attainment of freedom conceived as
power to act in accord with choice depends upon
positive and constructive changes in social arrangements.

We now have two seemingly independent philosophies, one finding freedom in choice itself, and the
other in power to *act* in accord with choice. Before
we inquire whether the two philosophies must be
left in a position of mutual independence, or
whether they link together in a single conception, it
will be well to consider another track followed by
another school of thinkers who also in effect identify
freedom with operative power in action. This other
school had a clear consciousness of the dependence
of this power to act upon social conditions, and
attempted to avoid and correct the mistakes of the
philosophy of classic Liberalism. It substituted
a philosophy of institutions for a philosophy of an
original moral or psychological structure of individuals. This course was first charted by Spinoza,
the great thinker of the seventeenth century. Although
the philosophy of Liberalism had not as yet taken
form, his ideas afford in anticipation an extraordi-
narily effective means of criticizing it. To Spinoza
freedom was power. The "natural" rights of an
individual consist simply in freedom to do whatever

he *can* do—an idea probably suggested by Hobbes. But what *can* he do? The answer to that question is evidently a matter of the amount of the power he actually possesses. The whole discussion turns on this point. The answer in effect is that man in his original estate possesses a very limited amount of power. Men as "natural," that is, as native, beings are but parts, almost infinitesimally small fractions, of the whole of Nature to which they belong. In Spinoza's phraseology, they are "modes" not substances. As merely a part, the action of any part is limited on every hand by the action and counteraction of other parts. Even if there is power to initiate an act—a power inhering in any natural thing, inanimate as well as human—there is no power to carry it through; an action is immediately caught in an infinite and intricate net work of *inter*actions. If a man acts upon his private impulse, appetite or want and upon his private judgment about the aims and measures of conduct, he is just as much a subjected part of an infinitely complex whole as is a stock or stone. What he actually does is conditioned by equally blind and partial action of other parts of nature. Slavery, weakness, dependence, is the outcome, not freedom, power and independence.

There is no freedom to be reached by this road. Man has however intellect, capacity of thought. He is a mode not only of physical existence but of mind. Man is free only as he has power, and he can possess power only as he acts in accord with the whole, being reinforced by its structure and momentum. But in being a mode of mind he has a capacity for understanding the order of the whole to which he belongs, so that through development and use of intellect he may become cognizant of the order and laws of the whole, and insofar align his action with it. Insofar he shares the power of the whole and is free. Certain definite political implications follow from this identification of freedom with reason in operation. No individual can overcome his tendencies to act as a mode or mere part in isolation. Theoretic insight into the constitution of the whole is neither complete nor firm; it gives way under the pressure of immediate circumstances. Nothing is of as much importance to a reasonable creature in sustaining effectively his actual—or forceful—reasonableness as another reasonable being. We are bound together as parts of a whole, and only as others are free, through enlightenment as to the nature of the whole and its included parts, can any one be free. Law, government, institutions, all social arrangements must be informed with a rationality that corresponds to the order of the whole, which is true Nature or God, to the end that power of unimpeded action can be found anywhere. It would be difficult to imagine a more complete challenge to the philosophy of Locke and the Liberalistic school. Not power but impotency, not independence but dependence, not freedom but subjection is the natural estate of man—in the sense in which this school conceived "the natural." Law, however imperfect and poor, is at least a recognition of the universal, of the interconnection of parts, and hence operates as a schoolmaster to bring men to

reason, power and freedom. The worst government is better than none, for some recognition of
law, of universal relationship, is an absolute prerequisite. Freedom is not obtained by mere abolition of law and institutions, but by the progressive
saturation of all laws and institutions with greater
and greater acknowledgment of the necessary laws
governing the constitution of things.

It can hardly be said that Spinoza's philosophy
either in its general form or in its social aspect had
any immediate effect—unless it was to render
Spinoza a figure of objurgation. But some two centuries later a phase of reaction against the philosophy of Liberalism and all the ideas and practices associated with it arose in Germany; and Spinoza's ideas were incorporated indeed in a new metaphysical scheme and took on new life and significance. This movement may be called institutional
idealism, Hegel being selected as its representative.
Hegel substituted a single substance, called Spirit, for
the two-faced substance of Spinoza, and restated the
order and law of the whole in terms of an evolutionary or unfolding development instead of in terms of
relations conceived upon a geometrical pattern. This
development is intrinsically timeless or logical, after
the manner of dialectic as conceived by Hegel. But
from the outside this inner logical development of a
whole is manifested serially or temporally in history.
Absolute spirit embodies itself, by a series of piecemeal steps, in law and institutions; they are objective reason, and an individual becomes rational
and free by virtue of participation in the life of

these institutions, since in that participation he absorbs their spirit and meaning. The institutions of property, criminal and civil law, the family and above all the national state are the instrumentalities of rationality in outward action and hence of freedom. History is the record of the development of freedom through development of institutions. The philosophy of history is the understanding of this record in terms of the progressive manifestation of the objective form of absolute mind. Here we have instead of an anticipatory criticism and challenge of the classic liberal notion of freedom, a deliberate reflective and reactionary one. Freedom is a growth, an attainment, not an original possession, and it is attained by idealization of institutions and law and the active participation of individuals in their loyal maintenance, not by abolition or reduction in the interests of personal judgments and wants.

We now face what is admittedly the crucial difficulty in framing a philosophy of freedom: What is the connection or lack of connection between freedom defined in terms of choice and freedom defined in terms of power in action? Do the two ways of conceiving freedom have anything but the name in common? The difficulty is the greater because we have so little material to guide us in dealing with it. Each type of philosophy has been upon the whole developed with little consideration of the point of view of the other. Yet it would seem that there must be some connection. Choice would hardly be significant if it did not take effect in outward action, and if it did not when expressed in deeds make a difference in things. Action as power would hardly be prized if it were power like that of an avalanche or an earthquake. The power, the ability to command issues and consequences, that forms freedom must, it should seem, have some connection with that something in personality that is expressed in choice. At all events, the essential problem of freedom, is, it seems to me, the problem of the relation of choice and unimpeded effective action to each other.

I shall first give the solution to this problem that commends itself to me, and then trust to the further discussion not indeed to prove it but to indicate the reasons for holding it. There is an intrinsic connection between choice as freedom and power of action as freedom. A choice which intelligently manifests individuality enlarges the range of action, and this enlargement in turn confers upon our desires greater insight and foresight, and makes choice more intelligent. There is a circle, but an enlarging circle, or, if you please, a widening spiral. This statement is of course only a formula. We may perhaps supply it with meaning by first considering the matter negatively. Take for example an act following from a blind preference, from an impulse not reflected upon. It will be a matter of luck if the resulting action does not get the one who acts into conflict with surrounding conditions. Conditions go against the realization of his preference; they cut across it, obstruct it, deflect its course, get him into new and perhaps more serious entanglements. Luck may be on his side. Circumstances may happen to be propitious or he may be endowed with native force that enables him to brush aside obstructions and sweep away resistances. He thus gets a certain freedom, judged from the side of power-to-do. But this result is a matter of favor, of grace, of luck; it is not due to anything in himself. Sooner or later he is likely to find his deeds at odds with conditions; an accidental success may only reinforce a foolhardy impulsiveness that renders a man's future subjection the more probable. Enduringly lucky persons are exceptions.

Suppose, on the other hand, our hero's act exhibits a choice expressing a preference formed after consideration of consequences, an intelligent preference. Consequences depend upon an interaction of what he starts to perform with his environment, so he must take the latter into account. No one can foresee all consequences because no one can be aware of all the conditions that enter into their production. Every person builds better or worse than he knows. Good fortune or the favorable cooperation of environment is still necessary. Even with his best thought, a man's proposed course of action may be defeated. But in as far as his act was truly a manifestation of intelligent choice, he learns something:—as in a scientific experiment an inquirer may learn through his experimentation, his intelligently directed action, quite as much or even more from a failure than from a success. He finds out at least a little as to what was the matter with his prior choice. He can choose better and *do* better next time; "better choice" meaning a more reflective one, and "better doing" meaning one better coordinated with the conditions that are involved in realizing his purpose. Such control or power is never complete; luck or fortune, the propitious support of circumstances not foreseeable is always involved. But at least such a person forms the habit of choosing and acting with conscious regard to the grain of circumstance, the run of affairs. And what is more to the point, such a man becomes able to turn frustration and failure to account in his further choices and purposes. Everything insofar serves his purpose—to be an intelligent human being. This gain in power or freedom can be nullified by no amount of external defeats.

In a phrase just used, it was implied that intelligent choice may operate on different levels or in different areas. A man may, so to speak, specialize in intelligent choices in the region of economic or political affairs; he may be shrewd, politic, within the limit of these conditions, and insofar attain power in action or be free. Moralists have always held that such success is not success, such power not power, such freedom not freedom, in the ultimate sense.

One does not need to enter upon hortatory moralization in order to employ this contention of the great moral teachers for the sake of eliciting two points. The first is that there are various areas of freedom, because there is a plural diversity of conditions in our environment, and choice, intelligent choice, may select the special area formed by one special set of conditions—familial and domestic, industrial, pecuniary, political, charitable, scientific, ecclesiastical, artistic, etc. I do not mean of course that these areas are

sharply delimited or that there is not something artificial in their segregation. But within limits, conditions are such that specialized types of choice and
kinds of power or freedom develop. The second
(and this is the one emphasized by moral teachers in
drawing a line between true and false power and freedom), is that there *may* be—these moral idealists insist there *is*—one area in which freedom and power
is always attainable by any one, no matter how much
he may be blocked in other fields. This of course
is the area they call *moral* in a distinctive sense. To
put it roughly but more concretely: Any one can
be kind, helpful to others, just and temperate in his
choices, and insofar be sure of achievement and
power in action. It would take more rashness than
I possess to assert that there is not an observation of reality in this insight of the great teachers
of the race. But without taking up that point, one
may venture with confidence upon a hypothetical
statement. If and inasfar as this idea is correct,
there is one way in which the force of fortunate circumstance and lucky original endowment is reduced
in comparison with the force of the factor supplied
by personal individuality itself. Success, power,
freedom in *special* fields is relatively in a maximum
degree at the mercy of external conditions. But
against kindness and justice there is no law: that is,
no counteracting grain of things nor run of affairs.
With respect to such choices, there may be freedom
and power, no matter what the frustrations and failures in other modes of action. Such is the virtual
claim of moral prophets.

An illustration drawn from the denial of the idea that there is an intimate connection of the two modes of freedom, namely, intelligent choice and power in action, may aid in clearing up the idea. The attitude and acts of other persons is of course one of the most important parts of the conditions involved in bringing the manifestation of preference to impotency or to power in action. Take the case of a child in a family where the environment formed by others is such as to humor all his choices. It is made easy for him to do what he pleases. He meets a minimum of resistance; upon the whole others cooperate with him in bringing his preferences to fulfillment. Within this region he seems to have free power of action. By description he is unimpeded, even aided. But it is obvious that as far as he is concerned, this is a matter of luck. He is "free" merely because his surrounding conditions happen to be of the kind they are, a mere happening or accident as far as his make-up and his preferences are concerned. It is evident in such a case that there is *no growth* in the intelligent exercise of preferences. There is rather a conversion of blind impulse into regular habits. Hence his attained freedom is such only in appearance: it disappears as he moves into other social conditions.

Now consider the opposite case. A child is balked, inhibited, interfered with and nagged pretty continuously in the manifestation of his spontaneous preferences. He is constantly "disciplined" by circumstances adverse to his preferences—as discipline is not infrequently conceived. Does it follow then that he develops in "inner" freedom, in thoughtful preference and purpose? The question answers itself. Rather is some pathological condition the outcome. "Discipline" is indeed necessary as a preliminary to any freedom that is more than unrestrained outward power. But our dominant conception of discipline is a travesty; there is only one genuine discipline, namely, that which takes effect in producing habits of observation and judgment that ensure intelligent desires. In short, while men do not think about and gain freedom in conduct unless they run during action against conditions that resist their original impulses, the secret of education consists in having that blend of check and favor which influences thought and foresight, and that takes effect in outward action through this prior modification of disposition and outlook.

I have borrowed the illustration from the life of a child at home or in school, because the problem is familiar and easily recognizable in those settings. But there is no difference when we consider the adult in industrial, political and ecclesiastic life. When social conditions are such as to prepare a prosperous career for a man's spontaneous preferences in advance, when things are made easy by institutions and by habits of admiration and approval, there is precisely the same kind of outward freedom, of relatively unimpeded action, as in the case of the spoiled child. But there is hardly more of freedom on the side of varied and flexible capacity of choice; preferences are restricted to the one line laid down, and in the end the individual becomes the slave of his successes. Others, vastly more in number, are in the state of the "disciplined" child. There is hard sledding for their spontaneous preferences; the grain of the environment, especially of existing economic arrangements, runs against them. But the check, the inhibition to the immediate operation of their native preferences no more confers on them the quality of intelligent choice than it does with the child who never gets a fair chance to try himself out. There is only a crushing that results in apathy and indifference; a deflection into evasion and deceit; a compensatory over-responsiveness to such occasions as permit untrained preferences to run riot—and all the other consequences which the literature of mental and moral pathology has made familiar.

I hope these illustrations may at least have rendered reasonably clear what is intended by our formula; by the idea that freedom consists in a trend of conduct such as causes choices to be more diversified and flexible, more plastic and more cognizant of their own meaning, while it enlarges their range of unimpeded operation. There is an important implication in this idea of freedom. The orthodox theory of freedom of the will and the classic theory of Liberalism both define freedom on the basis of something antecedently given, something already possessed. Unlike in content as are the imputation of unmotivated liberty of choice and of natural rights and native wants, the two ideas have an important element in common. They both seek for freedom in something already there, given in advance. Our idea compels us on the other hand to seek for freedom in something which comes to be, in a certain kind of growth; in consequences, rather than in antecedents. We are free not because of what we statically are, but inasfar as we are becoming different from what we have been. Reference to another philosophy of freedom, that of Immanuel Kant, who is placed chronologically in the generation preceding that of Hegel and institutional idealism, may aid in developing this idea. If we ignore the cumbrous technicalities of Kant, we may take him as one who was impressed by the rise of natural science and the role played in science by the idea of causation, this being defined as a necessary, universal or invariant connection of phenomena. Kant saw that in all consistency this principle applies to human phenomena as well as to physical; it is a law of all phenomena. Such a chain of linked phenomena left no room for freedom. But Kant believed in duty and duty postulates freedom. Hence in his moral being, man is not a phenomenon but a member of a realm of noumena to which as things-in-themselves free causality may be ascribed. It is with the problem rather than the solution we are concerned. How one and the same act can be, naturalistically speaking, causally determined while transcendentally speaking it is free from any such determination is so high a mystery that I shall pass it by.

But the *problem* as Kant stated it has the form in which it weighs most heavily on contemporary consciousness. The idea of a reign of law, of the in-

PHILOSOPHIES OF FREEDOM   263

clusion of all events under law, has become almost
omnipresent. No freedom seems to be left save
by alleging that man is somehow supra-natural in
his make-up—an idea of which Kant's noumenal
and transcendental man is hardly more than a trans-
lation into a more impressive phraseology.

This way of stating the problem of freedom
makes overt, explicit, the assumption that either
freedom is something antecedently possessed or else
it is nothing at all. The idea is so current that it
seems hopeless to question its value. But suppose
that the origin of every thought I have had and
every word I have uttered is in some sense causally
determined, so that if anybody knew enough he
could explain the origin of each thought and each
word just as the scientific inquirer ideally hopes to
explain what happens physically. Suppose also—
the argument is hypothetical and so imagination may
be permitted to run riot—that my words had the
effect of rendering the future choices of some one
of my hearers more thoughtful; more cognizant of
possible alternatives, and thereby rendering his future
choices more varied, flexible and apt. Would the
fact of antecedent causality deprive those future
preferences of their actual quality? Would it take
away their reality and that of their operation in
producing their distinctive effects? There is no
superstition more benumbing, I think, than the current notion that things are not what they are, and
do not do what they are seen to do, because these
things have themselves come into being in a causal
way. Water is what it *does* rather than what it is

caused by. The same is true of the fact of intelligent choice. A philosophy which looks for freedom in antecedents and one which looks for it in consequences, in a developing course of action, in becoming rather than in static being, will thus have very different notions about it.

Yet we cannot separate power to become from consideration of what already and antecedently is. Capacity to become different, even though we define freedom by it, must be a present capacity, something in some sense present. At this point of the inquiry, the fact that all existences whatever possess selectivity in action recurs with new import. It may sound absurd to speak of electrons and atoms exhibiting preference, still more perhaps to attribute bias to them. But the absurdity is wholly a matter of the words used. The essential point is that they have a certain opaque and irreducible individuality which shows itself in what they do; in the fact that they behave in certain ways and not in others. In the description of causal sequences, we still have to start with and from existences, things that are individually and uniquely just what they are. The fact that we can reduce changes that occur to certain uniformities and regularities does not eliminate this original element of individuality, of preference and bias. On the contrary, the statement of laws presupposes just this capacity. We cannot escape this fact by an attempt to treat each thing as an effect of other things. That merely pushes individuality back into those other things. Since we have to admit individuality no matter how far we carry the chase, we might as well forego the labor and start with the unescapable fact.

In short, anything that is has something unique in itself, and this unique something, enters into what it does. Science does not concern itself with the individualities of things. It is concerned with their *relations*. A law or statement of uniformity like that of the so-called causal sequence tells us nothing about a thing inherently; it tells us only about an invariant relation sustained in behavior of that thing with that of other things. That this fact implies contingency as an ultimate and irreducible trait of existence is something too complicated to go into here. But evidence could be stated from many contemporary philosophers of science, not writing with any thought of freedom in mind, but simply as interpreters of the methods and conclusions of science, to the effect that the laws leave out of account the inner being of things, and deal only with their relations with other things. Indeed, if this were the place and if I only knew enough, it could be shown, I think, that the great change now going on in the physical sciences, is connected with this idea. Older formulas were in effect guilty of confusion. They took knowledge of the relations that things bear to one another as if it were knowledge of the things themselves. Many of the corrections that are now being introduced into physical theories are due to recognition of this confusion.

The point needs an elaboration that cannot here be given if its full import for the idea and fact of freedom is to be clearly perceived. But the con-

nection is there and its general nature may be seen.
The fact that all things show bias, preference or
selectivity of reaction, while not itself freedom, is
an indispensable condition of any human freedom.
The present tendency among scientific men is to
think of laws as statistical in nature—that is, as
statements of an "average" found in the behavior
of an enormous number of things, no two of which
are exactly alike.   If this line of thought be followed out, it implies that the existence of laws or
uniformities and regularities among natural phenomena, human acts included, does not in the least
exclude the item of choice as a distinctive fact having its own distinctive consequences.   No law does
away with individuality of existence, each having its
own particular way of operating; for a law is concerned with relations and hence presupposes the
being and operation of individuals.   If choice is
found to be a distinctive act, having distinctive consequences, then no appeal to the authority of scientific law can militate in any way against its reality.
The problem reduces itself to one of fact.   Just
what *is* intelligent choice and just what does it effect
in human life?   I cannot ask you to retraverse the
ground already gone over.   But I do claim that
the considerations already adduced reveal that what
men actually cherish under the name of freedom
is that power of varied and flexible growth, of
change of disposition and character, that springs
from intelligent choice, so there is a sound basis for
the common-sense practical belief in freedom, al-

though theories in justification of this belief have often taken an erroneous and even absurd form.

We may indeed go further than we have gone. Not only is the presence of uniform relations of change no bar to the reality of freedom, but these are, *when known*, aids to the development of that freedom. Take the suppositious case already mentioned. That my ideas have causes signifies that their *rise*, their *origin* (not their nature), is a change connected with other changes. If I only knew the connection, my power over getting certain ideas would be that much increased. The same thing holds good of any effect my idea may have upon the ideas and choices of some one else. Knowledge of the conditions under which a choice *arises* is the same as potential ability to guide the formation of choices intelligently. This does not eliminate the distinctive quality of choice; choice is still choice. But it is now an intelligent choice instead of a dumb and stupid one, and thereby the probability of its leading to freedom in unimpeded action is increased.

This fact explains the strategic position occupied in our social and political life by the issue of freedom of thought and freedom of speech. It is unnecessary to dwell by way of either laudation or exhortation upon the importance of this freedom. If the position already taken—namely, that freedom resides in the development of preferences into intelligent choices—is sound, there is an explanation of the central character of this particular sort of freedom. It has been assumed, in accord with the whole theory of Liberalism, that all that is necessary to secure freedom of thought and expression, is removal of external impediments: take away artificial obstructions and thought will operate. This notion involves all the errors of individualistic psychology. Thought is taken to be a native capacity or faculty; all it needs to operate is an outer chance. Thinking, however, is the most difficult occupation in which man engages. If the other arts have to be acquired through ordered apprenticeship, the power to think requires even more conscious and consecutive attention. No more than any other art is it developed internally. It requires favorable objective conditions, just as the art of painting requires paint, brushes and canvas. The most important problem in freedom of thinking is whether social conditions obstruct the development of judgment and insight or effectively promote it. We take for granted the necessity of special opportunity and prolonged education to secure ability to think in a special calling, like mathematics. But we appear to assume that ability to think effectively in social, political and moral matters is a gift of God, and that the gift operates by a kind of spontaneous combustion. Few would perhaps defend this doctrine thus boldly stated; but upon the whole we act as if that were true. Even our deliberate education, our schools are conducted so as to indoctrinate certain beliefs rather than to promote habits of thought. If that is true of them, what is not true of the other social institutions as to their effect upon thought?

This state of things accounts, to my mind, for the current indifference to what is the very heart of actual freedom: freedom of thought. It is considered to be enough to have certain legal guarantees of its possibility. Encroachment upon even the nominal legal guarantees appears to arouse less and less resentment. Indeed, since the mere absence of legal restrictions may take effect only in stimulating the expression of half-baked and foolish ideas, and since the effect of their expression may be idle or harmful, popular sentiment seems to be growing less and less adverse to the exercise of even overt censorships. A genuine energetic interest in the cause of human freedom will manifest itself in a jealous and unremitting care for the influence of social institutions upon the attitudes of curiosity, inquiry, weighing and testing of evidence. I shall begin to believe that we care more for freedom than we do for imposing our own beliefs upon others in order to subject them to our will, when I see that the main purpose of our schools and other institutions is to develop powers of unremitting and discriminating observation and judgment.

The other point is similar. It has often been assumed that freedom of speech, oral and written, is independent of freedom of thought—but you cannot take the latter away in any case, since it goes on inside of them where it cannot be got at. No idea could be more mistaken. Expression of ideas

in communication is one of the indispensable conditions of the awakening of thought not only in
others, but in ourselves. If ideas when aroused cannot be communicated they either fade away or become warped and morbid. The open air of public
discussion and communication is an indispensable
condition of the birth of ideas and knowledge and of
other growth into health and vigor.

I sum up by saying that the possibility of freedom is deeply grounded in our very beings. It is
one with our individuality, our being uniquely what
we are and not imitators and parasites of others.
But like all other possibilities, this one has to be
actualized; and, like all others, it can only be actualized through interaction with objective conditions.
The question of political and economic freedom is
not an addendum or afterthought, much less a
deviation or excrescence, in the problem of personal
freedom. For the conditions that form political
and economic liberty are required in order to realize
the potentiality of freedom each of us carries with
him in his very structure. Constant and uniform relations in change and a knowledge of them in
"laws," are not a hindrance to freedom, but a necessary factor in coming to be effectively that which
we have the capacity to grow into. Social conditions interact with the preferences of an individual
(that *are* his individuality) in a way favorable to
actualizing freedom only when they develop intelligence, not abstract knowledge and abstract
thought, but power of vision and reflection. For

these take effect in making preference, desire and purpose more flexible, alert, and resolute. Freedom has too long been thought of as an indeterminate power operating in a closed and ended world. In its reality, freedom is a resolute will operating in a world in some respects indeterminate, because open and moving toward a new future.

WHAT IS REAL AND WHAT IS ILLUSORY
IN HUMAN FREEDOM

By Horace M. Kallen

I

IF the reality of a thing can be measured by the
magnitude and variety of the powers which are
invoked to restrain and to overcome it, Freedom is
the most real thing in the world, at once the maker
and the bondman of civilization, fettered by its
institutions, checked by its physical establishments,
entangled and cramped within its unwritten laws
and statutory enactments. But these, the jailers of
Freedom, also are its children, and the sure testimony to its real presence in the world. For, I cannot too often repeat, history defines the liberties of
men by no positive traits, only by the prohibition of
certain types of obstruction or interference: religious, civil, personal, political and the like. Thus
any action native or acquired, once impeded, then
*un*impeded, becomes a liberty; and it becomes a
liberty only through the withdrawal, usually the
forced withdrawal, of the impediment. An impediment, however, is not such unambiguously: jails,
which impede the characteristic actions of many
individuals, annul them as impediments to the

actions of a great many more. Liberty is involved
in paradoxes of which the meaning of the expression
libertine is the pregnant example. For the libertine
began as a saintly freethinker about God and the
good; he became a synonym for the profligate and
wastrel earth-bound by his passions. The saintly
freethinker was so because he had overcome impediments of church and state to his judgment regarding
the ground of the world and the desires of men; the
profligate is one because his judgment has passed
under the dominion of his greeds. Either may be
looked upon as free or bond, according to which
restraint it is felt more important at the time to
remove—restraint upon the judgment or restraint
upon the appetites.

Liberty, it follows, does not appear in the daily
life as a thing-in-itself, a positive character of experience or imagination like *red*, or *Captain Nemo*, or
space or *Lindbergh*. It seems to be always a thing
implied by its opposite; not a thing you can positively
put your finger on. Observing this fact, some
thinkers, like Immanuel Kant, have been led to deny
liberty altogether to the world of our experience
and to put it in an unseen, transcendental world;
others have been moved altogether to deny its reality
as an independent fact and to identify it with acquiescence in the causal necessities of natural law, like
Spinoza, or the statutory coercions of the institutions
of the state, like Hegel, or the economic determinism
of history and the imputed dialectic of matter like
Marx. Even Bergson, for whom Freedom does possess positive features which intuition can grasp di-

rectly in experience, is compelled, in stating this experience, to make use of negations, such especially as *un*predictability. Concerning Liberty, the oracles also of philosophy seem forever to say, "You never can tell."

On the other hand, concerning the measures of Liberty, the voices are clear and precise enough. True, this Freedom is never a secure possession, ever a conquest. True, its story as a light of the human heart is the story of an illumination never too strong, mostly intermittent; an ideal which neither individuals nor societies have often striven for or long kept. But these are precisely the reasons why current clamor over lost liberties seems to me no cause for despair. Never, since men began to record and to analyze their own doings has the idea of Human Freedom been so widespread, the concern about it so alert. The violence claimed against Liberty bespeaks its extent and importance. Those, again, are the growth of the past hundred years; the men and women who inhabit the civilization of 1928 are subject to far fewer restraints than their fathers and mothers of 1828; they are masters of many more abilities. Where their ancestors had to "take liberties" and "make free," they have the right and *are* free. This state has accrued to them with the discovery and analysis, rule for rule and detail upon detail, of the determinism which characterizes sequences in nature and events in history. Human freedom has been a function of the discernment of the compulsions within and upon humanity —and their use. The value of any propaganda for

Liberty seems to me to lie in this use—in the manner and the rate and the degree that these masters can be transformed into servants.

II

The compulsions against which the propaganda of Liberty is directed are, broadly speaking, of two kinds: the powers within, which predetermine the life-cycle and its qualities, physical and spiritual, of personality; the outer forces, in nature and in the human world, whose impact on the inward states makes a man's biography and establishes his value. If we choose to mean by heredity the potency of an ancestral past working upon a human being from the time it is born, then its heredity is the first and nearest limitation upon its freedom. It gives a man's life-line one inevitable direction and no other. It predetermines him for disease or health, a long life or short, idiocy or genius, honesty or knavery, gaiety or dullness, and so on. His endocrine balance, the structure of his nervous-system, already implicit in the germ-plasm he unfolds from, explicitly determine his adjustments with the world he lives in.

He grows up as a clock runs down, and there is no quality of his which is not capable of being measured.

On the side of the mind the measurers fall into three groups. One of these takes for its unit the reflex, native and learned. It measures the speed, the intensity and the duration of reactions to stimuli. Another takes for its norm a certain standard of intelligence,

different for different ages, and establishes I. Q.'s.
The third defines and measures temperament, the
lability or slowness of emotion. It is allied in its
presuppositions to the determinisms of the Freudian
psychology; determinisms which the Russian pupils
of Pawlow have succeeded in restating physiologically and measurably by means of experiments in
conditioning reflexes. All three groups presume
that the behavior of a human being is due to inherited traits of mind and body reacting singly or
in configurations and that he as individual contributes
nothing to this behavior. Nor can the environment
which acts upon it in any way alter it. Rather does
it transform the environment to its mode. All
arguments about racial superiority rest upon these
consoling presumptions regarding the inalterability
of inherited traits. The religion of eugenics, on
the other hand, has for its principal dogma the
alterations in human nature which may be achieved
by the manipulation of such inalterable inherited
traits. Thus, the already-living claim a power and
right to choose and fix the nature of the still-unborn.
Here Freedom is a use of determinism.

III

Of the powers that oppress us from without, the
nearest, the most intimate, are those of the family;
the inventions of psychoanalysis have already made
very familiar the mechanisms of family compulsion.
Then in their order come the other institutions of
society: the school, the church, the economic establishment, the state, and the general state of mind

of the community as that is embodied in the accepted ideologies of the arts and the sciences. Each of these institutions has been conceived as a rigid mold through which the plastic individual passes as he grows, and from which he enters into maturity, a synthetic reduplication of those who have preceded him. Over against the institutions that shape him he is presumed, in spite of his inalterable heredity, to be powerless. Whatever they may do to him, he can do nothing to them. His life moves ineluctably onward to foregone conclusions. Even his originations and inventions are predetermined and fall, as Prof. Ogburn so plausibly argues in his "Social Change," into conventional statistical patterns that point to the inexorable workings of some kind of social law.

Such a law is of course regarded as nothing primary and fundamental. It is presumed to belong to the upper levels of the architectonic of existence and to be reducible to simpler laws which are those of biology and chemistry and physics—ultimately of physics. Physics enters the social structure directly through machinery. Machinery is an unnatural mechanism incarnating the mechanics of nature. As an order, it stands between the plastic arrangements of human groupings and the chaotic rigidities of natural determinism. It is an organization abstracted from both; a pure mechanism, therefore the more thorough and inexorable in its compulsions. Where it exists, all life becomes, as we have already seen, remade to its measure.[1] Under machinery, its

[1] Above, p. 13, *seq.*

foundations lie—the laws and cataclysms of nature herself: space, time and causality. Beyond it and around it are the bacteria and the earthquakes and all the other forms and congeries of natural existences that hem us in and press us down; that give definition to our liberties as we work out beyond and overcome them.

Inheritance, which compels us from within, and society and nature, which compel us from without, have, since the middle of the 19th century, been envisaged in a philosophy of determinism that sees man as the passive and helpless plaything of blind inexorable forces which he may perhaps observe and understand but can in no way control. All that his freedom can under these circumstances consist in is, as Bertrand Russell once wrote in *A Free Man's Worship*, "to take into the inmost shrine of the soul the irresistible forces whose puppets we seem to be, death and change, the irrevocableness of the past, the powerlessness of man before the blind hurry of the universe from vanity to vanity. . . ."

Such a deterministic philosophy is usually called Materialism. But the great romantic Idealisms, the systems of Hegel or Schopenhauer or Bradley or Royce, optimistic though they are, also come to the same determinism. They reach it, however, in a different way. This way is the use of the dogma that all relations are "internal"—that is, that no one thing can exist unless everything else exists, that a flea-bite on the tail of a dog or a kiss on the lips of a light o' love requires the universe to bring it about or sustain it. Their universe is what James calls a block-universe. Its wholeness is the wholeness of all-at-once; none of its parts can be, or be anything, without all of the others; none can be really known unless all are known.

Machines, in their work, are like that, too. We may assemble each piecemeal, one part after another, but these parts must work together and simultaneously. Materialism conceives the world as an eternal, unassembled machine, the parts of which are all there together forever. Like Idealism, it is involved in the dogma of internal relations, though it did not start with this dogma as its first assumption. What it started with was the observations and generalizations of Galileo, the generalizations and discoveries of Newton. With those Newton drew a specific picture of the world as a machine. And he had a real man-made machine in mind. He conceived the universe after the analogy of a watch or a clock which would go wrong or run down without the occasional intervention of the watchmaker God. Newton believed that the universe couldn't go of its own motion; that unless God rewound it every so often it would run down; that God alone kept the laws of gravitation working infallibly, and not anything in the nature itself of the inert and passive mechanism of the cosmos. God, however, was a hypothesis that the sciences had less and less use for, an extra wheel that could only interfere with the smooth, uninterrupted running of the world-machine. This they envisaged as an eternal self-winding mechanism, each of whose parts so acted upon its neighbors as to keep them running, while the movement of the whole was assembed from the motions of the parts, and the motions of the parts were distributed from the movement of the whole. The laws of nature were the principles governing these movements. When we speak of natural law and the like today, we still have in mind this Galileo-Newtonian view of the structures and motions of the universe, their measurableness and predictability.

The elegance, the simplicity and the extreme usefulness of the model, demonstrated in the successes of physics and astronomy, could not fail to infect students of the composition and movements of society with a desire for an analogous quantification. But here the numbers and simple logical processes of mathematical form were inapplicable. The nearest the social sciences can come to resultants and tensors are averages and medians. With all the complications of statistics, predictability remains in the region of the abstract mathematical pattern: the social sciences can designate the form taken by a social mass: they cannot foretell the conduct of any particular individual in the mass. For all that, they quantify whatever falls into their categories and is susceptible to counting and correlations; business cycles and sun-spots or the phases of Venus; prices and privileges; Fridays and bad luck. Their ideal is, and most properly is, that sure precision of mathematical form and successful forecasting which the physical sciences won to, more than two and a half centuries ago, and which they have been refining and perfecting ever since.

IV

And here the usual irony steps in. While the social sciences become ever more imposingly mathematical under the impulsion of their Newtonian ideal, the physical sciences have begun to abandon the notion of the world-machine with its precisely cogged determinisms, its clock-like motions and forms. They have been turning toward a view of nature, of causation, of natural law which may involve more than mere deviation from the Newtonian system; which may involve its contradiction. In this other view, the laws of nature take on the aspect of statistical averages and there seem to be in nature no discoverable laws of another kind.

Thus the Newtonian physics presumes the reality of solid matter, hard, impenetrable crumbs of stuff, no two of which can occupy the same place at the same time. It presumes that this stuff occupies infinite, uniform objective tri-dimensional space which consists of points, through infinite, uniform, monodimensional time, flowing in equal instants. It presumes that the crumbs of stuff are at rest or in motion, and that motion is something different from the stuff, something that the stuff can take on or drop as a woman does a taxi. It assumes that this is accomplished according to fixed laws stateable as relationships between the mass of the stuffs, the space they move in, the time their moving takes. It assumes that these relationships are efficacious regardless of the nearness or remoteness of one mass to another in space or in time; that the law of gravitation, for example, holds as infallibly of you and Sirius as of you and the earth.

In the new view, the solid, impenetrable crumbs of matter are replaced by something wavelike, the parts of which, instead of being instant, are successive and enduring, so that the later phases interpenetrate with the earlier, as the partial vibrations of a string overlap with each other and coincide with the whole vibration or the partial phases of a man's biography overlap and interpenetrate with each other and coincide with his whole life. Since these vibrations *are* motion, motion is not something that they can take on and put off. Every new motion is an inward alteration, which must logically affect their characters as things—for example, their mass. They are happenings or events, however, not things.

And they are not happenings in a uniform empty space, such as is set forth by the geometry of Euclid. As a matter of fact, we never encounter such a space. The space we do encounter is non-Euclidean. It is shaped by the events that take place in it; its shaping *is* their taking place. Hence fixed measures, constant rules, become ambiguous. Bodies can be of two sizes at the same time and are of variable mass; distances between them cease to be fixed and inalterable; straight lines may be contemporaneously crooked, and the straightest straight line may be the route cut by a ray of light—the great circle called a geodesic.

So again, the notion of a single, uniform time elapsing eternally in equal instants is replaced by the notion of an indefinite variety of local and individual times, each the variable and idiosyncratic tempo of events as they take place. Time, hence, ceases to be an independent variable flowing evenly in uniform three-dimensional space. It becomes a factor in a four-dimensional complex, Space-Time, whence physics derives the coordinates by means of which it designates the sequence of events.

This sequence ceases to be determinable by action at a distance. It can be defined surely only as it eventuates from next to next. As events are separate and countable, there must be some sort of interval between them, the shorter this interval, the more instantaneous, the more "necessary," the connection; the longer the interval, the more doubtful the causal nexus. "Necessity" becomes a synonym for immediacy in the sequence of events.

Unities in the world of physics, hence, are now to be regarded as of what James calls the strung along, concatenated kind, in which there is no skipping of intermediaries, in which all genuine transition is from next to next. Determinism becomes identical with instant determination. But as events are at least numerically different one from another, intervals fall between them, which may be gaps of indeterminism. For example: the words that I say now have an influence on the words that next follow but what connection can anybody ascribe to these and the words I am going to say next year at about this season? What is the causal relationship between your breakfast on March 21st when you were five years old and your sitting in this room at this time.

You could, if you chose, interpolate between that breakfast and your present state a series of transitions, leading from the one to the other. But the connection so established would be romance, not science. With or without that breakfast, you would be in this room at this time. And at breakfast time then not even an astrologer could foretell where you would be and what you would be doing now. Yet any onlooker who knew you then might predict two or three possible actions any one of which might take place after you had eaten your porridge and drunk your milk. You might ask for more; you might have your face wiped with your bib; you might scrape back your little chair and run to the bathroom to have face and hands washed. The nearer the event the surer the prediction. But never an absolute repetition.

So in science. Sequence is sure where the interval is small. Causal law is the rule of this sequence: the equation which states it is a differential equation. The more universal its application, the more indeterminate its results. Modern physics, hence, is not apt to make generalizations about the state of the universe as a whole. It deals with chains of events rather distributively and severally, in their concatenated individuality. Its laws are in effect interpolations that bridge intervals—like the verbal continuity which links up and holds united the successive phases of a motion-picture. If the linkage is successful we feel that the end of the picture was determined by its beginning; if not, we perceive a sequence but do not recognize an impulsion or push;

causality has not filled in the gaps. Imagine all
nature to consist of countless discrete chains of
events of the type of the motion-picture, in which
the earlier with their intervals pass over into the
later. Each has its own time, its own space, its own
characteristic form of eventuation. A law of nature, which is a formula for all, is a photographic
compenetration, a statistical composite of their individualities. It is secondary, not primary; not initial
but eventual. The Space of Euclidean geometry and
ordinary mathematics, the Time of our clocks and
railway guides and calendars are similarly synthetic
and secondary. They are like the British Empire,
a very tenuous form of unity emerging from various
concatenations of inwardly differentiated and variously connected social and political organizations.

V

"But," you cry, "how can such things be, in view
of the atom that the new physics offers for our
belief! Granted that they hold of the macrocosm;
the vision of Newton remains true of the microcosm.
Certainly physics has abandoned the old atom as an
indivisible, impenetrable, immutable element, the un-
changing foundation of our changing world! But
what has replaced it? A complex atom in which
electrons and protons furnish the indivisible, impenetrable, immutable units, and in which these units
are related to each other like the planets to the sun.
As formerly through atoms, the energies and forms
and qualities of the world now are reached by

calculable, progressive, regular combinations of these units of positive and negative electric charges, moving with respect to each according to known laws. Has not Bohr shown us atoms with nuclei of protons and electrons like to the sun, with satellite electrons moving round them even as the planets move round the sun?"

Surely, surely. But every such scheme of the structure of matter is an interpolation. It is to the actual event which physics studies what the continuity is to the actual sequence of the cinematograph. It fills and rationalizes the dark and empty interval. The actual event which physics studies is a change in the atom. This change shows itself as wavelike radiation. To account for this radiation it was assumed that the planetary electrons are able to go round their centers only in two or three different orbits and not in the indefinitely many which the Newtonian mechanics permit. The intervals between the orbits were found to be definite multiples of the smallest orbit and are called quanta. Radiation, runs the tale, takes place when an electron jumps from one orbit to another—always from a greater to a lesser one. The radiation is measured and so the quantum ascertained. But the anatomy of the atom was invented to fill in the interval between the radiations. Still no one knows, no one can know, why the electron jumps from one orbit to another; why it jumps to this of its available orbits and not that; why the orbits between those in which it may move are never followed. The anatomy of the atom thus fails to fill in the intervals between the radiations.

The calculations of the German mathematicians Heisenberg and Schrödinger are said to have the effect of assimilating the Bohrian microcosm to the Einsteinian macrocosm. The atom would then again be without any spatial anatomy. The electron would be simply a point of reference in Space-Time for a radiation, the radiation would be a sequence of events with intervals; its quanta would be its pulse or beats, its actions.

The study of radiations leads to still other inconstancies. These appear as phases of the phenomena of radioactivity. In radioactivity it is not the planetary electrons which jump their orbits but the sunlike nuclei which break down. In the course of this disintegration elements like uranium or thorium or radium pass through phases. Some of these phases are momentary, others have the capacity to last endlessly. During some of their phases identical elements like the stable form of uranium have the same atomic numbers and different atomic weights. Some, like the intermediate forms of uranium, have different atomic numbers. The leads in which all radioactive series terminate (radium, actinium and thorium lead), have the same atomic number as lead mined from the earth, but their atomic weights all vary. Such leads are "isotopes." They are alike in every respect but their atomic weights; and many elements so-called, in no sense involved in the phenomena of radioactivity, have turned out to be mixtures of two or more kinds of the same thing: chlorine, for example, consists of two isotopes, xenon of as many as seven.

Why should the nucleus of an atom break down when it does and as it does? Why should electrons be practically imponderable and move discontinuously from orbit to orbit, while the radiations which such movements initiate are propagated continuously through their medium? Why should an electron be the name for one kind of electricity and a proton for an opposite, and each repel its like and attract its opposite? Are we not here at the walls of our world, at the brute data which have no beyond? It would be reasonable to say that we are—if we could be only sure that all these ideas are not inventions for the purpose of bridging intervals between events of experience. But whether we are or not, it is significant that when we reach such brute data we reach indeterminations, we reach chance and freedom. "Nature," says Bertrand Russell, in his latest book [1] on the subject, "seems to be full of revolutionary occurrences as to which we can say that *if* they take place they will be of several kinds, but we cannot say that they will take place at all, or, if they will, at what time. So far as the quantum theory can say at present, atoms might as well be possessed of freewill, limited, however, to one of several possible choices." As Eddington suggests, the orderly systems that we know and that we identify as the heart of the world are largely projections of our own heart's desire; most scientific laws of the past are conventions of measurement, rational because conventional and because conventional not likely to be

---

[1] The Analysis of Matter, p. 38.

real. It is when we come upon something by the methods of science which shocks our sentiment of rationality, which we find irrational, that we come upon reality. It is such irrationality that we come upon in the quantum and in the interior of the atom. "This world of the interior of the atom," says Sommerfeld,[2] "is in general closed to the outer world; it is not influenced by conditions of temperature and pressure which hold outside; it is ruled by the law of probability, of spontaneous chance which cannot be influenced."

VI

Spontaneous chance, probability, revolutionary occurrences, freewill, statistical averages—the irrational,—all this from masters in the field, deeply inured to the presumptions and attitudes of scientific determinism and mathematical certainty!

Does it not establish the likelihood that in Nature as a whole, determinism is the result of mutual determinations, a secondary thing, resting upon the interaccommodation of discrete liberties? "Ah," you reply, "but is there not a *law* of probability, a theory of chance?" Certainly, but what is this law? A rule of counting. A ratio of predictability. Complicate it mathematically as much as you please, that is what in the ultimate test it must come to—successful or unsuccessful prediction. A ratio can mean something if the number of possible instances is finite. Then a prevailing tendency in a sequence of events may—other things being equal—overcome a

[2] Atomic Structure and Spectral Lines (tr. H. L. Brose) p. 109.

counter tendency and repeat itself. But when we
deal with irreversible times and unbounded spaces
and all nature, we are not dealing with finite aggrega-
tions. That the chances are even that a coin will
fall heads or tails in an *infinitely long run* makes no
sense. There are no definite ratios of infinity.
Each event and item of it contains the brute and
arbitrary givenness of pure chance; it happens and
that is all. You cannot deduce anything from the
infinite, because it implies everything.

Theories of probability, hence, are secondary
elaborations of scientific method. Primary is the
act of sampling. Whenever we find a new law dis-
covered or a new quality discerned, we shall find
that the discoverer has taken a sample out of a more
or less heterogeneous aggregate of things, examined
it, described it, generalized his description and then
expressed his faith that the other items in this aggregate are of the same character, have the same
measurements and the same relationships as his
generalization. But the generalization is already a
transformation of the sample. The experiments
and experiences which now occur in confutation or
confirmation never quite coincide with the generalization or law. That is a mathematical limit which
experiment and experience ever approximate, never
attain. As Charles Pierce wrote, more than half a
century ago: "Try to verify any law of nature and
you will find that the more precise your observations, the more certain they will be to show irregular
departures from the law." Note: "the more precise," not "the less precise." So long as you deal

with nature wholesale, with gargantuan aggregates, with macrocosmic times and spaces, the laws hold pretty well: as soon as you bring them to bear on specific detail, something escapes them, something stands out and will not go under their yoke. You are compelled to nullify this with the insubordinate aspect of another instance . . . and another . . . and another. . . . You generate, in fact, though the imposing machinery of your mathematics may prevent you from realizing it, or your language habits may veil your ways of thought from you, a statistical composite. It is the constant amid the flux, and it has neither double nor avatar within it. It is a sign and a guide, not a governance. And it seems to be the final inwardness that our day assigns to the "laws of nature."

VII

With these things in mind, let us now once more take up the determinisms presumed to inhere in the nature of mind itself. Modern psychology may be said to sum itself up in the dictum that the mind is what the body does. The dictum states nothing new: it is an observation fundamental to Aristotle, who saw the mind related to the body as cutting to the axe. But the dictum inverts Aristotle, to whom cutting was a form or entelechy, generating the axe and justifying it as, he believed, mind generates and informs and justifies the body. But for modern psychology mind is a function and a mode of response. It comes to be when a living body with a nervous system, especially with a brain, reacts to

stimuli.   Indeed, if you think of reactions in terms
of conditioned reflexes and their integrations, mind
becomes very largely a function of the brain.
Changes in the brain are then critical events for the
history of the mind.   But brain changes are of a
very minute kind, of a kind that may assimilate
readily enough to the events which occur in the interior of atoms.   An indiscernible change in a single
associative cell, may hence be enough to turn the
course of history.   And such a change would belong
to the incalculable, the utterly chanceful and brute
and free.   It might be of the nature of a quantum
radiation, or even of radioactivity.   It might be the
physical content of the experience of freewill, so
often described and so often denied.   "On the basis
of physics itself" writes Russell,[3] reluctantly "there
may be limits to physical determinism. . . . Perhaps
the electron jumps when it likes; perhaps the minute
phenomena in the brain which make all the difference
to mental phenomena belong to the region where
physical laws no longer definitely determine what
must happen."   Perhaps.   I call to mind as a not
too dim analogy William James's discussion of the
energies of men: of unbearable crises met and overcome; of deep, deep levels of energy tapped and
poured out.   Between the new atom and certain old
an unfashionable notions of the qualities and behavior of mind certain analogies obtain.   But it is
faith and not knowledge that can at present—or
perhaps ever—convert these analogies into correlations or identities.

[3] Op. Cit., p. 393.

VIII

How shall we know where the kind of freedom which is today conceived to initiate events at the bottom of the world comes through at the top, granting for the moment the traditional vaunt that we human beings are the top? Directly we can never know, save perhaps in the feeling of freewill, and in the insurgences of energy. But indirectly, does not all evolution tell the tale? Which new species could be deduced from which, in that quality or power that makes it new? Darwin's "spontaneous variations" is, willy nilly, still an indispensable concept to biology. As Nietzsche well knew, you cannot deduce the Superman from man, or man from the ape. What is the ape to man? A reproach and a burning shame. Such is man to the Superman. How can one tell what the Superman will be like, being not a perfected man, but a negated man? And so man is a negated ape. With his coming, old things went on, but also something old was taken away, something new was initiated and set going. If there is repetition, there was also variation, and this variation was chanceful, contingent, unpredictable, like the discontinuous jump of the electron which initiates a continuous radiation as its act.

This congregation of beginnings and continuations, repetitions and variances, law and chance, is exemplified in as interesting a form as any by the paradox that the realization of freedom in the western world is a function of the acceptance of determinism in nature and in society.

Compare an individual of pre-industrial society
with one of our own times. How limited, how circumscribed, had his experiences to be! His vehicles
couldn't take him very far in a given time. The
places he could reach were fewer and less varied.
He was confined to few choices in his diet, his ward-
robe, his shelter, his amusements, his vocation. He
was more frequently and more painfully subject to
disease. He had fewer means of redress against
wrong. He had fewer avenues of escape from one
station in life to another. His span of life was
shorter. As compared with us moderns, the member of preindustrial society—any Russian or Chinese
or Hindu peer or peasant, living inland, will do as a
sample—was a bondsman to time and space, to wind
and weather, to disease and death, to his inherited
defects and acquired madnesses. Although the rich
are undoubtedly richer today, and the poor mathematically poorer, the poor man is in fact infinitely
freer from the restrictions and limitations believed
a hundred years ago to be absolute and inescapable;
infinitely richer in avenues and channels toward a
full and varied life.

Compare the presumptions with which the precise
study and the measurement of intelligence began
and the perceptions it is leading to. We are confronted with the transformation of an innate trait,
constant, invariant, uninfluenceable by learning or
environment, into a profoundly modifiable endowment, responsive in a notable degree to the action
of the environment.[4]   Indeed, the search after law

---

[4] *Cf.* especially "The Influence of the Environment on the In-

in the economy of our inheritance has converted all the rigidities of our nature into plastic and flexible traits not exercising an inevitable compulsion upon our destiny. By the knowledge of the causes of our being we win to freedom from their consequences if we choose.

Compare the presumptions of the old economics with the discoveries of the new. The old theory defines the processes of the economic establishment in terms of "law"—the "law" of supply and demand, the "law" of diminishing returns, Gresham's "law," Pareto's, and the like. Wherever its proponents can they give its laws a quantitative form, at least a statistical one. They will to believe that columns of figures and areas of graphs can provide veracious forecasts of what will happen when and where it does happen. At bottom, their ideal of science is that of the Newtonian physics. Their views and methods may be called scholastic and academic. Over against them we set the realists in economics. They see no universal determinations, no inevitable sequences, no laws. They study an economic chain of events with presumptions analogous to those of modern physics. Being realists, they are relativists, acknowledging eventuation only from next to next.

"My whole experience in the study of economic law," Dr. Leo Wolman writes me, "has led more and more to the conviction that it is impossible to discover any economic laws in the sense in which the

telligence, School Achievement and Conduct of Foster Children," by Frank N. Freeman and others in the 27th Yearbook of the National Society for the Study of Education, Part I, pp. 103 seq.

term was used in the older economics. Even in the field of money and prices where descriptions of phenomena have achieved much more precision than in other fields of economics it is found to be impossible to discover and describe so-called economic laws. In the hearing now being held before the United States Senate Committee testimony is being received from all of the leading experts of the country on the question whether the Federal Reserve Board can really regulate prices and the consensus of opinion seems to be that they cannot. Many of the witnesses appear to agree that the most influential factor in the American situation since the war has been the flow of gold into this country. But as for segregating the effect of gold movements from a multitude of other influences, and as for measuring the effect of any single force, the analysis proves to be quite inadequate.

"In some studies I have recently been carrying on with regard to the geographical differences in wage rates in the United States I find enormous differences in wage levels persisting for long periods of time. They cannot be explained in terms of underlying market forces which in the old theoretical economics were regarded as economic laws. They appear on the contrary to be the resultant of a large number of influences such as labor skill, managerial skill, attitude of the banks and other things. A recent study, for instance, of the automobile industry in New England comes to the conclusion that this industry which began in New England, then died there, and became localized in the Middle West was forced to leave New England because the bankers in that section did not have enough faith in the industry to advance sufficient capital in its early stage. Considerations like these were always operative and to summarize them into a single category called economic law is neither illuminating nor accurate."

IX

It is time to draw to a close. What shall we say is the upshot of this conspectus of Freedom and Determinism from the world of the infinitely big to the world of the infinitely little, and in the human heart? We see the pomp and circumstance of the world of our daily lives, with its surprises and monotonies taking shape out of congeries of concatenated and compenetrating events, that succeed each other and pass into each other as do the tones of a melody or the years of a life. These chains and sequences have limits, they begin and they end. They are acts which once born, die. When they are born, why or how, is not revealed; nor how, nor when, nor why, they die. Between their beginnings and their endings, the events that compose them are continuous; their sequence is from next to next, as the sequence of a life is, which may not skip the intervening years between five and twenty-five, but must pass through them all. In fact, there are no years to intervene until they have been lived, and they enter into and unite with the years they separate. Their span as an act may be described as a rhythm or quantum. Unless stopped, it goes on until it stops of itself.

Of human beings Metchnikoff said a long time ago that they have instinct toward death; it becomes manifest only when we die naturally, when the act of our living has actually spent itself of its own momentum. Then we enjoy dying. Our instinct toward death is merely the completion of that vibration of events which was initiated with our birth. Of course hardly any human beings die a natural death, and I cannot say if there is much non-human that does.

But within any given *going* sequence of events, subsequent initiations take place, novelties, spontaneities. These are reacted to as blockings, distractions, diversions, interferences. They must come to terms with what is already there: either by way of conflict or by way of accommodation or both, usually both, the terms attained take shape as a *modus vivendi,* a way of living together, which is a determination of the undetermined novelty and is the essence of law. That such determinations can be accomplished and are, is an assurance to Human Freedom: for the undeterminable and utterly spontaneous are not amenable to control and to use, which are the agencies of Human Freedom. It is earthquake and tidal wave, cancer and other unconquered disease, which we cannot control, that make us afraid and keep us bond. For mankind hence the discovery of determinism is the beginning of freedom. Our knowledge of the mechanisms which work the world we live in frees us from their compulsions. To know how a thing happens is to be the master of the event, to be in a position to transform a power that commands into a power that serves. This is why scientific determinism was, as we saw, the initiation of social freedom; it is what the whole of civilization rests on. This determinism is, however, of a nature quite different from that which the philosophers console themselves with. It is nothing static; no all-at-once. It is a strainful and *going* activity being constantly applied to things themselves undetermined, ambiguous and fluid. In effect determinism is nothing ready-made and finished, but a process of determination. It is the enterprise of rendering serviceable to human interests that in the world which would otherwise defeat those interests. And "that" points to nearly the total contents of experience. The processes of determination bridge the distances between the uncontrolled and uncontrollable chance comings in which events begin and chance emergences in which they deviate and are transformed. Both are objectives of determination, which binds them into a cohering world. . . .

We may say, may we not, that Freedom is a fact that physics records, that psychology feels. Confronted with Freedom as a fact, what can we do with it? Isn't it something of a White Elephant on our hands? Yes, it is a White Elephant and we can harness it up and make it work for us. What we can do with Freedom is to pass laws to restrain it. What else are laws for? Without liberties there could be no laws, whether in physics or in civilization. Laws are the ways in which free things come together and stay together. They are the consequences of the impact of liberties upon one another, mutualities of restraint which presuppose that which they restrain. Laws are also facts, more obvious and blatant because they are secondary, derivative, closer to the surface of things. In the universe they are cosmic habits. In the life of society they are customs, traditions, conventions, statutes. In the life of the individual they are personal habits.

Science and experience reduce neither to the rigid determinisms nor the brute spontaneities which the absolute logics of determinisms and indeterminisms imply. They show us rather biography-like chains of events in conjunctions of attraction and repulsion, conflicts and cooperations; establishing these conjunctions as lasting ways of being together; breaking them when the tension grows too great; or confirming them; and always deviating from them into this byway or another; so that during any later phase of these cosmic acts, there are more things and more different things than there were in the earlier. Where the breaks and the deviations take place is the fighting front of liberty; law is the rearward stretch. Freedom is thus the present point of change in a process whose past is determinism.

In a world so constituted, how can human beings not be operative factors? The new physics, indeed, installs them as such when it declares that the point of view of the observer is an essential in designating and placing an event. More specifically, civilization is the change we have actually effected in the earth and in ourselves for our own ends.

Items in the cosmic processes, human beings contribute their share of novelty and repetition to the incommensurable sequences of the world.

Insofar as the novelty they contribute is a brute freedom, a liberty inconsiderately taken with the tradition of existence, it is unpredictable and uncontrollable, and is a problem and a present trouble to the specific life in which it appears no less than to the residual environment which it challenges. Upon both its happening imposes adjustive alterations, countering action, which shall either destroy or naturalize its aliency and incorporate it with the established order, the going economy of whatever already *is* going and repeating itself. This is why novelties have such a hard time when they arrive and seem so little novel when they establish a freehold, even though they may succeed, by the adjustive changes they evoke in the environment they enter, in altering the environment as much as it alters them, or more.

Insofar as human activity is an upkeep of the tradition, an item itself in the cosmic repetition of items, it is as much the substance of "law and order" as anything else in the world. At the phase of Space-Time in which we find ourselves, living as we live and doing as we do, we are ourselves streams of events, modes of interplay of novelty and repetition, freedom and determinism, with some calculable consequences for us and many incalculable consequences for us and the world. Within the limits of birth and death, we do make our own fate.

Now this fate, which is ever a lived life looked at from its end and never foreseen from its beginning, comes into the perspectives and dogmas of logic and metaphysics and theology as something single, inevitable, ultimate. So seen, it is an illusion. It identifies the completeness of a review with the successive efforts of an endeavor, a thing ended with events going on. It confuses the composites and averages which are the unity of a law with the discrete contiguous successions of events which are the living of a life. It sets up the "continuity" in the place of the pictures. Its logical premise is the dogma that relations are internal. Its impelling emotion is the felt insecurity and thwarting of the flux of life, generating philosophies of unity—idealisms and materialisms indifferently—which abolish uncertainty, obstruction and the flux all together.

On the other hand Freedom, as utter chance without law, is equally an illusion. Like the notion of utter determinism it also is by a major intention a compensatory ideal. Living in a world which was not made for us, but into which we are born and in which we must struggle to survive, we find ourselves surrounded by countless other beings, each of which is no less intent upon its own activities. Lives collide, obstruct each other, impose upon each other limitations, adjustments, which are restraints upon the processes of eventuation whose sum is a biography. So we imagine a world which is congruent and serviceable to our lives instead of running counter to them. We define the environment as impotent to obstruct us or as reenforcing us. Or we conceive ourselves as being without an environment. When we do this we identify ourselves with God or the Absolute if we are idealists, or Nature with ourselves if we are materialists. In either case we have made Freedom by a logic of illation. And this made Freedom is illusion.

Not less illusion is Freedom which is a logical elaboration of the observation of utter spontaneity that can in no aspect and no way be assimilated to another event or personality or being. Such a spontaneity, if it enters our world leaves it as soon as it enters. It is wholly discontinuous. It cannot develop a past or generate a future. It cannot get into ways of staying with other things. Its nature involves an undiscoverable and solipsistic uniqueness which a Leibnitzian monad without preestablished harmony would have, or an idealistic monist God. When it occurs in the latter form, it becomes indistinguishable from the compensatory unity in which we are free by identification.

While, so far as our experience goes, the latter is ruled out as a background or environment for the world we actually live in, plural spontaneities are not. There is reason to believe that our world derives from just such entire chaos, from the slow formation through endless times of a cosmos in which initial variety and anarchy are taking on law and order in the sense of habits of being together with one another. Philosophically, pure Freedom and pure Determinism are symbolic elaboration of samples selected from mixed data, elaborations which are not descriptions of the data, but corrections of them, compensations against them. Sometimes one prevails in the history of thought, sometimes the other, according to the sort of thing a society at the time finds in its way and wishes to overcome. As instruments of living, both libertarianism and determinism are makers of Human Freedom. As facts of life, determinism is meaningless without freedom; freedom is unmanageable and therefore enslaving without determinism. Determinism is the continuity of the determinations of freedom; freedom is the initiation of rule and law. The latter is a function of the former, and they work together on human life.